Behind Closed Doors

Edward N. Costikyan

Behind
Closed Doors

✸✸

Politics

in the Public

Interest

A HARVEST/HBJ BOOK

HARCOURT BRACE JOVANOVICH

NEW YORK AND LONDON

Library of Congress Catalog Card Number: 66-12359
Printed in the United States of America

CDEFGHIJ

To My Wife Frances

Who Made Possible and Shared the Education
That Made Both of Us Proud
To Be Politicians

Acknowledgments

Many people contributed to this book, by their behavior, their examples, their advice, their help and counsel. Indeed, everyone who contributed to the political education of the author, and there were many who did so, is entitled to my thanks.

Most of all, I am grateful to the New Democratic Club and its members and captains over the years. They made it possible for me to be a political leader, and if I was a good one, they are entitled to the principal credit.

The ladies and gentlemen who have made up the Executive Committee of the New York County Democratic Party likewise are entitled to my thanks. I hope they will find what I have said about politics and politicians to be fair and true.

In addition, over the years, there has been a group of close political and personal friends who have helped and guided and advised, especially when the going got rough: Jean McCabe Angell, Bill and Freda Barlow, Jack Brickley, George Daly, Justin and Janet Feldman, Jerry Finkelstein, Charles J. Morrello, Dr. Walsh McDermott, Ed and Mary Reed, Harvey Spear, and Len and Mort Weber were the principal friends, advisers, and supporters to whom I wish to express my thanks.

My political secretary when I was county leader, Mrs. Lillian Halloran, and her able staff, Elsie Cortes and Vicki McGarry, made it possible to run a political office with a part-time boss. Without their devoted service, it could not have been done.

My law partners who had enough faith in me to carry me through the last few years when almost half my time was spent elsewhere have my special thanks. Mr. Robert Leavitt, who read the manuscript and identified the sentences fit for preservation in formaldehyde before they were printed has my, and, I am sure, the reader's, thanks.

And my secretary, Mrs. Sylvia Colodner, who typed my briefs, affidavits, speeches, and letters, managed my schedule, co-ordinated my activities, placated my clients, made sure I was where I was supposed to be, and placidly accepted the incredible problems created by having an absent-minded boss trying to be two or three or four places at once, holds a special place of gratitude.

To all of the above, and to the many others who helped, my deepest thanks.

E. N. C.

January 1966

Contents

PART THREE

PART FOUR

PART FIVE

PART SIX

Behind Closed Doors

PREFACE ✴ On Becoming a Tammany Sachem

At the age of thirty I was elected by the enrolled Democrats of my district in New York County as the Democratic district leader. I was, according to the press—which will not let ancient tradition die—a Tammany Sachem.

What is a Sachem?

What is "Tammany"?

What does a Democratic district leader do?

Nineteen years of the kind of education the established middle class gives its sons did not provide me with answers. College government texts could not do much more than warn me to beware of the bribers. A Protestant heritage was of little help, other than to leave me with the impression I was entering the nether depths. My mother's reaction was unmistakable: I had fallen among bad if not evil companions.

George Washington Plunkitt's counsel, delivered from a shoe-shine stand outside the old County Court House to an enterprising journalist, was the only "out of the horse's mouth" reference work extant. According to Plunkitt, a loquacious but unimportant Tammany district leader around the turn of the century, I should look for "honest graft," look for "opportunities" and take them, decry civil service for destroying the "patriotism of the young," and otherwise I was on my own.

Plunkitt wasn't much help.

Ed Flynn's good book—*You're the Boss*—while interesting, did not go far enough. Nor was there much guidance to be derived from anyone else who had ever put words to paper. The theorists had notions as to how politics worked and what political leaders should do. Lincoln Steffens, the journalist extraordinaire, warned me of the corruption to which the business community wished to subject me. The histories of the Society of Tammany, official and unauthorized, laid bare their version of the heritage of which I was becoming a part.

But the literature on American government includes very little, if any, genuine learning on how the political process really works. The contemporaneous press does little more than reveal the insights into the current political situation which skilled publicists decide the public should be told.

But none of this answered the question: What does a leader *do?* And how?

I soon discovered there were no businessmen lining up to bribe me. No franchises were for sale. If "honest graft" was available I failed to recognize it. I didn't have time to sit at a shoeshine stand and listen to others pontificate. The others weren't there anyway. And none of the Tammany Sachems whose ranks I was joining were anxious to sit down and explain the mysteries of political leadership to me. To the contrary, as a rather strange newcomer, I was hardly spoken to for months.

And no "opportunities," in Plunkitt's sense, were to be seen.

So after four years as a Democratic captain and club officer on the election-district level,* I began ten years on the county level as an assembly-district leader, during which I had to learn by doing.

As a district leader, I functioned as a member of the New York County Democratic Executive Committee (which consisted of 33 men and 33 women district leaders). To the press, the Executive Committee is "Tammany," and its members "Sachems."

For the last thirty-two months of that time I also served as county leader—to the press, "Tammany Boss."

In these capacities I participated in countless political decisions, including the nomination of candidates for governor, United States senator and other statewide offices, for mayor, judge, borough president, congress, council, state senate and assembly.

And now, after retiring from politics, I find the questions

---

* New Yorkers call the smallest political subdivision—a block or two—election districts (elsewhere they are called precincts) and the next largest subdivision—a group of at least 15 or 20 and as many as 80 election districts—an assembly district or assembly district part (other cities call them wards).

remain unanswered in any book of which I am aware: What does a political leader do? What is he supposed to do? How are political decisions made? What are the elements to be considered? What kind of people make the decisions? What are their motives? What beyond instinct, and general knowledge, guides the politician at work? Are there "rules of the game" and do they make sense? Is government served well or badly by politics and by politicians and their conduct?

Throughout this book, I use the terms "politician" and "political leader" to identify political-party officeholders—captains, district leaders, county leaders—whose basic activity is in the *internal* political structure—*not* public officeholders such as mayors, congressmen, legislators, and the like. The latter I refer to as "public officeholders."

Many political leaders are also public officeholders—councilmen, deputy commissioners, assemblymen. But their principal activity is internal politics—where no one is paid money—and the public office they may hold (or their private business) is secondary in political terms.

This distinction is an important one, and one rarely understood by outsiders. For although the public rarely makes the distinction, political leaders—that is, the party officeholders—and public officeholders are different breeds of cat, with different functions, different ambitions, different responsibilities. The party officeholder must have a far greater interest and concern in the institution he serves and its success than in his own personal fame. And he usually does. He works behind the scenes. He seeks party, not personal success. His satisfaction (and his power and prestige) come from seeing people he has found and developed in public office.

The public officeholder, in contrast, places his *own* name, his *own* success, his *own* future first. He must. For it is *his* name which appears on the ballot. It is his mistakes and his successes upon which the voters pass judgment, and success or victory to him turn upon his personal victory or defeat. It is no comfort to a candidate for public office to be told that a district that for twenty years had been lost by margins of 65–35 percent and 60–40 percent was only lost by 51–49 percent. But the political leader can look at such a result as a sure sign of effective political organization, progress, and a harbinger of future success.

The political leader derives his satisfaction from finding good candidates, developing good issues, running effective campaigns, closing the losing gap or raising a winning one. The public officeholder derives his satisfaction from winning—by any margin, but the bigger the better.

The party officeholder is more concerned with a party record, a party image, a party victory. Even if his own local candidate doesn't quite make it, the increased vote in the area contributes to the over-all victory. The public officeholder must be more concerned with his *own* record (of independence from the party, sometimes), his own image, his own victory. As a result, the two kinds of politicians are quite different in approach and attitude, and although on occasion a party officeholder moves over to the ranks of the public officeholder, the occasions are rare.

I was a party officeholder type, not a public officeholder one. I never ran for public office, although I was frequently urged to. But I regarded myself as a talent scout, not as the talent, and I frequently chided associates who always managed to end the search for a talented candidate for public office as soon as they looked in a mirror.

I learned of the difference between party officeholders and public officeholders by watching them at work. Books don't talk about this aspect of politics anymore than they talk of other aspects. Perhaps one reason is that no one can write effectively on such subjects if he is currently a participant in the process without destroying his current effectiveness. And usually the retired politician is either unwilling or unable to reveal the inner secrets. Perhaps he harbors secret hopes of a return to power. Like most politicians, his desire to continue his political career may persist until long after his political career has been ended by the voters. Hoping for a return to power, he keeps silent. What is equally common is that retirement never takes place and the politician remains in office until death ends his career.

But the secrecy also breeds myths.

The nature of politics and politicians is to reach decisions privately. This often leads the public to believe that secrecy is a screen to shield wrongdoing. It usually isn't. Generally it shields a desire for privacy, as well as some confusion, some dissension, and some selfishness. The secrecy exists, however, because the natural habitat of a politician at work is behind a closed door. And while, on occasion the shut doors shield misconduct, usually they simply protect a process that cannot function well at a public hearing, any more than a mother can be sensibly delivered of a child in Macy's window.

In *The Last Hurrah,* Edwin O'Connor tells a fine political story. But whenever the politicans retire to discuss "tactics," the door is closed to the novelist and to the public.

I believe politicians would be well advised to open that door, and that politics would thus be well served. What goes on behind it is normally perfectly exposable to the light of day. Only the mystery is destroyed. But, like magicians, politicians like to smile enigmatic smiles after a startling political result. For mystery breeds respect. And respect breeds power. And power is the principal asset and persistent natural goal of the politician.

The speculators of the press speculate. "Informed sources" instead of people reveal the inside story—usually inaccurately. The general repute of the politician suffers, fewer able men and women participate in politics, the parties suffer, the government suffers, and the cycle goes on and on.

And so, why not answer the questions: "What does a district leader do?" "What does a politician do?"—fully and fairly?

Well, why not?

For the truth generally reflects well on the men and women who find a fascination in political activity and devote themselves to it as a full-time occupation or preoccupation. Not all are saints. Few, if any, are rich. And, with rare exceptions, the political process functions well because of their activity.

Am I breaching confidences? I don't think so. For this book does not reveal secret misconducts or confidential disclosures, or attempt to even old political scores.

Rather, I hope to show the political process at work, political pressures in action, political leaders seeking solutions, the ways in which compromises unite disparate forces, and the realities of politicians at work.

This is not a "kiss and tell" book on New York politics. It does not attempt to reveal how a paper bag of money was left unclaimed in a taxicab, or why Senator Lehman broke with Carmine De Sapio, or how Mayor Wagner became a reformer. Indeed, but for the particular local environment, and the names and dates, it is a story of how American urban politics works, why politicians act as they do, how they achieve their results.

I should, however, add a few personal notes to reveal the personal biases and attitudes that affect the appraisal in these pages.

At the age of thirty, as a new Tammany Sachem, I was (and am now even more so) a Democrat. I feel an attachment to the institution of the Democratic Party which is similar to my pride in my Armenian and Swiss heritage, my family, my law firm, and my church.

I feel pride in the party's accomplishments; I feel unhappiness and sometimes disgust and anger at its stupidities. I revel in its victories; I am unhappy when it fails.

I count as victories those occasions when it stands for high principles, though the voters may not agree, and I count as defeats the occasions when it seeks the lowest common denominator, even though the majority of the voters may accept such a solution.

But it is *my* party. I feel a responsibility for what it does and what it doesn't do; I believe it has the capacity for imaginative and effective government. And I have long since despaired of achieving good government without the assistance of a good political party.

Perhaps, in some other era, the Republican Party might provide that assistance. But in our day and age, as I see it, it is the Democratic Party which is concerned with solving our governmental problems before they become crises, with seeking out the problems before those afflicted by them either are prostrated or organize a march on City Hall, and with developing solutions which harmonize both the problems and the solutions into the tapestry of our democratic heritage.

I suppose I am also a liberal. Certainly at the age of thirty I would have so described myself. Today I am less concerned with labels, and more concerned with human problems and human solutions to them, and with the rate at which the problems are solved.

But in the traditional spectrum of political thought and labels, I must acknowledge the liberal classification. I must make this clear, because most of the description of political activity which follows is silent as to traditional liberal-conservative classifications. Indeed, most political activity, in the internal party organization, lacks any overt manifestations of the political coloration of the objectives. And much of what I experienced could as well have taken place in a party whose political objectives were quite different from those of the Democratic Party of New York County.

But that does not mean that the activity had no politically classifiable objective. For I was part of and I led a liberally oriented political institution and, especially when I led it, I believe that our objectives were ascertainably to the liberal side of the spectrum. That being so, however, the political techniques I learned and the political experiences I engaged in have a value independent of the political coloration or classification of their objectives. It is that value in which I have become increasingly interested over the years.

Thus, when there is discussion of what man or woman was nominated or ought to have been nominated, I have not attempted to analyze the qualifications of the candidates in terms of liberalism or conservatism. In fact, never, to my knowledge, was the political coloration of candidates a significant factor in choosing between them. For the New York County Democratic Party is a liberally oriented institution and so were its available candidates. Our problems, rather, related to degrees of competence, and understanding: to finding and selecting the man or woman who *ought* to be in public office and could win an election.

Finally, I must acknowledge that I found a fascination in political activity. I liked almost all the people I dealt with—even those with whom I disagreed and against whom I fought. The man I first defeated for district leader lives across the street and we never meet without stopping to discuss what is going on.

I liked the negotiation, the argument, the persuasion, the planning, the maneuvering. I liked dealing with problems that affected many people and on some occasions helping to solve them. I liked planning campaigns, and finding out what bothered people, and helping to formulate programs that appealed to them.

I liked helping to get action out of government. I liked being involved in the process of government in what was, to me, a most meaningful way, while at the same time pursuing a career at the law which was my principal enthusiasm.

In short, despite the occasions when political activity was disappointing—because people didn't behave the way they really should have, or elections that should have been won were lost, or personal rebuffs brought gloom and loss of self-confidence, or for any other reason—for me, politics has a fascination and excitement which make it simultaneously addictive and nourishing. I believe it's good for the people in it and, despite all those who criticize politics and politicians, for the country.

With this preface, and from these biases, and with these attitudes, I find there are for me recordable answers to several persistent questions: What does a politician do? How are political decisions made? What *is* the nature of the political process? Is it a good thing or a necessary evil?

Part One

The
Political
Environment
New York County,
1945–1965

Introduction to Part One

Every politician functions in a particular environment, with its particular political history, its particular terminology, its particular problems, its particular forces of change at work.

New York County's Democratic party organization was founded in 1789 as the Society of Tammany or Columbian Order. It somehow survived for almost 180 years, despite its own mistakes and the onslaughts of its enemies. From 1945 to 1965, it was going through an unusual metamorphosis, which most of its members, including the author, did not and could not fully understand while it was happening.

If this book, however, is to make sense to the nonpolitical reader, and if it is to have any effect, the nature of the environment must be first explained, the nature of the currents of change must be pointed out, the author's particular position in that environment should be noted, and the nature of the opposition parties ought to be briefly outlined, since no political party exists in a vacuum.

This, then, was the political environment of a Democratic politician at work in New York County from 1945 to 1965 in the oldest—and at times most disreputable—continuous political institution in the Western Hemisphere: "Tammany Hall."

1* Who Speaks for Political Purity?

✿✿

The Anti-Political Good-Government Tradition in New York

When James Bryce visited the United States in the 1880's, he noted that while our federal and state governments had demonstrated great competence in managing their affairs, generally our cities were badly governed.

Growing, sprawling, teeming with new arrivals mostly from Europe, far larger than the established European cities which had long been able to manage their own affairs, American city governments seemed grotesquely unsuited to their tasks.

The most obvious symptoms of this mismanagement were apparent in the activities of political leaders in New York City—Boss Tweed, Honest John Kelly, Richard Croker, not to mention Fernando Wood, mayor of the city, who, with the forty-man Board of Aldermen, soon became known as "Ali Baba and the forty thieves."

The political leaders took advantage of the incompetence of city government without restraint. Government privileges were bought and sold. New courthouses cost ten times their value. Alliances between the underworld and political leaders were common knowledge.

Soon the symptom of poor city government became the target of good-government forces. Good government and political-party government were antagonists. A political leader was, by definition, a lower form of human being—untrustworthy, likely to be

mysteriously wealthy, probably allied with underworld characters, and certainly not to be emulated.

How the political parties—especially Tammany Hall—survived
generations of public criticism and public exposure to be returned
to power again and again is an exceedingly complex tale. In part,
the longevity is attributable to the extent of alienation of new
citizens from the old Americans who dominated good government movements; in part to the loyalties earned from these new
citizens by the political bosses; and in part to the reforms that
good-government forces occasionally forced through—civil service, public bidding, independent school boards—which limited
the opportunity for political leaders to get into trouble.

But the machines survived until the New Deal, immigration
legislation, good-government reforms, and a host of other factors,
including population mobility, economic mobility, and World
War II, destroyed the bases upon which the old machines
existed.

During this long period, the good-government tradition and
heritage in our cities became almost entirely an anti-machine,
anti-political-leader one. "Reformer" was a term of opprobrium
within the machine, and reformers looked elsewhere for political
success and governmental progress.

They looked to the occasional creation of an ad hoc political force which would sporadically "throw the rascals out" and
enjoy four years or so of steadily deteriorating governmental
power, until the machine returned to power.

In New York, this tradition became known as "fusion." Three
times in this century it succeeded—in 1901 when Seth Low,
president of Columbia University, became a one-term mayor, in
1913 when John Purroy Mitchel became a one-term mayor, and
in 1933 when Fiorello La Guardia became a three-term mayor.*

Each time the coalition behind the successful candidate was
an unstable one, each time it magically deteriorated. On one
occasion a new alignment was created within the fusion movement, assigning different power positions to different groups
within the coalition. This was in the case of La Guardia in 1937

---

* For reasons stated later, the Lindsay victory in 1965 was not an example
of a genuine fusion victory.

and 1941, when the American Labor Party, La Guardia's own newly created party, replaced the Republican Party as the dominant force within the coalition.

In the other two successful fusion movements, 1901 and 1913, the coalition died within one term—two and four years respectively.

One reason was the absence of any political skills in the managers of the coalition. Being anti-political in orientation, and being convinced that the symptom of bad government—venal political leaders—was its cause, the fusionists disdained the political arts. Efficiency and nonpolitical administration would produce good government. The introduction of political skills would produce bad government.

And so each of the leaders of fusion—until La Guardia—destroyed his own coalition—out of principle. Lincoln Steffens described the phenomenon magnificently in *The Shame of the Cities:*

. . . Certainly Mayor Low is pecuniarily honest. He is more; he is conscientious and experienced and personally efficient. . . . Is there a demand for Mr. Low? No. When I made my inquiries—before the lying had begun—the Fusion leaders of the anti-Tammany forces, who nominated Mr. Low, said they might renominate him. "Who else was there?" they asked. . . . Mr. Low's is not a lovable character. But what of that? Why should his colleagues love him? Why should anybody like him? Why should he seek to charm, win affection, and make friends? He was elected to attend to the business of his office and to appoint subordinates who should attend to the business of their offices, not to make "political strength" and win elections. . . . Mr. Low is the ideal product of the New York theory that municipal government is business, not politics, and that a business man who would manage the city as he would a business corporation, would solve for us all our troubles.

Because of this anti-political attitude, each reform-fusion movement carried within it the seeds of its own destruction. Each became a temporary protest movement, and each ran its course—until La Guardia.

La Guardia was the first fusion mayor who was principally a politician. He was anti-machine in orientation—even his own party's machine, which he had frequently opposed and which had frequently opposed him. In Congress he had aligned himself with the Midwest Progressives—La Follette and Norris—and he had within his volatile makeup a good deal of the Midwestern Progressives' animosity toward any form of power—whether of political machines or political leaders or businessmen.

Initially, La Guardia was a shaky leader of the 1933 fusion coalition (others like Judge Samuel Seabury and C. C. Burlingham were far more powerful). But La Guardia gradually assumed control, reshaped the coalition, created his own political party—the American Labor Party, which consisted largely of nationally oriented Democrats dissatisfied with the local democratic machine—and, using his broad patronage powers, built a personal machine, loyal to him and able to support him effectively each time he ran.

It was only when he lost the support of this personal machine towards the end of World War II that he decided to abandon an attempt to be re-elected, and announced his retirement in 1945. By that time the original fusion movement which had elected him in 1933 against a divided Democratic Party was long since dead. Efforts in 1945 and 1949 to revive "fusion" behind different candidates were total failures, and the Fusion Party in 1957 and 1961, by then little more than a letterhead and a negotiable instrument, endorsed the Democratic incumbent, Robert F. Wagner.

And yet La Guardia fortified the anti-political-leader bias of the good-government tradition. His tirades against "tin-horn gamblers" and "two-bit politicians" deepened the public association between politicians and evildoers. In retrospect, his administration became a myth—a myth which equated good government with the absence of political leaders in government. But it was a myth in both respects.

The government in question was simply not that good. For example, the failure of the La Guardia administration in the field of education—the tremendous lag in school construction and the steadily decreasing quality of education in underprivileged areas—laid the groundwork for the explosive educational, employment, and civil rights problems which have beset the city ever since.

There was an equation of "honest government" with "good government" during the La Guardia years—an equation of doubtful validity. Dishonest government is bad government, but honesty in government in and of itself does not insure good government.

The second fallacy in the appraisal of the La Guardia years was the notion that La Guardia government represented government conducted in the absence of political leaders. For La Guardia was himself one of the most astute politicians ever developed in New York. A fantastic vote-getter, a shrewd utilizer of manpower, a careful dispenser of patronage, La Guardia carefully kept the political parties alive, but barely so,—sufficiently strong to help win re-election for La Guardia but insufficiently strong to dominate those elected.

In this, La Guardia became the prototype for Mayor Robert F. Wagner of New York, Richard Daley of Chicago, and David Lawrence of Pittsburgh—the public-officeholder who was also the political leader.

Despite all this, La Guardia left the good-government tradition and theory where he found it—firmly oriented against political leaders, political machines, and political parties. While he privately incorporated the function of the political leader, the political party, and the political machine into his administration and made them extensions of his own personality, he publicly railed at the politicians.

And so the spokesmen for good government remained antipolitical in orientation and in utterance. The Citizens Union, the City Club, and various other custodians of the good-government tradition maintained their aloofness from the political machinery. They patiently awaited the day when the dominant Democrats, who had recaptured control of the mayoralty in 1945, would again so decline in public esteem, so fragment themselves in internal disputes, and so misgovern, that another upsurge of anti-political-leader reform would create a new fusion movement to restore good government to New York City.

As we shall see, however, during the twenty years from 1945 to 1965 the good-government tradition, in younger hands, began to seek a more permanent and more meaningful existence. With a slight but significant amendment of the good-government philosophy, it sought expression within the dominant Democratic Party. This deviant good-government tradition asserted the following propositions:

1. Political leaders were not bad per se—only bad political leaders were.

2. The principal fault with prior political leadership had been excessive autocratic control by too few men of the political machinery.

3. Prior "good-government" efforts had failed because they were sporadic, impermanent, and outside the established political machinery. These efforts, to be permanently effective, should be directed at internal party reform—to replace the rascals with honest men, not to attempt to eliminate the role of the political leader entirely.

And so for the next twenty years the good-government tradition metamorphosed. The spokesmen for political purity were no longer solely political mavericks, attacking the political machinery, but more often than not holders of political office attacking other political-officeholders.

"The Reform Movement," dedicated to party control, became the official good-government spokesman, and acquired the kind of sanctity the editorial writers had previously accorded only to anti-political-party fusionists.

From time to time editorial writers vainly called upon the reformers to abandon their Democratic Party orientation and to strike a blow for good government by "joining" a fusion movement. ("Creating" would have been far more apt, since without the Reform Democrats there was no fusion movement to join.) In 1961, these editorial pressures reached their zenith, but after some hesitation, the reformers stuck to their theory and remained within the Democratic Party and supported Robert F. Wagner for re-election.

The major cause of this new good-government movement was

Adlai E. Stevenson, the Democratic candidate for President in 1952 and 1956. Stevenson was essentially a good-government man. An intellectual, a gentleman, an idealist, he set out to prove, and he did prove, that an honest man could remain honest within the context of the obligations created by whole-hearted devotion to a political party.

His excellence, although occasionally dimmed, endured despite the accommodations which a political existence occasionally required. And his defeats led many of his admirers to believe there was something wrong with a political party which could not produce a majority vote for such a magnificent, honest, intellectual, articulate, witty—almost perfect—human being.

These followers decided to follow his example: to plunge into the political maelstrom, to replace the hacks who had failed, to school themselves and their followers in the techniques of political action. As he was loyal to the institution of the Democratic Party, so were they. As he had demonstrated the possibility of the good-government tradition functioning in the context of an organized political party, so would they. As he had engaged in the political drudgery of campaigning in primaries and general election, so would they. As he had engaged in political maneuvering without destroying his integrity, so, by God, would they.

By the time of Governor Stevenson's death, many of his followers had installed themselves in significant party offices throughout the country. New York's reform movement was staffed, almost to a man, with Stevenson supporters. And the people of the country at large had come to an increasing awareness of the compatability of political activity with integrity.

One curious aspect of the phenomenon was the extent to which the Stevensonians far exceeded their mentor in practical political awareness, tactical understanding, and skill by the time Stevenson died. He had come to political activity for the first time in 1948—at the age of forty-eight. He plunged in, cold. From the good-government tradition which he represented, he tended to view politicians as enemies, as a bit outside the pale, as objects of suspicion. Indeed, because I was active in politics, there were occasions when we seemed to be talking a different language although I was one of those stimulated by Stevenson's example, and although I was one of his law partners.

I came to feel, moreover, the same frustration with him which an older generation of politicians had been reputed to feel. This was especially true in 1964 when Stevenson was sometimes a possible candidate for U.S. senator from New York—and sometimes not. Only at the last moment, when it was too late, did he become convinced he ought to accept the nomination—but by then it was not possible to get it for him. The absence of political skill in a man who came to politics at the age of forty-eight was clear to me, then thirty-nine, who had come to politics at the age of twenty-six because of Stevenson's example. I believed (and believe) that if only he had been more comfortable in the political environment, we could have put him over.

But even though his followers may have surpassed him in their understanding of political activity and grasp of political techniques, he remained an inspiration to those who sought to translate the good-government anti-political tradition into an internal political program.

The end result in 1965, the year of Stevenson's death, was a deep division in the New York good-government tradition. Part of it was committed to the new Stevenson tradition of good government via the political structure. Part of it—usually older voters who grew up on the La Guardia brand of good government—remained uncommitted to the new tradition, although not unfriendly to it, but basically anti-party in orientation.

And yet 1965 was an ideal year for a resurgence of the old fusion tradition:

. . . the Democratic Party was deeply divided, its wreckage strewn all over town;

. . . the city's problems seemed even more overwhelming than usual, with a profound budget deficit already in existence and an even more difficult series of deficits to be faced;

. . . the Republican Party had produced an extremely attractive vote-getter—John Lindsay—who had managed to put together a tri-party slate (Republican, Liberal, and Democrat) which gave at least the traditional appearance of a fusion slate.

On the other side of the coin:

. . . the Fusion Party, the organizational heir of the good-government tradition, announced its support of Paul Screvane, one of the Democratic aspirants;

. . . the Reform Democrats, while split between two candidates, William Fitts Ryan and Paul Screvane, remained committed to the Democratic Party, and the Democrat who joined the Lindsay slate, Milton Mollen, was not part of this reform movement in any way.

Nevertheless, after a twenty-year hiatus, an effort was being made to ascertain whether enough of the old good-government tradition had survived to produce a majority for a personable candidate, running with a tri-party slate against a badly divided Democratic Party.

The end result was an inconclusive draw. The Republican-Liberal "fusion" candidate for mayor, John Lindsay, was elected by a narrow margin. But along with him the people elected, by far more conclusive margins, Democrats Frank O'Connor and Mario Procaccino to the Number-2 and -3 spots in the city government, and an overwhelmingly Democratic City Council.

The good-government tradition thus remained half-committed to each approach—the old and the new—but fully committed to neither.

This inconclusive result fairly reflected the twenty years of metamorphosis in the Democratic Party and the good-government tradition which preceded the election. And it accurately mirrored the confusion of the electorate as it sought a path to better city government.

2. The Decline and Fall of Tammany Hall

❋❋

The Translation of the Good-Government Tradition into Political Terms and Its Application within the Democratic Party

Shortly after World War II, a change began to roll through the oldest and best-established political organization in the Western Hemisphere—the Democratic County Committee of New York County.

The origins of this political instrument are shrouded in the mystery of a secret society that was incorporated in 1789. Its name was the "Society of Tammany or Columbian Order," and its original purposes included, beyond philanthropy (which was sometimes notoriously private), the preservation of Indian lore, the celebration of the Fourth of July, and the destruction of the aristocratic Hamiltonian notions which threatened genuine democracy.

Its Jacobin outlook led it into political excursions and by 1800—in the Jefferson-Adams presidential campaign—it had discovered the secret of urban political success: a block captain in every block in charge of getting all favorable voters to the polls.

It spawned what is now the Democratic Party of New York County, and so close was the identification between the society and, the party that to this day the party is referred to by those rhetorical traditionalists, the reporters who cover New York politics, as "Tammany." This is true although the society is moribund, Tammany Hall is now the headquarters of a local of the International Ladies Garment Workers Union, and there is no connection between the Society of Tammany and the Democratic Party.

But immediately after World War II no one bothered to make any distinction between the two: their divorce was a recent and private one.

Of course, the society's membership and leadership was and still remains secret. The party, in contrast, in 1946 was governed by approximately 35 executive members (men) and 35 co-executive members (women) who made up the Executive Committee. By 1953 the number was reduced to 33 of each, and by 1955 both titles were abolished, and a male and a female district leader, theoretically equal in power, were each elected by the enrolled Democrats of the 33 assembly districts or parts * of assembly districts which made up New York County.

These district leaders were the unpaid local directors of the Democratic Party—a man and a woman together responsible for their area. Under them served enough captains to cover every election district (or precinct, as this division is called elsewhere), and each assembly district or assembly district part had its own regular Democratic club, which was the local party headquarters.

In 1946, most of these clubs were regarded by their members as private membership and social as well as political organizations. Many were modestly wealthy, owning their own headquarters and possessing substantial investments. Newcomers to the Democratic Party—as voters—were welcome, but not as members of the local club—at least, not unless some member sponsored them. Certainly no one coming in "off the street" was accepted without inquiry.

Once in the club, a lengthy period of probation was appro-

---

* In most cases, the party rules divided assembly districts in halves or thirds, called "assembly district parts," and each part had its own leaders and organization. In 1965, of 16 full assembly districts in New York County, each of which elects one assemblyman in the state legislature, 3 were not divided, 9 were divided into two parts, and 4 were divided into three parts. Reapportionment altered these figures somewhat by increasing the number of subdivisions from 33 to 39.

priate before the new member was accepted, let alone heard from.

Then the squalls of change hit the institution. Returning veterans, their political awareness stimulated, were not content to beg for admission. Once admitted, they were not satisfied to sit silently and wait their turn, especially while nonveterans— who had joined the club and advanced in the political vacuum created by the war—exercised the power, were listened to by the higher-ups, and helped make the decisions that affected everybody.

In 1949, the clash between these two forces produced three minor explosions. On the West Side, Franklin D. Roosevelt, Jr., himself back from the wars, ran in a special election for Congress against the candidate of the district leaders. With the help of his own personality, his name, and a host of young people who felt themselves excluded from the regular party clubs, Roosevelt won.

Second, on the East Side, in the "Silk Stocking" * Ninth Assembly District, a group of disenchanted young men and women, many of them veterans, seceded from that district's regular Democratic club to form an insurgent club, the Lexington Democratic Club, and to run candidates for district leader.

Third, emboldened by the success of the Roosevelt candidacy, his supporters sought to form a countywide, over-all organization of young, anti-organization Democrats for the purpose of electing a borough president—elected countywide to represent the county in one of the city's two legislative bodies, the Board of Estimate— and other officials. This group called itself the Fair Deal Democrats.

Of these three outbursts, the first was quickly accepted by the district leaders, who welcomed Roosevelt back into the bosom of the party as its newest and most exciting congressman. The third outburst was demolished by a combination of ineptitude within the Fair Deal Democrats and shrewdness in their or-

* Basically Park Avenue, Madison Avenue, Fifth Avenue, and Lexington Avenue, from about Fiftieth Street to Ninety-sixth Street, although from time to time the lines have been changed. This, however, is the heart of the silk-stocking district.

ganization opponents. The Fair Deal Democrats expired as rapidly as they were born.

Only the second outburst—the Lexington Democratic Club—survived. In 1949 it lost a primary election to elect Democratic district leaders in the Ninth Assembly District South, but by 1953 it had won the leadership in the entire Ninth Assembly District.

The Lexington Club laid the groundwork for the so-called reform movement, which in 1961 destroyed the old Democratic Party structure and created the terminology which permeates any discussion of New York County politics during the ten years from 1955 to 1965.

When the Lexington Democratic Club was founded in 1949, it had created no ideology of "reform." Indeed, the label "reform" did not attach to the Lexington Democratic Club and its followers until later. At its inception, however, the Lexington Democrats made membership control of important decisions the cornerstone of their club. Club membership was open to all Democrats. Secret ballots at duly called membership meetings would elect club officers, nominate candidates for public and party office, and decide which, if any, candidates nominated on a higher level would be supported.

Financial reports were to be made to the club members periodically, and the treasurer's accounts would be audited annually. The district leaders would no longer decide party policy in the County Executive Committee on their own authority, but would first consult the club membership (or club Executive Committee if time were short) and vote as instructed.

Substantively, the Lexington Club had an interest in public issues and a willingness to discuss them which far exceeded the interest of most of the existing district clubs.

What would have happened to these notions in the absence of the 1952 Stevenson candidacy is impossible to tell. But that candidacy stimulated a host of young bystanders to become activists as they plunged into the political arena in an effort to elect their hero.

After the Stevenson defeat, a surprisingly large number of these newcomers remained active. New local clubs sprang up throughout the heartland of Stevenson supporters, the Middle East and West sides of Manhattan. To all of these Stevensonians, the Lexington Club's theories made sense. And so they organized on Lexington Club lines, and ran candidates against the established Democratic district leaders and clubs in their areas.

By 1955, three clubs in the thirty-three leadership districts—all of them composed mainly of Stevenson enthusiasts—had won their elections, and these clubs and their leaders were the official "regular" Democrats in their areas. A fourth club was sympathetic to the Lexington Club approach. By 1957, four of the thirty-three leadership districts and clubs accepted these principles, and the fifth remained sympathetic. Each of these five clubs had won a primary fight in which their leadership candidates had defeated incumbents who represented clubs that rejected these notions, looked to their leaders for guidance, and accepted a high degree of party discipline.

Throughout the period from 1949 to 1957, New York County had been headed by Carmine De Sapio, a district leader from the First Assembly District, South. Elected county leader by the other district leaders in 1949, he had varying reactions to the Lexington Democratic Club and its ilk. Initially, he fought the Lexington Club, but by 1953, recognizing he could not lick it, he decided to try to get along with it and its leaders and members as best he could. As late as 1957 his relations with the Lexingtonian clubs were not bad. Indeed, he was on reasonably close terms with two of the five clubs, moderate terms with two, and very unclear and hesitant terms with the latest arrival.

Not so with many of the other leaders. They saw in the Lexington Club and its bedfellows an ultimate threat to their own survival. Clubs that rejected the Lexington idea of club democracy called themselves "regulars." The new clubs were initially called "insurgents," and then, by 1958, "reformers."

In 1958 the wind that had been blowing since World War II reached hurricane force.

Within three years De Sapio was replaced as county leader and as a district leader; his close ally, Michael Prendergast, the state chairman, was removed. The new Democratic clubs became known as "reform clubs" and ultimately as "The Reform

Movement"; their number climbed from 4 clubs and leadership districts to 8 in 1959, and in 1961 to 15, with 30 leaders out of the 66 in the county, casting a little short of a majority of the votes on the County Executive Committee.

The reformers had a central fund-raising and campaign co-ordinating organization called "the Committee for Democratic Voters" (the CDV). This committee was founded in 1959 by Mrs. Franklin D. Roosevelt, former Senator Herbert H. Lehman, former Secretary of the Air Force Thomas K. Finletter, and the leadership of the Lexington Club. By 1962 the reform movement had elected one congressman out of four in New York County, one state senator out of six, and two assemblymen out of sixteen. How this all happened is a subject for a book in itself.

Why did Senator Herbert H. Lehman in 1958 forget his life-time of party regularity to turn on Carmine De Sapio after De Sapio directed the nomination of Frank S. Hogan for United States senator over the objections of Governor Averell Harriman at the Buffalo convention?

Why did De Sapio fail to start fighting for his political neck until it was already wrung?

Why did the public increasingly accept and credit the attacks upon De Sapio as a boss?

Why did regular clubs and leaders insist on resisting the in-evitable modernization of the party which the reformers pro-posed, until more and more of the regulars and their candidates were defeated by the voters?

Finally, why did the regulars blindly follow De Sapio until he was totally defeated in 1961?

The answers to these questions are undoubtedly fascinating. For the purposes of this narrative, however, the important point is that 1961 marked the end of the hurricane stirred up after World War II by the returning veterans, and the beginning of new and different competing forces—forces which have yet to exert their full power.

By January 1961 reform was riding a wave.

First, the new Democratic administration in Washington, while privately repelled by the theories, occasional arrogance, intractability, and growing self-righteousness of the reformers,

nevertheless made clear its dissatisfaction with the state chairman, Mike Prendergast, a close De Sapio ally, and cut New
York State (including De Sapio) off from federal patronage and
federal recognition.

Second, the 1960 primaries had dealt De Sapio serious blows
in key primaries in which reformers defeated his candidates.

Third, Robert F. Wagner, the incumbent Democratic mayor,
himself in some political trouble, faced an election campaign
for a third term, and recognized the liability of De Sapio's support. Indeed, he discovered through the magic of polling that
he could easily (according to the poll, anyway) win re-election
if he ran against De Sapio's candidate, but was in serious trouble
if he ran as De Sapio's candidate.

In addition, there had been a growing coolness between
De Sapio and Wagner since 1958, when Wagner, as well as
Harriman, had objected to the De Sapio-sponsored nomination
of Frank Hogan.

Fourth, the reform movement was growing rapidly, as *new*
newcomers to politics scented De Sapio's coming demise and
sought to defeat his district-leader supporters while the chances
were good. Almost half of New York County had reform clubs
either challenging incumbent regulars or already successful.

And so, in February 1961, Wagner declared war on De Sapio.
First, he engineered the selection of his candidate, Domestic
Relations Judge Edward R. Dudley, for Manhattan borough
president to fill a vacancy over De Sapio's choice. In doing so,
he demonstrated political muscle of which not even his admirers had suspected him capable.

Next, Wagner publicly denounced De Sapio and demanded
his resignation. He had previously cut off De Sapio's access to
city patronage.

And then Wagner began wooing the reform movement. Former
Senator Lehman, officially a member of the "Board of Advisers"
of the CDV but actually (with Mrs. Roosevelt and Thomas K.
Finletter), the leader of the reform movement, was happy not
only to welcome the mayor aboard but to make him the skipper.

Some of Lehman's supporters, however, were less happy. Coming from democratically operated clubs, they reflected much

rank-and-file unhappiness with Wagner's administration, with Wagner's earlier failure to embrace them, and the continued vitality of the earlier fusion idea.

Until late May, committees of reformers were, in fact, exploring the possibility of running a fusion candidate against Wagner.

But the wooing went on, and Wagner met again and again with Lehman and the reform district leaders. At the end of June, Wagner announced his candidacy with running mates of his own selection.

Not until late July was the organized reform movement, i.e., the Committee for Democratic Voters, formally, if only theoretically, behind him. Even then many reform clubs held back—refusing to circulate designating petitions for Wagner for fear of hurting their own local candidates. But by late August reformers scented victory on Wagner's bandwagon and rushed to get aboard.

And on primary day, September 5, 1961, the mayor won. On the ballot with him and also successful were twenty-eight * reform district leaders in Manhattan, the home of Tammany.

Reform had triumphed, and the bosses were dead!

* Two other reformers ran independently and won.

3. Reform Triumphant!

✿✿✿

Its Basic Objectives Achieved

But Its Trademark Captured

Its Proprietors Confounded and Then Confused

Its Followers Institutionalized

Because of the marginal voting system used in the Executive Committee of the Democratic County Committee, which allocated a full vote ($\frac{1}{2}$ to the male and $\frac{1}{2}$ to the female leader) to a full district, and $\frac{1}{3}$ or $\frac{1}{2}$ vote to assembly district parts where full districts were divided into parts, the reformers in September 1961 had $6\frac{5}{6}$ votes out of 16, or $1\frac{1}{6}$ short of a majority.*

The regulars had a majority of $1\frac{1}{6}$ votes.

At this point, the mayor had the power to dictate De Sapio's successor as county leader. For the regulars who had survived the primary were prepared—indeed, eager—to accept Wagner leadership, within reason. And it was expected that the reformers would likewise accept the mayor's guidance.

This was the context in which I was elected county leader.

The reasons were both simple and complicated.

The simple reasons were as follows:

First, my club was a reform club—one of the earliest of such clubs. And so my reform credentials were technically valid—

---

* These $6\frac{5}{6}$ votes were cast by 30 leaders—a gain of 14 over 1959. All but 9 of them were newcomers. Of the 16 incumbents in 1961, 5 retired from politics and 2 defected to the regulars and were replaced by reformers.

and as part of the "image" of a new Democratic Party the mayor wanted a reformer as county leader.

Second, I had been an early supporter of the mayor as a candidate for re-election, while almost all the other reformers were relative late-comers. As early as December 1960 I was committed to the notion that the mayor's participation in the drive to unseat De Sapio was essential. Almost every other reformer had resisted this notion until the bitter end.

Third, even before Wagner had declared his candidacy, my club had publicly declared its support of his candidacy.

Fourth, I had worked with the mayor over some period of time, and he trusted me.

Fifth, neither of the two declared candidates for county leader—J. Raymond Jones, the regular, and John Harrington, the official reform candidate—satisfied all of the conditions the mayor felt should be met.

And, finally, the regulars—who constituted a majority—viewed me with less suspicion and more confidence than they did any other reformer, since during my six years as district leader I had apparently earned a degree of respect from them.

And so after five months of delay, during which my candidacy slowly developed as a "compromise choice," I did nothing on its behalf but sit, wait, and keep my mouth shut.

Complicated reasons lay behind the reform opposition to my election. While my candidacy developed, opposition to it hardened, and then became bitter.

The reasons were complex:

First, although I had played a role in creating the Committee for Democratic Voters, neither I nor my club had ever formally affiliated with it. Indeed, we had on repeated occasions rejected such affiliation, despite great pressure upon us to join. We did so essentially because we believed that affiliation with a group publicly dedicated to the defeat of various other members of the Executive Committee, with whom we were committed to work as fellow members of that Executive Committee, would destroy any effectiveness we might possibly have as party leaders within party councils.

Secondly, I rejected the notion that in the performance of my duties as Democratic district leader of the Eighth Assembly District South, I should be controlled by any supra-district organization whether it was called the Society of Tammany or the CDV.

Third, I had publicly expressed my disagreement with other reformers from time to time—specifically in 1959 at a County Committee meeting of some 3,000 committeemen.* On that occasion, by some legerdemain which I have never understood, a reform committee called to plan reform floor strategy on the evening of the County Committee meeting ended up by nominating a slate of officers for the County Committee consisting of candidates for district leaderships who a week earlier had all been defeated by the enrolled voters of their districts. I did not see how I could vote for such a slate. I was angered, in addition, at what seemed to me to be deceptive tactics in calling the meeting that chose them. I said all this—and more—publicly that night. My speech became known as "the plague on both your houses" speech.

This public manifestation of disagreement with "the reform movement" reflected deeper divisions. I saw two years of party leadership ahead—until the next election for party leadership— during which the elected leaders either could try to work together and possibly achieve something or could start off by declaring war on each other and achieve nothing. I favored the first course and so did a substantial majority of the sixteen elected reform leaders. The CDV, containing a preponderance of reformers who had not yet been successful, preferred the second course.

In 1960, I compounded the situation by participating in and

---

* The County Committee consisted of three or four Democrats per election district. Until 1955, the county committeemen from each assembly district or assembly district part elected the district leaders. After 1955, the district leaders were elected directly by the enrolled Democrats in the district, but the county committeemen remained as the theoretical ultimate source of party power.

In fact, the County Committee delegated most of its power to the district leaders, under the party rules, and, except for a few vestigial functions, meets once every two years to elect officers and readopt or amend the party rules.

helping to organize a "third force" of liberal, reform-oriented Democrats who, like me, rejected the growing rigidity and intransigence of the CDV. This ultimately unsuccessful gambit, although it drew me closer to a middle-of-the-road approach to party reform (which ultimately prevailed), gave me a status similar to that enjoyed at Communist Party gatherings in the 1930's by liberals and radicals who rejected Stalinist Marxian theory. I was a deviationist, a more dangerous enemy than the regulars whom the CDV were basically out to destroy.

Finally, I had been a "loner" as far as CDV activists were concerned, a rejecter of "reform discipline," an advocate of the successful tactic of enlisting Mayor Wagner in reform ranks and thereby defeating De Sapio, and one of those who made it possible, so it seemed, for the mayor to steal the reform label and platform which the reformers had so laboriously invented and developed while the mayor sat on the sidelines.

The arguments against me were aptly summarized the night each reform candidate was asked to explain to his co-district leaders why he should be chosen. When I got through and all the speeches were over, one of the leaders said to me regretfully:

"Eddie, it's clear you are the best qualified for the job, but I can't vote for you."

"Why not?" I asked.

"Because of that speech you made in 1959 at the County Committee meeting."

I shrugged: if he felt I was the best qualified candidate, but he couldn't vote for me, it was, I thought, really his problem, not mine. Everybody had the same problem, and within the reform caucus (a misnomer, since its decisions were not binding) I lost gloriously.

To the reformers, internal discipline was regarded as the most important factor in the drive for reform—and I had rejected that notion. To me the prerequisite to success was not internal discipline, but rather a more politic flexibility, a less monolithic approach to the problem of achieving basic reform.

The extent of my rejection by my fellow reformers did not become clear until the very last moment. Months passed between the night the reform leaders voted for John Harrington

(late September 1961) and the day I was elected county
leader (March 2, 1962). In the interim, there was far more
flexibility in attitude than was publicly manifested. Several of
the reform leaders privately volunteered to act as my campaign
manager among the reformers, each undertaking to deliver between 2 and 3 votes. All they wanted to know from the mayor
was that the mayor really wanted me.

And so I arranged meetings for these putative campaign
managers with the mayor. A day or so after one of the meetings
an amused Robert F. Wagner called me.

"Some campaign managers you've got," he said.

"What happened?" I asked.

"One of them arrived with X, Y, and Z [naming three of my
nonadmirers] and the four of them spent an hour and a half
telling me why you shouldn't be county leader and why your
campaign manager should."

After that I left my campaign managing to Robert F. Wagner.

The regulars, in contrast to the reformers, however, had some
degree of confidence that I would not use my power to destroy
them. They quietly accepted the mayor's guidance.

And so, by a vote of 9⅔ (all regulars except me and my co-
leader) to 6⅓ (all the rest of the reformers), I became the
reform leader of an organization in which my support came from
the leaders against whom I had been fighting—the regulars—and
my opposition from my co-reformers who were united to a man
against me!

By then "reform" was seeking new meaning. The goal of
opening the clubs to all Democrats who wanted to join them
was largely won—and the few clubs and leaders that refused to
accept this, and other reform doctrines such as club democracy,
were soon defeated and replaced.

Their replacements were called regulars or reformers, depending solely on whether they formally affiliated with the Committee for Democratic Voters, by now the proprietor of the
reform trademark.

During the next 2¾ years, the regulars remained loyal to the
mayor (and to me, as *his* leader). The reformers were sometimes ready to support me or the mayor, or both. Sometimes

they were not willing to support either of us. Sometimes they
were united, sometimes divided. Throughout the period they
were seeking new ideological content for the label "reform," but
at the same time becoming unconsciously more "regular" in their
increasing disregard of securing democratic club decisions to
validate their positions, and in their increasing willingness to
"go along" with the mayor.

By late 1964, when I resigned as county leader, the distinction
still remained, in theory, but in fact it was blurred, indistinct,
only occasionally apparent, and neither side was any longer
monolithic. Indeed, the West Side reformers and the East Side
reformers were by now almost two separate groups. The "reform
movement," whose ideology in 1955 could be described as against
autocratic political leadership, seemed more and more against
political leadership of any kind.

And the regulars had divided into two groups—the "Uptown
group" consisted of leaders north of 110th Street, including
Harlem, East Harlem, Washington Heights, and Inwood, and
the "Downtown group" consisted of the Lower East Side and
Lower West Side leaders.

From what has been said, it is clear that the words "reform"
and "regular" had different meanings during the period covered
by these chapters. In the years before 1959 the term "reform"
was generally used to describe any insurgent candidate for
district leader whose club had a "Lexington-type" constitution
(membership control, open financial reports, control over the
leadership by the club's executive committee and membership). With this small-d democracy went a series of other
distinguishing marks: regular monthly meetings of the membership to hear speakers on subjects from air pollution to U.S.
foreign policy in Ghana, forums, countless committees made
up of members dealing with whatever problems they wanted
to deal with (mental health, art tours, United Nations hospitality,
problems of the aged), and a degree of self-righteousness.

These clubs asserted a doctrine of party discipline that
shocked the traditional Democratic Party worker—that discipline
flowed from the bottom up—that the leader followed the dictates
of the club—and that "the word" did not come down from the

top. This idea, more than anything else, shook and shocked the party establishment, in essential implication (though hardly in scale) much as the Protestant Reformation shook the Catholic Church. It is interesting, moreover, that most reform clubs in the pre-1959 period resembled in organization and in operation the organization and operation of Congregational-type churches. In contrast, the county leader's nickname was "the Bishop," and, like a bishop, he at times selected local district leaders and installed them in local regular clubs. When early reformers mixed with the then regulars, it was as if the Unitarian churches had suddenly become part of the Episcopal or Catholic churches.

The differences between the early reformers and the regulars were differences of cultural background, education, economic status, attitude—attitude about the function of politics and about leadership, and about organization and discipline and responsibility. There was, however, an additional highly significant difference between early reformers and regulars which made it possible for them to get along at least a little bit—the difference between youth and age. To a great extent, the reformers were young and the regulars older. And the difference in age made it possible for the early reformers to listen and learn, and for the regulars to talk and teach. As we learned, so we taught our strange doctrines. Some understanding was created, but never approval. Open warfare was not declared, except in a few isolated cases (of which I was once a victim).

This exploratory era came to an end in the period from 1959 to 1961—as the CDV led by Herbert H. Lehman gradually asserted control and dominion over most of the reformers and created "The Reform Movement" out of most of them. Hence the second wave of reform—a new generation, and a new rebellion. Until 1959, the four successful reform clubs in Manhattan had gradually accommodated themselves to the realities of political leadership. While adhering in principle to the ideal and forms of democratic control, the leaders increasingly exercised their own judgment in the County Executive Committee—and afterwards reported back to their clubs. Often they had instructions from their clubs on pending county business, often they did not. They realized—and so did their club executive committees and membership—that it was not always feasible, especially in nonlocal matters—to convene the clubs to pass upon each and every question.

The new wave of reformers were loud in their acceptance of the theory and practice we had spawned. At times they glorified it *ad absurdum*. They entered the new-wave rhetoric in an absolute fashion. Underneath their advocacy lay an important political calculation. In their view, the "reform" of the party was to be accomplished not by reforming the old-liners but by defeating them, each and every one. In the words of Mendelssohn's Elijah, "Take them down to Kishon's Brook and *there let them be slain!*"

Of the 8 leaders who constituted the reform bloc in the 66-member Executive Committee in 1959, only 2 were still in office after the 1961 primary—the author, and Alice Sachs from the Ninth Assembly District. All the rest had quit or, in two cases, moved on to greater rewards. It was in this situation that the new wave of reform arose—by now organized into a "reform movement."

The objectives of the new reformers were quite different from those of their predecessors, who had the same label. Where we pre-1959 reformers had emphasized club control, small-d democracy, functioning as part of the existing Democratic Party, and dealing with our regular counterparts as equals, the new reformers had other notions. For example, the separate Reform Democratic clubs and their leaders were organized into one entity—the CDV—and united decisions were taken through that one entity. Moreover, the notion that a democratically operated club was the essence of reform was dropped. Instead, affiliation with the CDV became the keystone of reform identity.

The objective of second-wave reform in New York County was simple, clean, and blunt: control, not by making alliances with regulars, but by defeating them. Indeed, "compromise" was a dirty word, "moderation" was a sin, and, as one of my good friends within the second-phase reform movement told me, "When I asked my co-reformers 'But what *do* we stand for?' I was told: 'For God's sake, never raise that question or we'll be up all night arguing, we'll get nowhere, and we'll fall apart.'"

Some may feel that this is an unfair characterization of the second-phase reformer. I don't think it is.

"But weren't they for ending court patronage?" No. A minority of them were, but a majority were not, and many sought it until the day I resigned.

"But weren't they for a nonpolitical judicial selection system?" No. A *different* minority of them were, but a majority were not, and almost all of them sought judicial nominations for their supporters until the end of my term as county leader. This includes the chairman of the CDV (who wanted such a nomination for himself *) and two others who would so endow their spouses.

"But weren't they against patronage?" No. Only one club out of fifteen—the Village Independent Democrats from Greenwich Village—was, and it *alone* of all the clubs neither sought patronage nor would participate in the process. While the VID used to drive me crazy with their notions about politics and government (and me), at least I had to respect the club and its leaders for their integrity. They meant privately what they said publicly.

I can honestly find no unifying ideological concept in the second wave of reform—not even the concept of a democratically operated club—other than the notion that out of unity comes strength and out of strength would ultimately come control.

For example, while the second-wave reformers voted against me to a man when I was elected county leader, so far as I have been able to ascertain only one club took a vote on the issue— and that club voted to support me! But its leaders disregarded the vote and followed the CDV line by voting against me.

As a result, the "reform movement" took on some of the aspects of the old Society of Tammany. Like the society it was a closed group, to which admission was a privilege and not a right—a nonparty group, which sought to control party affairs.

What about the term "regular"? It followed that the shift in the meaning of the label "reform" produced a corresponding shift in the meaning of the term "regular." Until 1961, "regular" meant adherence to the notion of party discipline—and, therefore, adherence to the county leader—which has been previously

---

* And ultimately got it, after I resigned.

described. After 1961, when the second wave of reformers arrived, "regular" became a looser and a looser term, eventually encompassing everyone—with the possible exception of the author (I tried to retain my credentials as a first-generation reformer)—who was not part of the "reform movement." Included among the "regulars" were some like Tom Lenane, whose first-rate Fifteenth Assembly District North Democratic organization adopted and enforced the Lexington Club constitution, lock, stock, and barrel. In my days as a reformer, that alone would have admitted Lenane to the group. But in the latter day of reform, he was fought by the reform movement and labeled "a regular."

If in the ensuing pages the author sounds like a regular from time to time, it is because in one sense I was a regular: I never joined the second-wave reform movement. If at times I sound like a reformer, it is because I believed myself to be one, though I was unwilling to trade one kind of discipline from the top, directed at the objective of maintaining political power—that of the Bishop—for another kind of summit discipline directed at acquiring power in the service of an ideological liberation whose content was imprecise. What is the point of trading one form of bossism for another?

For the most part, the terminology of "regular" and "reformer" is used in this book in the sense that the terms were used after the second wave of reform gave the words new and popular or, as trademark lawyers say, secondary meanings.

The Shift of Power to the Mayor

While all of this activity was occupying the internal political stage, there was a co-ordinate movement within the public sector to increase the power of the city's chief executive. As the power of the political leaders declined and that of the major public officeholder—the mayor—increased within the political sphere, a similar movement took place in the area of government power. New Yorkers, concerned with the apparent immobility of city government and concerned with its apparent inability to deal with and solve the city's problems as they arose, accepted the theory that the fault lay with the city charter, which unduly limited the mayor's power.

A new charter was enacted in 1961. It heaped power on the mayor—power which thereafter was principally used to raise salaries for city officials, to quietly approve projects thought necessary which had aroused public resistance, and to minimize the power of every other public officeholder. The result was to concentrate in the hands of one man—the mayor—more political and governmental power than was in the hands of any other American public officeholder with the exception of the President of the United States.

By 1965, therefore, the political leaders accorded all power to the mayor. The City Council, though it was trying to establish itself as an independent legislative body, remained a rubber stamp for the mayor. The Board of Estimate, a supervisory legislative body of seven men and one woman (including the mayor), set sail in the same boat (on any issue, the mayor could control the votes of six of the eight members, who together cast 16 of the 22 votes). Taken together, these facts meant that in the hands of one man rested almost all the political and governmental power in the city. Despite this concentration of power, the capacity of the city to deal with its problems as they arose was not improved; the backlog of unsolved problems was not diminished. Citizen unrest, which had looked to the removal of "the bosses" and the passage of a new charter with hope, was if anything more profound. Yet each step in this process of concentration—the destruction of bossism, the increase in the chief executive's power—was logical in light of the myths about government, about politics, about politicians which our post-Civil War, anti-urban, anti-immigrant, Protestant culture has inculcated in all of us. But, somehow, none of these steps solved the basic problem.

In 1965, the party and government leader, Robert F. Wagner, decided not to run for re-election as mayor. Since he had amassed a virtual personal monopoly of Democratic political power, his sudden decision to withdraw from the race left a political vacuum. Only a primary race could fill it. A primary was inevitable because the political monopoly that had sustained Wagner, had required by its very nature that no other Democratic Party personality flourish in any serious way in the city. Thus if the electorate was to find a Democrat to replace Wagner, there was no other way to find him than through the wasteful primary process.

Twelve years of Democratic Party control in a Democratic city should have produced several acknowledged leaders in addition to the retiring mayor. There should have been men whose qualities of leadership and length of experience would obviate the necessity of a primary even in a party divided between regulars and reformers. This was not the case because the party had long since surrendered control of its future in pursuit of one Democrat's career. In that pursuit, Robert F. Wagner came to dominate the entire local political spectrum, and permitted the party to crumble beneath him. This did not become apparent in public or external politics until his withdrawal from the 1965 mayoralty race. It had been apparent for some time in the internal politics of the party.

In the Wagnerian vacuum, the old-fashioned anti-political fusion movement rose phoenixlike from the past. Neither the new charter nor the Reform Democrats had solved the city's governmental problems. Perhaps a return to an older notion—fusion—would. Accordingly, a replica of a fusion ticket—one Republican, Congressman John Lindsay, for mayor, one Liberal, Professor Timothy Costello, for president of the City Council, and one Democrat, Milton Mollen, for comptroller, was put together. It represented, basically, an affiliation between two of the other three political parties in New York, the Republicans and the Liberals, in the hope that together, with a ticket headed by an attractive young man, and facing a divided, squabbling Democratic Party, they could do what each had failed to do alone: capture City Hall.

And so in 1965 politics in New York had arrived at this curious condition: after four years of reform triumphant, reform seemed defeated and disunited, and the good-government tradition was ready to return to its old home of anti-political, fusion-based good government.

4. The Political Competition for Purity

✳✳✳

The Other Political Parties in a Democratic Town

In New York City, every political party, including the Democratic Party, seeks to hold itself up as the Party of Purity. Since
the other three parties are rarely in power, they rarely have the
opportunity to demonstrate either purity or lack of it, but they
are free to talk purity.

And they do!

Except in a fusion year, none of the other parties—the Republican, Liberal, and Conservative parties—is a serious factor,
in the sense that none seriously seeks to obtain and exercise
political power for and by itself.

This axiom of New York City politics is no reflection upon the
leadership of the other parties. For that leadership is as skilled
in the arts of politics as the Democratic leadership, and therefore is realistic enough to accept the fact that all the parties
other than the Democratic Party are minority parties, and act
accordingly.

The Republican Party

The Republican Party leadership has repeatedly demonstrated
its natural political interest in winning the mayoralty, but the
rest of the party, dominated since World War II by upstate-
oriented leadership (Dewey and then Rockefeller) has been
unprepared to threaten its upstate base by making the govern-

mental moves that would give its New York City candidates the
material with which to win.

The examples are legion. Since World War II the Republican
formula for state aid to local education has awarded almost
twice as much to each child outside the city than to a child in
the city. Since the turn of the century, the formula for apportion-
ment of the state assembly and senate—a Republican con-
trivance that insured upstate Republican rural domination of the
state until the U.S. Supreme Court declared it unconstitutional—
has best demonstrated the Republican Party's anti-urban (and,
recently, suburban) bias: in 1964 one upstate district with only
about 14,000 residents had one assemblyman. A New York City
district with ten times the population had the same representation.

As a result, New York City citizens, correctly, do not trust
Republicans to do right by the city. Generations of discriminatory
treatment in taxes, state aid, representation, and a general anti-
urban bias have created deep-seated voter resistance to Republican candidates, and have made city-wide victory for even a
Republican personality boy a difficult objective and an unwelcome assignment.

Only when a Democratic administration becomes impossible
for the voters to swallow is there a chance for a Republican.
This was the case in 1965, but even in that year, the Republican
Party was unable to field a Republican ticket. Its candidate,
John Lindsay, was unwilling to run as a Republican, and a
makeshift Republican-Liberal-Democrat ticket was fielded in an
effort to eliminate the liabilities implicit in running in New
York as a Republican.

Normally, the city Republican Party concentrates upon local
legislative victories (a handful of congressmen, assemblymen
and state senators), and looks to the state government for its
political support.

Operationally, the Republican Party also differs from the
Democrats. The currents of change that hit the Democratic
Party in 1949 did not even brush the Republican Party until
1963. Even then, the air hardly moved strongly enough to

flicker the curtains in an open window. Until 1965, the Republicans still elected their district leaders by the indirect system which, in the Democratic Party in 1965, survived in Bronx County and nowhere else. In 1963, the Republican Party began to adopt direct-election rules for 1965, but with fear and trepidation.

Nor have the Republicans attracted the energy of the vigorous and energetic post–World War II generations. I used to kid my Republican counterpart about his soft life and threaten to send over a contingent or two of reformers to stir things up. "Now, Eddie—now, Eddie," he would say, "not that—not that."

The Liberal Party

Far more important to the Democratic Party is the Liberal Party. It is an outgrowth of the American Labor Party, which was created in 1936 at President Roosevelt's instance to provide Democrats with a non-Republican line on which to support Fiorello La Guardia, a fusion, nominally Republican mayor. The American Labor Party was a political success. It was a home for anti-Tammany Democrats, liberals, intellectuals, labor groups, left-wingers, and, later, Communists who felt unwelcome in the regular Democratic Party organization dominated by the Society of Tammany.

In 1944, the division between anti-Communists and Communists within the ALP had become so sharp that the party blew apart. The anti-Communists left the ALP and formed the Liberal Party. In less than ten years the ALP was dead.

The Liberal Party was hailed as a great step forward. Led by a mixture of intellectuals (Adolf A. Berle, William Kirkpatrick, Paul Hays) and labor leaders (David Dubinsky, Alex Rose) it steadily forged ahead. With an enrollment (or membership) one-quarter to one-fifth the size of its vote, it grew in power and respectability. In 1965 its enrollment in the city was a nominal 62,000, but with duplications and deaths and removals, not reflected in the registration rolls, it was closer to 55,000. Its

1961 vote, on a slightly higher enrollment, was 211,000. Many enrolled Democrats, independents, and Republicans vote on the Liberal Party line to demonstrate both their support of Democratic candidates and their rejection of the Democratic party organization.

In 1951, the Liberal Party won a city-wide election for president of the City Council; but in 1953, emboldened by its 1951 success, it ran the same candidate (a registered Democrat, Rudolph Halley) for mayor—and lost. Meanwhile, the Democratic Party was opened to the new mood of reform, and young idealists who in other days might well have turned to the Liberal Party, to demonstrate their distaste for old Democratic organization politics, piled into the Democratic Party and into the reform movement—intent upon changing the old from within, not upon defeating it from the outside.

The birth of the reform attitude—internal rather than external reform—substantially limited the Liberal Party's future. Instead of becoming an independent party capable of electing its own candidates, which had seemed possible in 1951 and 1953, it has become a tail for someone else's kite. For, as the Democratic Party found itself teeming with noisy, youthful, idealistic reformers, the Liberal Party continued on its well-planned, middle-aged, and ordered way, its enrollment shrinking, its leadership aging, its cadre of captains disappearing, and its few local clubs fossilizing.

By 1965, the Liberal Party no longer had district clubs, district leaders, or election-district captains in most parts of New York City—let alone the rest of the state. Nevertheless, while its attractiveness for new young blood was minimal, it still managed to draw a fair number of Democratic votes on election day, as well as those of independents and Republicans, but even the number of switching voters was diminishing. Indeed, in 1960 the Liberals drew over 400,000 votes for the Kennedy ticket—about the margin of the Kennedy victory in New York State. By 1964 its state-wide vote, in an election won by Johnson by over 2½ million votes, was only 350,000. And this poor result was achieved despite an intensive and expensive advertising campaign urging the voters to cast their ballots for Johnson and Humphrey on the Liberal, as distinguished from the Democratic, line.

Such marked decline aside, the Liberal Party is an important factor, especially in close elections. The Liberal nomination, however, is no longer uniformly regarded by voters as a stamp of purity upon, and badge of respectability for, a Democratic or Republican candidate. The reason for this skepticism is that voters aren't stupid. Since Liberal endorsements have increasingly been the obvious product of factors other than the purity and quality of candidates, the voters have come to realize it. To stay alive as a "balance of power," the power must be occasionally exercised for the benefit of Republicans in districts where it makes a difference. So on the local level the Liberals endorse a Republican or two, or sometimes run a Liberal Party wheel-horse in order to neutralize votes in a situation where if the Democrat were endorsed, the Liberal line would bring victory.

The process is routine practical politics and worth illustrating. In 1964, in the Sixth Assembly District in Manhattan, whose Republican district leader was also the Republican county leader, the Liberals ran their own candidate and pulled enough votes away from the Democratic candidate to assure the re-election of a Republican assemblyman of rather conservative stripe—a man who supported Barry Goldwater! The reason was not ideological; it was practical politics. The Liberal Party needs special legislation in Albany to stay alive as a state-wide party; it needs Republican as well as Democratic friends and it does what is necessary to sustain political friendships.

On the city level, occasionally it runs its own candidate, as it did in 1953, or joins up with the Republicans, as it did in 1965 in endorsing John Lindsay for mayor. But usually it joins Democrats, and on the state level it has yet to endorse a Republican.

Under the surface, the Liberal Party functions as the most efficient patronage-securing and -dispensing political party in New York City. This is because it bases its patronage requests and demands upon the proportion of the votes cast on its line. Since it may draw as many as four or five times as many voters as members, it finds it easier to satisfy the patronage demands of its relatively few party members. Five to one, or even three to one is a nice margin to operate on and the Liberal Party activists are well cared for.

Finally, the Liberal Party still provides a safe escape and refuge for anti-organization Democrats who prefer the badge of purity to the sword of internecine battle. It holds itself up as—and, in fact, is to some extent—an external restraint upon abuses of power within the Democratic Party.

As a result of the existence of the Liberal Party, the liberal wing of the Democratic Party finds itself weakened by the absence, *within party councils,* of those who should be making their voices heard within the party *before decisions are made* instead of afterwards. The Liberals are outside the Democratic Party and their absence creates a conservative imbalance within the Democratic Party, with the result that the party sometimes produces a candidate or program that is unpalatable to the liberal wing of the Democrats as well as to the Liberals.

The Liberal Party now exists in large part as a monument to the past, to the days when there was no way in which the Democratic Party could be revitalized because of the control exercised over it by the Society of Tammany. It exists in large part to satisfy the patronage demands of its small group of activists. It exists for what I call the "1930's liberals"—liberals who are still fighting the liberal battles of that era. It exists because its members, like the members of any organization, pride themselves on its past achievements. And it exists because its experienced leadership knows how to keep it alive.

Sooner or later, its leadership will change and its membership will, one hopes, realize that the cause for the creation of the Liberal Party in the first place—the nature of the Democratic party organization from the 1860's to the late 1930's—has been dealt with within the Democratic Party. The sooner that day comes, the better served will be the objectives the Liberal Party was created to achieve and has purported to serve. Indeed, it is high time for the Liberal Party members to return to their ideological home—the Democratic Party—and to lend a hand in the completion of that party's transition into a modern political institution.

It is indeed ironic that the divorce between the Society of Tammany and the Democratic Party, and the formation of the Liberal Party—which was basically protesting the Tammany-Democratic marriage—both took place in the same year.

The Conservative Party

The latest addition to New York's political parties is the Conservative Party, formed in 1962. It corresponds—at the opposite end of the political spectrum—to the Liberal Party in that it consists of conservatives who regard the Republican Party as far too liberal for conservative tastes. Like the Liberal Party vis-à-vis the Democratic Party, it seeks to affect Republican Party decisions by the threat of withholding conservative Republican votes—either by running a Conservative candidate to draw off Republican votes or by boycotting the election.

Its existence reflects the longstanding unhappiness of conservatives with the New York Republican Party's attempt to accommodate itself to the twentieth century. And as the New York Republican Party came more and more to represent the liberal wing of the Republican Party, its conservative members, firmly anchored to the laissez-faire doctrines of 1890 Republicanism, became more and more disenchanted. Sometimes they stayed home, rather than vote for Republican "apostates" (as they considered them) such as Tom Dewey ("that well-known radical") or Nelson Rockefeller ("We'll show him he can't win without us") or Senator Jacob Javits ("He's really a Democrat in disguise, and we'll pull enough conservative votes away to let the Democrats win").

These attitudes began to take political expression in the 1957 mayoral election, when Vito Battista—an echo of the grand little manner but not the substance of La Guardia—in an election that was hopeless for the Republicans anyway, created his own Taxpayers Party and ran for mayor. About 70,000 protesting conservatives preferred to throw their votes away on Battista than on the Republican candidate (who lost by over 900,000 votes), Bob Christenberry—then a hotel man, but later New York's amiable Postmaster.

And then came the Conservative upsurge. In other states, followers of William F. Buckley, Jr., *The National Review,* Barry Goldwater, and the John Birch Society went to work on the flabby Republican Party structure. In New York, however, the Republican Party was not flabby, and under Dewey's and Rockefeller's rigid control, the right-wing fringe got nowhere. This was so because there was no political vacuum within the Republican Party for conservatives to fill. Hence, the independent party gambit. Launched in 1962's gubernatorial election in order to steer hundreds of thousands of Republican votes away from Rockefeller, the Conservative Party laid an egg. Its statewide total was 150,000 votes—hardly enough to represent a significant political party in a state of almost 18,000,000 inhabitants.

Meanwhile, school integration problems in New York City and the negative response of many voters to the so-called "busing" program (in which school district lines were redrawn in a very modest number of cases so as to eliminate a handful of wholly segregated school districts), gave a new impetus to conservative organizations. Parents and Taxpayers (PAT) was created and became the focal point of conservative resistance to the school integration program and to "busing."

Many of the leaders of this organization were childless, but they were vocal. Mrs. Rosemary Gunning, a childless, motherly-looking type, became as familiar a face on television as her counterpart, public school boycotter the Rev. Milton A. Galamison (who was a parent, but his child attended a private school).

By 1964, the PAT-conservative-Taxpayers types found the Conservative Party to be their ideological home. Their hero, Barry Goldwater, had won the Republican nomination for President, over the stubborn resistance of New York's Republican Governor Rockefeller and the liberal New York Republican Party.

Sensing an opportunity to make headway with conservative Republicans, the Conservatives nominated Goldwater too, and prepared to run him at the head of their ticket (nominating with him some certified Conservative candidates for Senate and

House). If they had had their way, the Conservatives would have pulled a high percentage of Goldwater voters onto the Conservative line, lured by the Goldwater name and a slate of Conservative candidates who, unlike most Republican candidates, really supported the Arizonian. But the plan was thwarted by a maneuver which should commend itself to the Democratic Party in its relations with the Liberal Party. Under the Electoral College system specified in the Constitution, voters do not vote for candidates for President and Vice-President at all. They actually vote for a slate of electors, whether the names of the electors appear on the ballot or not, committed to vote for particular candidates for President and Vice-President. The *electors* with the highest number of votes are elected. They in turn meet to vote for *their* candidates for President and Vice-President six weeks after election day.

The Democratic and Liberal Parties have run the same 41 or 43 electors for years. It is basically a group of Democrats with a handful of Liberals. Since the same group is running on both tickets, the combined Democratic and Liberal vote "for President and Vice-President" is totaled, and the electors each receive the combined total. The Conservatives proposed essentially the same arrangement to the Republicans: all the Conservatives wanted was permission to run the Republican electors on the Conservative line as well as the Republican line, so that the Goldwater electors would receive the total of the combined Republican and Conservative vote. Without such consent the Conservatives could run their own slate of electors for Goldwater. But this would only hurt Goldwater, since two different slates of electors would divide the Goldwater vote between them, and neither slate of electors could possibly win.

The Republicans refused.

The Conservatives countered with the threat to name Clare Boothe Luce as a candidate for the U.S. Senate against incumbent Republican Senator Kenneth Keating, thus insuring his defeat.

The Republicans still refused—threatening to withdraw Republican support of Goldwater completely by having the Republican electors refuse to vote for him.

And the Conservatives gave in. They ran *no* candidate for President, and their state-wide impact was minimal.

In taking this course, the Republican Party leadership was undoubtedly affected by the results of the Democratic-Liberal alliance on Presidential candidates in 1948 and thereafter, which enabled the Liberal Party to build and maintain itself at the expense of the Democratic Party by capturing otherwise Democratic votes—and later, as in 1965, to attempt to deliver those votes (or those it could hold) to the Democrats' mayoral opponent, Republican Congressman John Lindsay.

In 1965, the Conservative Party reverted to its "spoiler" role by nominating a uniquely unbalanced city-wide ticket—all Conservatives and all Irish—headed by William Buckley, editor of the conservative *National Review,* and including Mrs. Gunning of PAT. Like the Liberal Party, it hoped to show that its votes constituted the balance of power in city elections, and therefore that its views should be recognized and given weight by the Republicans. Like the Liberal Party, it hoped to take advantage of the anti-political good-government tradition in New York City, by taking its supporters out of the Republican Party and creating an independent political party to protect their interests.

Its vote did not represent the balance of power. Lindsay won without it.*

The prognosis for close Republican-Conservative relations is accordingly not very promising. And the prognosis for the Conservative Party achieving its objective of becoming a Conservative balance of power, like the Liberal Party, is doubtful at best.

* Probably the Conservatives drew more Democratic votes than Republican ones, thus possibly *electing* Lindsay rather than defeating him.

Part Two

The Politician
in His Own Fiefdom

Introduction to Part Two

While it is true that the essential function of a politician is to make decisions and to form alliances in order to make the decisions effective, no political leader is in a position to be a participant in the performance of this function unless he is prepared to devote an inordinate amount of time to three basic activities in his own local area—his club, his constituents, and his campaign machinery. These three basic areas of activity will consume anywhere from 66 to 99 percent of the leader's time—depending upon how effective he is in delegating his authority and how efficient in staying on top of his remarkably miscellaneous job. Attention to these duties, staying close to "his people" is essential if the political leader is to maintain the base from which he can move out to promote candidacies and policies and to make alliances. Unless these three activities are properly handled, politicians from other areas will look with amusement, skepticism, or contempt at his proposals.

These activities are never exotic. They involve prosaic, time-consuming chores, all of which must be handled with good will, patience, and meticulous care. Anyone who does not experience such activity is not a real politician; he is a caricature—a mechanical and theoretical, rather than a genuine, political animal.

During a period of twelve years, I learned how to run a club, deal with constituents, and supervise campaigns. My telephone number, never unlisted, was well known. I spent every Monday and Thursday night—with some absences towards the end—at the headquarters of the New Democratic Club, first an insurgent Democratic organization and then the Regular Democratic organization of the Eighth Assembly District South in Manhattan. In addition, usually at least one other night a week was similarly occupied. During campaigns I put in four to five nights a week plus parts of Saturday and Sunday.

The club was my base, my political home, the place where I met people who were or became political associates. A conservative estimate of the time spent on this local political organization for a twelve-year period is a minimum of ten and as many as thirty hours a week—until I became county leader and assumed other responsibilities. Even then I remained as district leader (as I had to be eligible to serve as county leader) and tried to appear at least one night a week at my club.

What is all this time spent doing? Mostly the wholly unexciting detail of running an organization and making friends for it. No earth-shaking decisions are made, no headlines are created, no misconduct is plotted. Instead, the leader acts as chief executive of a hodgepodge volunteer enterprise: he meets, helps, comforts, and befriends his constituents; and he plans, oversees, and directs every party campaign in his area.

And he relies principally upon his captains to do the political job. They are his troops, his people, his infantry. My wife has always been my best captain. I have asked her to write about what a captain does before I try to explain the leader's role.

5 * The Captain in the Election District

by Frances H. Costikyan

☆☆☆ ☆☆☆ ☆☆☆ ☆☆☆ ☆☆☆ ☆☆☆ ☆☆☆ ☆☆☆ ☆☆☆ ☆☆☆ ☆☆☆ ☆☆☆ ☆☆☆ ☆☆☆ ☆☆☆ ☆☆☆ ☆

When a member of one of the new Democratic clubs in New York City is appointed a district captain by his club's campaign manager, usually the first view he has of his district is a pack of three-by-five index cards containing the names and addresses of the voters for whom he is to be responsible. As he shuffles through the cards, experimenting with pronunciations for these names of strangers, the captain himself is not at all sure he wants the job. He takes his first walk around his new district with map in hand, wondering "who lives here?"

In the old Tammany days, a political captaincy was a much-prized honor. It was conferred on a club member only after long years of service in the clubhouse. The old-line captain had probably grown up in the district assigned to him, or at least had grown up in the area and was familiar with the sort of people who lived there. Such a captain became a figure of respect in his district (or else he didn't keep the job) and would build up a following among his voters loyal to both his party, his leader, and to him. Ultimately several hundred people would follow his direction on election day, and vote for which-ever candidates he told them to.

When we were new in politics, it was this phenomenon of the "regular" captains that seemed to us the most reprehensible. They controlled the vote. After we had been in politics for some time, those of us who were captains and who had gotten to know our districts well, who were liked and trusted by our voters, discovered that we too could control a goodly number of votes. In fact, many voters did not want to be bothered with long

57

explanations and arguments. Time and time again we would be told, "If you're for him, it's okay with me."

Whether we liked it or not, one of the "reforms" we had brought to our district was that instead of the voters taking the word of men and women they had known all their lives, they now voted on the recommendations of comparative strangers.

This extraordinary relationship of trust between people who scarcely know each other is fundamental to the reform movement of the 1950's and 60's in Manhattan. It is primarily in the Manhattan districts where there is most residential movement, where nearly everyone is a stranger, that the new captains and the new clubs have been able to win the leadership in the Democratic Party. On the East Side, the old six-story walk-up buildings are coming down to make way for the twenty-story luxury apartment buildings; on the West Side, middle-class voters are on their way to the suburban dream house or the East Side duplex in the sky. One of the roots of our reform movement is its rootlessness.* Perhaps this is partially responsible for the lack of pragmatic reality, or even any positive definable goal for the reform movement.

The so-called reform captain is not firmly tied to politics or to his party. Unlike the traditional captain, he expects no tangible rewards for his efforts. What is more, he can give few tangible rewards to his constituents. Generally he is not looking for a job in government, although some do develop a deeper fascination for public service and go on to take positions in government. When they do they find themselves at odds with many of their fellow reform-club members who consider all governmental jobs "patronage" and thus "evil." † The modern welfare state, with

---

* Theodore White notes this developing pattern of political action in *The Making of a President, 1964,* when he points out that it was the influence of strangers ringing the doorbells of the lonely newcomers in California that decided the Republican primary of 1964 in favor of Barry Goldwater.

† It has always seemed to me self-defeating for us reformers to hope to reform government while simultaneously believing that putting our people in government guaranteed corruption. Elections supply less than 10 percent of those who work in government, civil service another 80 percent. If we are seriously interested in improving government, we *must* be able to urge the selection of people whom we regard and trust to the remaining 10 percent, which are appointive positions.

its care and concern for the less-advantaged citizen, has robbed the captain of much of his traditional function in the community. Instead of finding jobs for "his people" and helping them out in time of trouble, the captain's function has been reduced to steering his constituents through the maze of government bureaus to the appropriate agency.

Just as the reform captain has few really powerful pressures to tie him to politics as a profession, he has almost no compelling ties to his party. Party loyalty per se is considered a bad thing, and he is often indiscriminant in his use of his ability to "sit this one out" when he disagrees with party decision, or even join the opposition—as witness the large number of reform "Democrats for Lindsay" in the 1965 mayoral election campaign. It is hardly necessary to point out that such an attitude does not build a strong party. True, most reformers do not want a strong party, they just want effective government. What they miss is the vital connection between effective government and strong party leadership backed by a strong organization.

A Modern Political Captain's Function

The new function of the political captain is to *educate* his voters and to get the greatest possible vote for his candidates and party. He must explain the whole system of primary elections, and acquaint the residents of his district with the names and histories of their local officeholders. New York City is so vast, and the newspapers are so busy with "big news," that there is seldom space to mention state assemblymen and senators, city councilmen, and city-court judges. In addition, our citizens come from all over the nation and world, and are accustomed to a wide variety of political systems.

The captain must work to build up the registration for his party, get valid signatures on petitions to get his party's candidates on the ballot, prepare his voters for the election, and then see to it that they get to the polls.

Organizing to Canvass

How does the modern captain go about doing this?

When I was first given my district on East Forty-sixth Street in Manhattan, in the spring of 1953, I was handed my batch of cards listing the Democratic voters and a long green petition. On the petition were the names of the Democratic county committeemen pledged to our candidates for district leader (district leaders were then still elected indirectly by the county committeemen). I was to get signatures on this petition from at least 5 percent of the enrolled Democrats in my district, so that my county committeemen would be eligible to appear on the primary ballot for the primary election in September.

The cards were in alphabetical order. They had been made up from the voters list bought from the Board of Elections for eight dollars a copy. These lists are made up each year, and contain the names of all registered voters, their addresses, and party preference if they have indicated any on their registration.

After looking through the cards for several minutes, hunting for names of people I might know (my district included the block on which I and my husband had been living for the previous three years), I started sorting the cards by buildings—all of 246 East Forty-sixth Street together, for example.

Later I learned to arrange the cards within each building by apartment numbers. At the top of the pack would be the top-floor apartments, then the next floor down, and so on, all the way down to the first floor. When I canvassed a building, I would climb to the top floor and work my way down, peeling the cards off from the pack as I descended, and writing little notes on them as I went along: "seems friendly," "definitely against us," "likes cats," "maybe." As the years went by, the information on these cards began to pile up: "signed petition, 1953," "voted primary, 1954," "likes Ike, 1956, but maybe we can hold." By then, though, the notes were really not necessary to me. The names on the cards were no longer the names of strangers. I was more familiar with each voter's political attitudes than with those of my own social acquaintances.

What does a political captain have to say when he rings the doorbell?

Each captain develops his style out of the deepest resources of his personality. I am a little more enthusiastic and wide-eyed when on the campaign trail than in real life. I dislike taking the new young captains out with me for a training mission, for I am shy about having them see me in the captain's role. You must be charming, and firm, without appearing forward. You want the voters to remember both you and your candidates, since some will come to the polls out of a developing loyalty to their captain. You must be well informed on your candidates and issues, and articulate in defining them, for you are always "on" when you are canvassing. You never have the slightest notion what question you will be asked, and you have to learn how to stick to your principles, but not belligerently—you must know how to guide your voter gently off an issue that is troublesome and on to something you can both agree on.

I remember one of my most loyal and faithful voters, a woman who was enthusiastic about our program for reforming the Democratic Party but was even more concerned with the fate of the city's pigeons. In the primary fight of 1961, she was extremely resistant to the whole Robert Wagner slate because his running mate, City Council President Paul Screvane, had come out in favor of a program that would endanger the flocks of pigeons overcrowding the City Hall area.

We trod delicately around this problem on my first visit of the year. I obtained her signature on the petition for the Wagner slate on the basis that this was just to get these people on the ballot, so they could be voted on in the election, which was the only fair, American way. Later, when I called on her just before primary day, she was still pretty annoyed at Mr. Wagner for picking Mr. Screvane. But she compromised by agreeing to vote for all the ticket but Paul Screvane. This I am sure she did in part out of her friendship for me.

The district captain is in a unique spot to hear from the voters themselves what it is that makes them finally decide their choices. Those of us who are captains in East Manhattan are especially privileged to watch this decision-making process because a majority of our voters do not vote a straight party ticket.

They follow the election closely. From tenement to penthouse they are remarkably aware of the issues developed during any given campaign.

But in the last analysis, it seems to me, they vote on the basis of a visceral reaction to the candidate as they feel his personality, the personalities of his supporters, and the general mood of the campaign as the press (I include radio and TV here) has presented it to them.

By a week before the election, most of them have decided whom they like and don't like, and no amount of arguing will change them. Your only hope is to save the vote for someone lower down the ticket, or obscurely situated in the middle of the ticket, like a judge—though, strange as it may seem, an attitude towards the various judges usually filters through too, based, in part, on the Citizens Union recommendations, on the newspaper recommendations, and various outlets of public support.

But our voters almost never vote on the basis of a single issue or even several issues, be they economic, ethnic, or what you will. The issues are important only in the way in which they contribute to the whole pattern of the campaign. In the end there is an almost mystical meeting between voter and candidate. The voter can vote for a candidate about whom he has doubts, but not for one he just plain doesn't like.

Techniques in a General Election

In general elections the problem of canvassing for an entire ticket is a most difficult one. So often the voter is violently opposed to one particular candidate, which tends to turn him against the whole Democratic Party. The captain must try to save his vote for as many Democrats as possible.

In the good old days, I've been told, the captains tended to concentrate on the local candidates, but as most of us who belong to the newer clubs joined out of an identification with the Democratic Party on the national and state (occasionally city) level, we are usually most at home when talking of the Presidential, senatorial, and congressional candidates.

The technique is to start at the top of the ticket and move down in the discussion. If the year was like 1956, when almost all the Democrats in our district were for Ike, we would probe just a little farther to see if some loyalty could be found to save the vote, and then quickly slide on to the next candidate, the next and the next. Sometimes out of sheer exasperation the voter would agree to come back to the party for the assembly candidate, perhaps just to shut the captain up and show his friendship (and his independence) at the same time.

When canvassing Republicans in a general election, the captain is more inclined to start from the bottom of the ticket. He must open with a remark such as, "I know you are a Republican, and I'm sure you know as much, or more about the national (or state) issues as I do, but I thought you might be interested in hearing about some of our local candidates. It is so hard to get information about these people in the newspapers, and you never see them on TV." That, plus a sort of cheerful, wistful smile usually whets the curiosity, and the captain is invited in to sit down for a chat.

One year my co-captain, Aileen Schwartz, and I switched enough votes for our assemblyman this way to win a district which had had a deficit of sixty votes for the Democratic assemblyman, and to turn the deficit into a sixty-vote plurality. Unfortunately, things didn't go as well in the rest of the assembly district—our candidate lost anyway.

Techniques in a Primary Election

In a primary campaign, when calling on a voter for the first time, the captain frequently becomes a political science teacher. Often it is necessary to explain what a primary is—in New York State, the system whereby the enrolled voters of a political party elect their party officials, nominate many of their public office-holders, and elect delegates to political and judicial conventions.

The petition system must also be explained, for many voters come from other states with other methods. And then, finally, the captain gets to talking about the candidates he is working for.

After the first couple of nights of campaigning, I usually work out two main lectures. One short, snappy, and appealing to the voter's devotion to the democratic system and his eagerness to do his part to keep it working. This may sound a little like Fourth-of-July patriotism, but I believe in what I am saying, and have found most voters are also excited by this one great adventure all Americans share—the right to choose our elected leaders. Then, for those voters in whom I detect an interest in what I am doing, who ask questions about the club, and who seem likely prospects either as club members or possibly even workers, I have a much longer, fuller spiel. Sometimes I may not get a co-worker with the "long talk," but I usually do get a voter who will actually get himself to the polls and will stick with me through the years.

The trick is to try and size up the person and decide whether he is worth a half an hour, or whether it would be better to see three other people in the same amount of time. The hour of the evening makes a difference too. If it is 9:15 and you are tired and not too much in the mood to go through it all at the door of another stranger that night, you are much more inclined to expand on your topic. Usually you are also offered a drink. I make it a point never to drink liquor while canvassing, but I've had a lot of lemonade and coke and a lot of good political talk on a hot August night.

Adventures I Remember

To canvass in New York City in the middle East Side is to live the Arabian nights. You never know when an apartment door opens what adventure waits, or what will be demanded of you as a canvasser.

During our registration drive in 1956, when we made a complete canvass of our district apartment by apartment, hunting for fallen away Democrats as well as new voters, I remember being invited into a tenement apartment by a tall, gorgeous, sweet-smiling young Negro girl who looked about seventeen. In her dimly lit living room there was a black-and-white Picasso print on the wall, and a golden baby played on a zebra-striped rug in front of a make-believe fireplace, which sent red shadows dancing over the walls from a piece of cellophane revolving on a lighted spit. Who was she? I never found her again.

In another walk-up I found three young men in khaki shorts, sitting literally on orange crates, who invited me in to share their argument on Kafka.

Once, after climbing a particularly rickety pair of stairs on Second Avenue where the banisters seemed slick with grease, I entered a brilliantly lit kitchen. The yellow linoleum on the floor sparkled, and the refrigerator shone. Three jolly little children clustered about their smiling mother and father. Only the father spoke English, but he listened seriously to my talk of reforming the Democratic Party and the need for new leadership. He came to the polls on election day without being "pulled."

And late one evening in a dingy, rent-controlled, eight-story elevator building, a door opened on an apartment that looked like a black-white-and-gold Venetian palace interior. I was greeted at the door by a heavy-set woman in a white crepe dress and a startling head of orange-red hair.

She listened to me explain petitions and the fact that since she was a registered Democrat she was eligible to sign our petition and to vote in the primary, and when I was done she called out "What do you think?" It was then I first noticed the top of a man's head visible above the back of a white velvet armchair that stood with its back to me. A swarthy arm appeared holding a cigar and, as the ashes were flicked into a crystal ashtray, a voice replied, "Sure, sign it!"

We went through the awkward ceremony of signing. Ball-point pens don't write on paper held up against a wall, so I usually carry my petitions on a clip board. Since the petition is much longer than the clip board, all sorts of folding motions have to be gone through as the petition and board are handed to the voter. Also, it is necessary that he sign his name precisely as it appears in the Registration Book (with or without middle initial, for example) and that words like *East* and *Street* be written out in the address; so the captain is in the uncomfortable position of having to tell an adult how to write his name and address.

When my hostess and I had finished, I glanced at my card and noticed there were two names listed here, obviously a man and wife. I made a halfhearted inquiring gesture in the direction of the chair. The red head shook just perceptibly. We were two women who understood about husbands, and I said a warm but quick good-bye. The bubbly young couple across the hall asked me if I had tried their neighbor. They were slightly awed when I said I had. He was reputed to be a member of the "Mafia."

But mostly there were the lonely ones: the old couple who never went down to the street and were glad of the company of a stranger; the mother whose children were asleep and whose husband worked nights; the old widows whose children came home only to borrow money.

In all my twelve years of canvassing I never knew a moment of personal concern. To be sure, I never canvassed the disintegrating rooming houses at night. Almost everyone was friendly in the daytime. Sometimes the door would be shut in my face on the first visit (sometimes I wrote angry letters to those who a quick glance had convinced me really ought to listen, and invariably they did later), but usually by the second visit mine would be a familiar face and we could talk.

Working Districts Other than Your Own

Sometimes a veteran captain is asked to go to work for a specific campaign in a district other than his own. The Lexington Club sent over several of its most experienced captains to help my husband in his first campaign for district leader in 1955. They came in and worked for about three weeks, and got to know their assigned areas almost as well as they knew their home districts.

Several of the leaders south of us sent in captains to work against us in the primary election of 1957. But these gentlemen arrived on primary day itself. None of the names on their lists

were familiar to them. They frightened us at first. They were
bigger than we were. We were not sure enough of ourselves to
know what they could do to our vote. But they ended up by
helping us, though we could not know this at the time, because
they pulled more Democrats to the polls—most of whom turned
out to be for us. I've always thought that some of the enrolled
Democrats they bullied to the polls may have voted for us for
no other reason than to revenge themselves on the heavy-
handed strangers.

In 1965 I came home from the country the first week in
August to help my co-captain, Aileen Schwartz, qualify our
Sutton Place district—the district to which I had been assigned
after we had moved to Fifty-third Street. It took us one evening,
working separately, to round up enough old friends in our
respective giant apartment buildings to get the required 5
percent of enrolled Democrats to sign our petitions so we could
become county committeewomen * and contribute our share of
signatures to our district leaders. There was a hot primary fight
for mayor going on, but we had decided not to confuse our local
issue with that problem until after the petition period.

We got back to the clubhouse with our petitions, and were
informed that there were some five new districts that remained
to be qualified; they had just been assigned to our club as a
result of the 1964–65 redistricting.

We agreed to go to work on this problem, and so once again
we were confronted with new territory. But this time we had the
techniques to tackle it. These districts turned out to be almost
entirely big buildings with vigilant doormen, and just a few
tenements tucked in here and there. The obvious approach, we
both felt, was to telephone first, make appointments to see a
dozen or so Democrats in a building, and then go out like fisher-
men and haul in the signatures.

But we reckoned without the reaction of the people.

It was August. A great many people were away on vacation.

---

* We were uncontested, and the law has been changed so that those candidates for public nomination or party office who are qualified for the primary
but are uncontested shall be deemed nominated and elected upon the filing
of the required number of signatures on a designating petition.

The area had obviously never been worked before, and most of those we called had never heard of a petition. Those who were receptive had never heard of us, our club, or our leaders. A goodly number of these voters, moreover, were fed up with the Democratic Party in New York, and already planned to support the Republican candidate for mayor, John Lindsay, in the general election. The result was some of the most difficult canvassing I have ever done. Several times I was hung up on. One man told me he couldn't be bothered with me now, he was mixing martinis. Another told me he never concerned himself with local politics.

The situation was ironic, since most of these voters lived in apartments with enormously high rents, indicating comfortably high incomes and—I would assume—staggeringly high taxes. Enlightened self-interest should make them concerned with public officials who spend so much of their money. Yet they were, for the most part, utterly frivolous in their response to this "news" from the world of local politics.

Aileen Schwartz, who is most attractive, quick, and has a lovely voice, did get one gentleman to let her come over and witness his signature if she came right then. So she dropped her program of lining up several people and rushed out of her apartment, up the street, and into a gorgeous river-view domicile, where several guests sat around in sumptuous armchairs listening to a pianist. The maid introduced Aileen to the master of the house, who let her run through her account of districts, leaders, one of the first reform clubs, and finally signed her petition. She gently remarked that she noticed there was also a "Mary ——" listed at the same address, only to be told that the lady couldn't be disturbed at the moment because she was playing the piano. Aileen commented afterwards that the worst of it was she had to act as if such an excuse were a perfectly reasonable one, as she made her exit as gracefully as possible.

We finally qualified the district, but we had to go out into the streets and climb the tenements, where only one out of every four listed Democrats was at home; but there were at least one out of two whose memories went back to when there had been a powerful Tammany club and who would sign.

Canvassing by Phone

It goes without saying that canvassing in person is infinitely more effective than a telephone campaign. As any salesman can tell you, it is much harder for people to say "no" face to face. A personal visit gives the voter a chance to size up the worker, to ask questions that bother him in a quiet conversational tone, and actually to look at and sign the petition, which on the phone can only be described to him. These truths also apply when canvassing for the actual election, for much the same reasons. While no signatures are sought at that time, the canvasser usually has some literature about his candidates, and he can reinforce his arguments by pressing a brochure into the hands of the voter.

Most captains have discovered that those who live in the lower floors of the walk-ups (which are the slightly more expensive apartments) and the lower floors of the high-rise buildings (which are the slightly less expensive apartments) are much easier people to talk to. The very poor on the top floors of the walk-ups and the very rich on the top floors of the elevator buildings are too reluctant to commit themselves to anything as public or "controversial" as politics, or too uninterested, to be bothered with us.

More and more politicking is being done these days on the telephone. All of us veterans use it to remind our veteran voters that we will be looking for them at the polls on election day, and campaign managers are coming more and more to depend on it almost exclusively. Enter any congressional, state senatorial, or assembly headquarters, and you will see long tables lined with telephones where volunteers sit dialing from endless lists of unknown registered voters. It helps, but it will never replace the captain system of the personal door-to-door canvass for any candidate lucky enough to have loyal supporters who will hit the street for him.

Introducing Your Candidate to Your Voters

Occasionally, on a very local campaign, the captain will be asked to take the candidate for assembly or state senate canvassing with him. The notion is that this gets the word around the district that the candidate has been there. And although only a few people actually see him on a given night, he somehow seems closer.

This technique has been modified in recent years as the candidates have taken to going on walking tours through a neighborhood. The captain is called upon to round up some of his faithful voters to make sure there are enough bodies along the route to make it look successful. Everyone who is on the street at the time or who shows up of his own accord improves the occasion.

One technique of bringing the candidate to the voter that we have used with great success is the house party. We find a voter in a given apartment house who will donate his time and apartment for a cocktail or coffee party to meet the candidate. Invitations are sent out to all voters in the building and in the neighboring buildings. You figure you will get approximately 10 percent return on your mailing. If you want ten voters, you mail out a hundred invitations.

This is costly both in time and money, but it is very useful, especially for local candidates and in district-leadership campaigns (when half your voters don't know what a district leader is); in these campaigns you have to do a good deal of educational work. Often these house parties bring in new club members and workers. To make the most of such recruitment side effects, a captain should arrange parties fairly early in the campaign.

A Captain for Costikyan

During my husband's first campaign for district leader—my second campaign as a captain—we would both come home from work each evening and have a little supper of bread and soup in our hot dining area (our toughest battles were always fought through New York's torrid July and August, for the September primary). Then we would gather up our materials for the evening and I would head for my buildings, Eddie for the club.

I had one big apartment house with an elevator, 140 East Forty-sixth Street. To get by the elevator men I had to telephone one of the Democrats in the building first and make an appointment to see him at a specific time. Once in the building, I could usually slip down the stairs and ring quite a few doorbells before one of the elevator operators would see me and ask me to leave. Eventually I developed two able lieutenants in the building—a copywriter and food expert, Elinor MacNaughton, who joined our club and served on our executive committee until she moved out of the district, and an accountant, Lawrence Traubner, who with his wife, Bernice, also joined the club and became a stalwart of the "loyal opposition" in club councils. Elinor MacNaughton and the Traubners took over much of the job of getting signatures in 140, where we were all aided by the house switchboard operators, Betty and May.

As the campaigns went by and we came to know the voters by sight, one of us would sit in the lobby of 140 at about 5:30 P.M. and catch people as they came home from work. At about 7:00 we'd go home for a bite to eat, leaving a list with Betty. The mailboxes for 140 were in the same room as the switchboard, and Betty could keep track of who had come in by checking those who stopped by to get their mail before going upstairs. After supper we'd get the list back from Betty and sally forth to mop up the building. During our final primary fight for leader in 1959, Betty was so firmly with us that several times she took delight in directing our opposition captain to some of the really argumentative residents in the house, who were likely to tie him up for some time with their talk. A financial remembrance to Betty and May was always included in our "election day expenses." Anyone who lives in an apartment building is used to tipping doormen for getting taxis, handymen for changing ceiling light bulbs. This is the accepted way of saying "thank you" between tenant and staff—though our gratitude to Betty and May was such that the couple of dollars we gave as a tip was merely a token of our feelings.

For me, the secret of winning a primary battle, and ultimately of getting out a big vote on election day, was to plug
away until every voter on my lists had been found and talked to.
It didn't matter where I found him, at his door, on the stairs, in
the supermarket, just as long as we had our innings together.*

People in New York City work such different hours. There
would always be a little pile of dog-eared cards with notes such
as "not in 8/17, 9:00 P.M.," "not in 9/9, 3:30 P.M.," until I finally
would find the voter in at 10:00 A.M. on a Saturday. Invariably
such a voter would be among the first to the polls on election
day, with a big grin for me as I waved a couple of fingers at him
from my spot as a "poll-watcher" on a bench beside the table for
election inspectors. Often it has turned out that those who lived
the most offbeat lives, whose occupations kept them quite out of
the mainstream of the community, became my most loyal and
most knowledgeable following. Whenever we would get a request from our leaders to take soundings in our district, to find
out what "our people" were thinking about a certain candidate
or an issue, these were the people I would head out to find first.

The Captain and Campaign Issues

It is the captain who first knows what the issues are that are
bothering people in any given election, and he is the first to have
to articulate the answers. Part of the frustration of being a captain is the difficulty of getting the higher-ups to come through
with useful responses to the issues.

I remember how, in the Presidential election of 1956, we
discovered one of the things that was really disturbing our otherwise loyal Democrats. Since we live in a Republican area in a
Democratic town, we usually concentrate on Democrats, even in
general elections. Our purpose is to hold their vote, for it is our
experience that Democrats are far more likely to vote for the
man than the party. The problem was the position of the Democratic Presidential candidate, Adlai Stevenson, on atomic testing.

* See Chapter 29.—E.N.C.

He had come out against it quietly early in April, and loudly in October. After his first speech people were sure that this policy would weaken us as a nation vis-à-vis Soviet Russia.

Captain after captain came back to our clubhouse wanting to know what Stevenson's objection to atomic testing was based upon, and how it could be explained to the voters. We, and our leaders, bombarded the Stevenson headquarters and the Democratic National Committee for some sort of a piece on this matter —but none was forthcoming.

One evening in September we were talking with some friends from a neighboring club, who told us they had the same problem. One of them offered to introduce us to a scientist friend of his who might be able to explain it all. Eddie and I spent a fascinating evening with a young man named Bud Gibbs and learned something about the terrors of radiation, and the "half-life" of atomic particles. Together the three of us wrote a one-page explanation of these phenomena coupled with a political pitch for Stevenson. We had thousands mimeographed and our captains stuffed them under doors throughout the district, figuring the information would be useful to Republicans as well as Democrats. The piece was later copied by the New York State Stevenson people, and, we were told, was even used by the National Committee.

This sort of a dramatic discovery and response to an issue doesn't happen very often, but a wise campaign committee always keeps its ears open for captain reaction.

In 1958, when Governor Harriman was running for re-election against Nelson Rockefeller, and the press was talking about nothing but "bossism" and De Sapio and the "bossed" Buffalo convention, Elinor MacNaughton called me up one day and said she had found an issue for us in her building: rent control.

To get the full implication of her discovery, it is necessary to give a quick profile of 140 East Forty-sixth Street. It is a large building of some two hundred very small apartments. The rooms are small and dark. They are either studio or one-bedroom arrangements with tiny kitchens. The corner of Forty-sixth Street and Lexington Avenue is a very convenient midtown location. The building is rent controlled. Apartments in it, therefore, are highly prized. Most of the tenants are single people or older couples. Most of the latter are Republicans who live on tiny pensions and Social Security. One of the bitter laughs we got out of that building was the discovery that all these older people were such loyal Republicans in part because they were convinced the Social Security system had been created by Republicans. Many of them had become eligible for their Social Security checks under the administration of Governor Thomas E. Dewey, and since the checks are sent out from a New York office (of the federal government), these grateful voters gave Dewey the credit.

Rent control, however, was another matter. In New York City it has been maintained through the political muscle of the Democratic Party in the city and state, and this fact is well known. In her canvassing, Elinor MacNaughton had discovered that these elderly people were genuinely concerned that if Rockefeller were elected governor, rent control might suffer. Otherwise, they were for him one hundred percent.

Within the next few days, Governor Harriman (who had undoubtedly been getting similar reports from other parts of the city) began talking about rent control in some of his speeches, and as the campaign wore on, he talked of it more and more. It was the kind of intimate pocketbook issue that could get people's mind off the abstractions of "bossism."

The Reform Captain Discovers He Is a Veteran

As the campaigns began to pile up, I found that my voters were as pleased to see me again as I was to see them. We would catch up on the year's news, they would ask questions about what was going on, and I would ask their opinions. Sometimes they would have problems that needed to be referred to a lawyer or to our leader, and we would go together to the club. They became "my people." They belonged to me and I belonged to them. A good captain becomes very possessive about his district, and resents it bitterly if any outsider is sent in, say, by an independent citizens' committee for some particular candidate.

Each building becomes a part of the captain's "turf" and when, as in our area, buildings are so frequently being torn down, and new ones put up in their place, it is hard to take the change. This provides an additional reason for the fact that the new clubs have been winning in the areas of change. Not only does the old captain lose the friends he has made in the buildings that have been torn down, but he resents the new people in the new buildings. I have known this resentment myself. When we ourselves moved to a new apartment too far from Forty-sixth Street for me to continue comfortably with that district, I was glad that I did not have to canvass the new building that had sprung up where once had been 238 and 242 East Forty-sixth Street. They had been two of my really "good" buildings, and housed many friends. I still exchange Christmas cards with one family, the James Lugers, and see others on the street from time to time.

As a captain, I sometimes took new citizens to take their literacy tests. I remember one couple from Poland particularly (they later showed up on the voting lists as registered Republicans), and one charming Puerto Rican bride I helped over her stage fright at the literacy test. She then gave me her recipe for beans.

I listened to many, many stories of trouble. One old lady wanted my help to get her son out of a state prison for the criminally insane. There was another faithful Democratic middle-aged lady who folded patterns for a pattern company. She longed to return to her home in Hawaii, but she couldn't leave her beautiful daughter alone in New York. The daughter worked as a dancer in the Hawaiian Room at the Lexington Hotel, and she became a loyal Democratic voter as soon as she turned 21.

Perhaps one reason the captain becomes so embedded in his district after relatively few contacts with his people is that he sees his constituents in their most unguarded moments. One gets used to meeting strangers in their bathrobes at their apartment doors. After a while, one even becomes casual at discovering them in their pajamas or in their underwear. I don't think we'll ever get accustomed to having the door opened by a voter who is stark naked (this has happened), though most of us have witnessed a signature scrawled by a hand on the end of a long wet arm—which, with a partially hidden face and a section of bath towel, is all we see from our side of the hall door.

We have often unwittingly betrayed husbands and wives politically to each other. It is a foolproof way to start family arguments. I remember one young bride who had married a very proper, Brooks-Brothers-suited advertising man who hoped to rise in his Republican-oriented agency. She had wanted to retain a little of her past, so had registered as a Democrat, figuring he would never be the wiser. Of course, I had no idea of this situation when I rang the bell and asked for her. (My records told me the husband was a Republican, but many families are split politically, and we cannot stay away from *all* of them.)

Her secret was soon out, and there was hell to pay.

One of my fellow captains, Bill Barlow, has a story he loves to tell about the time he climbed to the top floor and asked if the husband was home. The Republican wife listened from the kitchen and then with much waving of arms and many decibels, informed her husband that under no circumstances was he to sign anything. The whole scene got so unpleasant that Bill decided to leave well enough alone and retreat. He said good-bye and started down the stairs. One the way he found a more receptive family at home; he was invited inside to talk and get their signatures for the nominating petition. When he got to the street some minutes later, there was a man waiting on the stoop who he thought looked familiar. It was the husband from the top floor. He reached over and practically snatched the pen and petition out of Bill's hand, saying, "I'm not going to let any fat old bag tell me what I will sign and what I won't sign."

As time passed, I became genuinely taken aback at discovering that when I brought a petition around my people were not interested in reading it. The fact I brought it was enough. They were eager to sign. After a while I stopped insisting that they listen to me tell what there was to tell about each of the candidates listed, and contented my conscience by reading off the names before I let them sign. A captain would be less than human if he did not accept this shortcut. It is a compliment. The gathering of petitions, after all, is a routine that palls with time. In fact, though I never went so far, I have always secretly envied what I was told was the technique used by Alice Sachs, leader in the Lexington Club's Ninth Assembly District. She would ring the doorbells of her regulars and announce cheerfully, "Today's the day we sign petitions." Her reported record for one night was forty-eight signatures—a formidable performance by any standard.

An experienced captain in one of the old-time clubs can often take a day off from work to get petitions; sixty or more a day is good, but not spectacular for such a fellow. Most of us in the new clubs have jobs we can't get away from or small children that keep us busy during the day, and so almost without exception, we have to do our political work at night. We get home from the office, grab a bite to eat, and hit the trail from, say, 7:30 or 8:00 P.M. until 9:30 or 9:45 P.M. Sometimes we skip dinner, work straight through from 6:00 to 9:30, and eat afterwards. This works the best, because most people, if they are home in the evening at all, are home at dinnertime. But it is very hard on the canvasser.

The captain usually has a good "feel" of how the election is going. To be sure, this sixth sense is strongly based on the general character of his district, but even in our heavily Republican area we can get the drift of the whole campaign by seeing how our Democrats are reacting.

The Loss That Hurt the Most

The most painful election for me in my twelve years as a captain was the Presidential election of 1956. Most of us in the New Democratic Club had gotten into politics as a result of an overwhelming admiration for Adlai Stevenson, and we had accepted his defeat in 1952 as one of those colossal mistakes a democratic society sometimes makes. We had come down out of the remote citizens' campaign headquarters into the precincts. In order to be prepared for Stevenson's second try for the Presidency in 1956, we had gone to work hoping to change the party from the bottom up. Though we were an army of zealots, we had worked hard and earned the trust of our voters. They listened to us with respect and friendship and were willing to take our lead on thorny issues that puzzled them. We felt we were making headway, that we had a chance of holding almost all of our Democrats. We had mounted a major registration drive. We mailed out some 80,000 pieces to 20,000 voters of all persuasions. We had found Democrats who hadn't voted since Al Smith, and even a few disenchanted Republicans. Our club executive secretary, who worked a good twelve hours a day without pay that campaign, had voted for Eisenhower in 1952 and was working for us as her personal penance for that error.

But then came Suez. The whole world froze, and so did our voters. Instead of getting mad at our President for his administration's part in the blundering among old allies, people became afraid to "change horses in midstream." Night after night I would go out and come home tired and desperately discouraged. I remember one night I said I thought I'd stay home and sew, but my husband (who was serving his first term as Democratic district leader) told me bluntly I had to go out.

"How can you keep sending me out when you know it's hopeless?" I asked him.

"You think it's difficult to face those voters who are against you," was his reply. "Think of how it is for me, who has to keep trying to encourage the captains, who are my friends, when I know it is almost impossible. But we must do our best. If this election is lost, even though we have done the best we could, we will be able to sleep, because we will know it was not our fault. But what if it is close, and we lose by just a few votes?"

As we entered the final week, there was a slight note of encouragement in the air. The world situation had calmed down, and my Democrats were once again willing to listen, and a few, out of loyalty to me and to the Democratic Party, told me "okay," they'd go for Stevenson.

Then came election day.

We lived on the top floor of a small, rent-controlled apartment building, and our bedroom window looked out on Forty-sixth Street. I remember coming home at one point in the day for a bite to eat, and stopping to look out the window and watch some of my voters from the buildings across the street, walking down toward the school where they were to vote. I watched them meet each other (many had lived in the neighborhood since childhood) and stop to chat. There was one point when two little knots of people were gathered on opposite sides of the street, and I knew them all. Then they broke up sharply and walked firmly towards the school. Somehow I knew—perhaps by the shift in the way they carried their shoulders—that they had decided to vote against me. And they did.

The results on the machine proved it to me. We were slaughtered. Not quite so badly as in 1952. But we hadn't been working there in 1952.

Getting Out the Vote

About a week before election day, either for a contested primary or for a general election, I would write a letter to my Democrats. The letter itself would be mimeographed, but addressed by hand, with a handwritten greeting: "Dear Mr. and Mrs. Luger," and a personal signature. In one page, single-spaced, I would try to remind my voters of the candidate, the issue, whatever was the big thing to remember that year, and wound up by saying how much I looked forward to greeting them at the polls, Primary Day, September 14, at the school on Forty-sixth Street between 3:00 and 10:00 P.M.

The night before election day, I and all my fellow captains, would go around our district with "hall cards"—printed cardboard cards with the hours the polls would be open next day and the address of the polling place for each building, the names of our Democratic leaders of the district, and the name of the Democratic captain. These cards were scotch-taped up in the hallways, just above the mailboxes if possible, and placed beside the table lamp in the halls of buildings with doormen. My son Gregory's first political assignment was following me around my district carrying these cards, when he was about three. Now, he and his sister Emilie both go around with me, and they also help if we have any last-minute literature to stuff under doors.

Usually, in the last few days of a campaign, the campaign manager gets anxious to get whatever literature is left out of the clubhouse. We hand it out with shopping bags in front of supermarkets and stuff it under doors. This is done on the theory that it's not doing any good piled where it is, and just might serve to refresh some voter's memory by turning up at his doorstep.

The morning of primary day (or the afternoon before a general election when the polls open at 6:00 A.M.), I would settle down with all my cards and lists, cull out the "nos" and "don't knows," and compile a typewritten list, still by apartment houses (though now by alphabetical listing of names again) of all the "sure" and "maybe." This list would include telephone and apartment numbers, and I would make four copies.

We would have a watcher, either a recruit from my district discovered during the canvassing period or a club member, assigned to my poll, who would sit at the poll taking down the names of every voter who came in. Then, if the watcher had time, he would cross out the names of these voters on his copy of my list. The club would usually provide me with a runner, and we would commandeer some sympathizer who lived on a low floor near the polling place to let us use his apartment and telephone as a command post. We would always offer to pay for the overcalls on that phone for the month out of campaign funds, but usually the owner was happy to contribute that as part of his donation to the club.

Once the polls open, the captain's job is to "pull" the vote. We would make desultory efforts in the afternoon, but I soon found that all that did was tire the workers out. The real push would begin about 3:00 P.M. on a general-election day when the polls close at 7:00 P.M., and at 6:00 P.M. on primary day (when people are just home from work) when the polls close at 10:00 P.M. The runner would go to the poll, compare his copy of the master list with the watcher's list, and cross off the names of those who had voted on his copy. (Since all the lists were exactly alike, the runner didn't even have to read the names, just cross off, say, the first six under 246 East Forty-sixth, skip one, strike the next two, etc.). Then he would hurry back to the command post, cross off these same names on the copy of the list there, so the worker on the phone could get busy calling those who had not yet come in.

This process would be repeated every half hour or so. Meanwhile, another runner or I would head out to climb the stairs in search of those who had no phones, and either remind them in person or leave messages under their doors if they were not at home. While we were at it, we would also leave notes under the doors of those who had not answered their phones. We would keep right on with this operation until about ten minutes before 10:00 on those primary nights when the contest was really hot. As a rule we would all be quite spent by about 9:20. It would become harder to decide who might be worth another prod. We would be deflated, absorbed by our failures—those voters we had not succeeded in "pulling."

It is astonishing how deep is the impact of one irritated lady who answers her phone sharply and says she cannot possibly vote today because she has dinner guests. Of course, we do become as grateful as long-lost puppy dogs to those sleepy voices that say "Oh, I'd forgotten all about it," and then turn up as golden living bodies, sockless and Democratic, five minutes later at the polls. But most reformers at bottom are not the traditional extroverted political types. We are compulsive introverts of some sort, who overcome our natural shyness by ardor for the cause. It takes us years to learn not to be overly sensitive to the way voters react to us.

It is those who refuse to vote, who are too lazy to vote, who welsh on the franchise, that fill our thoughts, as we watch the last-minute voters file slowly through the schoolroom. Suddenly there is a bustle of the policemen. It is ten o'clock and the time has come to close the doors.

Election Day

All through the hours of voting, there have been four election inspectors—two duly enrolled Republicans, two Democrats—assigned to each poll by the clubhouses and certified and paid by the Board of Elections. They are the ladies and gentlemen the voter finds seated at the tables, checking the voters, taking the signatures, supervising the vote. They work a total of about seven days a year, during registration week and election days, for which they are paid less than a dollar an hour—if you include the hours after the polls close when they count the vote and fill out the endless forms demanded by the Board of Elections and the Police Department, forms dreamed up by some far-out Rube Goldberg consumed by a passion to prevent fraud. Sometimes it takes until two or three in the morning to finish the paper work, especially if all four inspectors are serving for the first time.

Often the inspectors are slow and a bit dull, but in prosperous times in a silk-stocking neighborhood it is hard to recruit men and women to take on this grueling job. Not only are the forms fiercely complicated, but the light to work by is atrocious, and the inspector has to be willing to take a good deal of abuse from members of the public, who seem to feel that somehow the world owes them a brilliantly competent election board. The hours are long, and the pay very short. It is just about impossible for any-one with a regular nine-to-five job to be an inspector unless her boss lets her take off the necessary time. Many of our club members serve as inspectors as a public service, and all of us captains have sat in for our inspectors during coffee breaks, dinner hours, and the time they are allowed by law to return to their home districts and cast their own votes.

During the days of registration and election, the captain must jolly the inspectors along, bring them coffee, sometimes send them home in a cab. A happy board gets its work done more efficiently. The lines of voters move along and voters are less likely to go home in a huff. The count at the end of the day goes more quickly. Most of the captain's expenses involve the Election Board, and either we pay this out of our own pocket or, quite properly we feel, we are sometimes reimbursed out of the club's allotment from the county Democratic headquarters.

Once the doors of the polling place close, the ritual of "taking the count" begins. The committee that designed a horse and produced the camel instead also devised the systems and forms for recording the vote in New York County. The whole process operates on the theory that carbon paper has not been invented.

During registration and election, three people on the board are at all times recording different parts of the same information on different papers and cards. Two different numbers are given to each voter, and invariably there is a mix-up that conscientious, tired, irritated ladies spend hours trying to straighten out after the doors are closed.

In the not-so-long-ago days of the paper ballot in primary elections, each ballot had to be unfolded, piled up face down, and then turned over one by one to be scrutinized by inspectors and watchers for each candidate. Sometimes howling arguments between exhausted antagonists would ensue over the validity of the marks on the ballot. When we started out, only an X with its cross within the box next to the candidate's name was valid. I remember watching dozens of my votes go down the drain because my college-trained voters were too busy to study the directions at the top of the ballot, and just went cheerily down the page making dainty little checkmarks for the New Democratic Club slate.* This whole problem has been mercifully eliminated by the voting machine which is now used throughout the city in primaries.

The polls close, the inspectors take their positions, one Republican, one Democrat (one with flashlight), at the machine. The other two inspectors sit at the table, forms spread before them, ready to take down the figures. The front of the machine is locked so no further voting can take place, and the lock is sealed with a little piece of metal with a number on it. This number is recorded on the inspectors' tally forms. The number on the public counter is recorded, and *it* is locked and sealed with a piece of metal whose number is also recorded. Then the machine is opened, and the vote is called out loudly by one of the inspectors at the machine. The other inspector doublechecks while the rest of the board and the captains write the totals on their respective tally sheets, the inspectors' for the official count, ours for our club and candidates.

This is the eternal moment, this time in the night when those little numbers being called off from the machine by a tired

* A friend from Brooklyn also reports that there was considerable resistance among some Jewish voters to making a "cross" on the ballot, and that accounted for many checkmarks and lost primary votes.

voice tells us what the months of work, the hours and hours of talking in doorways, in living rooms, on the street, have added up to. There are few satisfactions in life greater than carrying your district.

We do what we can to help the inspectors with their sheets, but usually they shoo us away once the vote is recorded on the first set of forms. Our duties complete in our district, we head back to the club to give our figures and get the full returns for all the districts in the club. In our district, for our club, this has always been a joyous trip on primary night and on national-election night in 1960 and 1964. Since we work in a basically Republican stronghold, we have had to develop the all-important strength of the veteran politician—essentially the ability to bear frustration and disappointment—and snap back the next morning ready for more. Our job in the big elections has been to hold down the margin of our loss.

At the club, we turn in our figures to the campaign manager, who has a huge chart ready to receive them. We check the over-all picture so far, and then fall into eager talk with our fellow captains about how the vote has gone. We tell tales of the hard ones, and together we curse the ones that never showed. We are a band of brothers. We have done our best.

Several times, after my husband was elected county leader, a group of captains from our club would go over to the county headquarters to see how things were going there. But invariably we would stick together. The political enthusiasts who had spent the day at work, or shopping, or picnicking, or at the races, and who had now gathered at the county headquarters with others of their sort to watch the results, were too fresh-faced for our company. We had nothing to say to them. The front-line infantry soldiers probably would have little to say, at the battle's end, to the staff officers and generals back at HQ. They have been fighting a different war.

Our curiosity about how things went in Brooklyn or Ohio, the Bronx or Illinois, Staten Island or California, Queens or Pennsylvania, was dimmed by exhaustion. Our minds were pre-occupied with the details of our own day in the district.

That night, win or lose, we would sleep the sleep of the just.

6 * The District Leader in His Domain

✳✳

The Club, the Constituents, the Campaign

The Club

Every local political leader in an urban area must have a permanent headquarters to which supporters and suppliants alike may go to see him. In New York County, there are in normal circumstances thirty-three such local headquarters.* They are the regular Democratic clubs of their respective areas.

Each club pays for its own rent, telephone bills, mailings, insurance, typewriters, addressograph and addressograph plates. It must pay for whatever social events it sponsors, and for its own charities.

The hardest organization in the world to manage and lead is such a volunteer organization. Neither executives nor envelope-stuffers are paid. Dereliction in duty cannot be controlled by discipline nor by the threat of discharge. Even if the miscreant is a public employee by reason of the club's help, there is little that can be done; the city will not fire people because they fail to get out a political mailing or to ring doorbells even after they have promised, or even volunteered, to do so.

Once one of our club leaders insisted that at a particular elec-

* In 1955 the party adopted rules which, defying all natural law, declared each district would be headed by two co-equals, one male and one female. In 1963 in three districts, the male from one club and the female from its opposition club won. So in those districts there are two co-equal headquarters, making the county total 36 for 33 leadership districts. But the number may vary every two years. In 1965, due to reapportionment the total was 39 districts.

tion *every* captain be at his polling place at 6:00 A.M. sharp. We were then still an insurgent club. Our captains had no real function to perform at 6:00 A.M., since our Regular Democrat counterparts had their own staff of captains ready to handle early morning election-day details such as making sure the polls opened on time. Our captains knew it, and few were inclined to rise at 5:00 A.M. in order to show the flag when no one else would be awake to see it. I knew this, and declined to issue the 6:00 A.M. directive.

"But they *have* to come," I was told.

"What if they ask why, and there's no good reason to be there?" I asked.

"Then fire them."

"Yeah," I said, "fire them and then what do we do?"

To this there was no answer. There was no waiting line of anxious applicants begging for appointment to a captaincy. In fact, over half the districts then had no captains. This is the unanswerable problem when one seeks efficiency in a modern volunteer political party—if you fire someone, then what do you do?

Even if every public jobholder who failed to carry out his political duties could be fired, one still could not maintain discipline. The maximum percentage of jobholders among the captains and workers in any club in New York County is about 35 percent—and that is very unusual. More often it's between 10 and 20 percent and frequently less. Even if job threats could insure discipline in this minority, little would be achieved. A 35 percent container—like a sieve—carries little water.

These being the facts, other techniques must be used. Appeals to idealism, personal friendship, supposed obligations—all of these are among the tools. But essentially the leader must create a spirit that can produce a desire to follow through among his supporters. To sustain such a spirit is the heart of the matter. Even with it, running a club of this kind is a difficult and perpetually challenging task. The investment of time is incredible. Privacy, to a considerable extent, evaporates.

Budgets vary—from as low as $4,000 to as high as $30,000 a year. Memberships vary—from under 200 to over 4,000. The number of voters represented varies from under 10,000 to over 50,000. The degree of activity varies. In each case, the leader's responsibility is to keep the local headquarters open and functioning. Prospective new members must be sought and, once inveigled into the headquarters, welcomed. Someone else may have done the inveigling, but the leader had better personally show his happiness at their presence.

The headquarters usually looks dingy and needs repainting, which means money or labor or both. The leader must be prepared to see that the money or labor is there (or do it himself).

The Membership Committee is planning a new-member's party. The leader must be available.

The club's bank account is low and someone must be stimulated to set up a fund-raising affair. The leader's counsel is sought as to the best money-raising device to try this time.

Regular monthly membership meetings require a continuing supply of reasonably interesting speakers on important issues. Can the leader get the commissioner of correction or housing or something?

There is a growing feud between two key officers in the club. Will the leader talk to them and straighten them out?

Complaints are flowing in (to the leader) that club members are not receiving club mailings. The leader finds out that two volunteers, each looking to the other, have fallen five months behind in keeping the membership lists current.

So-and-so has moved out of the district, and no one is handling such-and-such committee. Does the leader have any ideas as to who might take over?

The treasurer has been away, the bills for annual dues (usually five or six dollars, with optional higher amounts for "sustaining members") have not been sent out, and the treasury is low. Where can we find some funds, borrowed or otherwise, for last month's rent?

The theater-benefit committee must put down a thousand-dollar deposit by next Tuesday. Can the leader suggest ten people to be asked to lend a hundred apiece?

And so it goes. The leader is always the first and last resort.

A good leader delegates—and then redelegates when the

original delegatee flops. As a result, as time passes, more and more of the internal work is undertaken by the club president and other officers. But still the problems continue, and when they remain unsolved on the way up, they end in the leader's hands.

Every problem—paint, heat, rent, telephone, mailing costs, repairs, robberies, fires, insurance, location, cleaning—at one time or another are the leader's ultimate responsibility. Indeed, the hallmark of a real political leader is whether he has swept out his own clubhouse—*while he was the leader!* There's nothing like it to stimulate the club members and, if I may say so, to clean up the headquarters the way they should be cleaned up.

The final club problem is *knowing* the members. They come and go. There are as many as a hundred new members a year. A leader who wants to survive must make sure that he spends enough time learning who they are, and meeting them, becoming *their* leader as well as the club's!

The Constituents

The second major area of the leader's activity is dealing with constituents. Depending upon the area serviced, a leader may have a heavy or light load of constituents *every* Monday and to a lesser extent, Thursday night, fifty-two weeks a year.

In some areas of New York, fifty to a hundred constituents arrive each week for help from the leader. In areas like mine, the number has varied—five to ten a week at the beginning, when the area was 60 percent tenements; one to two a week at the most now that the district is 80 percent middle, upper-middle, and luxury housing.

What do these people want?

Basically they want help with problems that are frequently impossible to solve and frequently quite simple.

Tenant disputes with landlords were once the bulk of our problem: the apartment hasn't been painted in six years; there's no heat; the plaster is broken; we need new windows; there are no lights in the halls. Sometimes it's worse: the landlord wants a rent increase; the building is going to be torn down and the landlord says I've got to get out; I was late on the rent and I have this eviction notice.

These problems, calling for various degrees of activity—from a phone call or a form to representing a tenant in court—are handled as the problem demands, either by the leader or his associates.

I always insisted that if anything more than routine form-filling or telephoning was necessary, one of the attorneys in the club assume the personal responsibility of becoming the attorney for the complainant—or else let someone else do the job.

On only two occasions did a constituent ask me to "talk to the judge," both times about a housing matter. One was a landlord. The other a tenant. In both cases I said no. In both cases, justice was done. Indeed, the tenant, who won her case without inter-vention, became a committed party worker and a firm believer in a nonpolitical judiciary.

There are constituents with problems in the criminal courts. A sixteen-year-old son was arrested; one of the club members, who was a good criminal lawyer, took that one on—and the boy was acquitted. The sister-in-law of a club officer was arrested for shoplifting and was on her way to night court when the leader was advised. The leader dropped everything, went to court, and ultimately worked out a disposition with the com-plaining witness.

A local neighborhood hotspot had repeated trouble with the State Liquor Authority, whose inspectors seemed to be harassing the place looking for a shakedown. Did the leader know anyone at the S.L.A.? He didn't, but he knew a leader who did, the complaint of harassment was made, and the harassment ceased.

A constituent on welfare had violated the rules, taken a part-time job, and picked up an extra three hundred dollars over a four-month period. Welfare had found out and was demanding he repay the three hundred, but he didn't have it. There were criminal charges pending. Could the leader help? He could. A couple of phone calls to the appropriate authorities in the Wel-fare Department resulted in the obvious conclusion that the money simply wasn't there and that it wouldn't help anyone to send the man to jail. (That was over ten years ago—and the man has been in no trouble since.)

A constituent had lost his job in an advertising agency at the age of forty-five, his unemployment insurance had run out, so had his savings. Wasn't there some place his obvious talents could be used? There was. A city agency needed a skilled economic researcher at $6,500 a year.

A constituent had taken a civil-service exam and passed it, but an ancient matrimonial dispute had led the appointing authority to reject him. Could he get a chance to explain the whole matter in person? He could (though he didn't get the job).

A group of constituents were fighting the installation of a commercial parking garage in a residential building. Could the leader appear at the hearing before the zoning authority? He couldn't, but the club president could.

The residents of a building were going crazy because of excavation for a new apartment house across the street. The racket started at 7:00 A.M. every day, including Saturdays. Could the leader get the contractor to lay off on Saturdays? He could.

A constituent wanted to organize a program to plant trees down one street. Would the leader get permission—and some money—from the landowners? He would.

A taxi driver had three moving-traffic violations and was about to lose his license. Can we help? Not much.

A family found their welfare allowance wholly inadequate. Could the leader help? He could, if only to the extent of speeding a review of the allowances.

And so it goes, week in and week out, year after year.

A relatively small number seek jobs; many—often proprietors of single-man enterprises—seek relief from jury duty; once the general counsel of a major oil company (a Republican, by the way, although we never asked anyone their party affiliation—a constituent is a constituent) sought help because a new street light had been put up outside his third-story bedroom window on Beekman Place. It was shining in his eyes all night. Couldn't a shield be placed on the back of the light? It was—and it was carefully adjusted one evening, while the venerable gentlemen stuck his head out the window and shouted directions to the man on the ladder.

In other districts the problems will differ. Getting new street lighting; placing traffic lights where constituents—not traffic engineers—think them necessary; dealing with school location and other education problems; securing better parks, or getting existing parks cleaned up; law-enforcement problems and better police protection.

Indeed, every variety of problem that affects his district finds its way to the district leader. A composite of the problems brought to district leaders is a composite of the problems that affect the city.

In a tiny percentage—far less than one percent of the problems, in my experience—something illicit is sought: the fixing of a case or the calling-off of an inspector who insists that a sidewalk be repaired. In twelve years of handling these problems, I can remember only one case where I was offered a pay-off, three cases where communication with a judge or hearing officer was sought, and one other case of proposed misconduct. That's a low percentage, in light of the legends about politicians.

As a general rule, no one who asks for help from the club is expected to pay for it. Indeed, the ranks of former politicians are heavy-laden with unimaginative types who thought it appropriate to receive a slight token of appreciation for each favor undertaken, let alone satisfactorily performed.

The requests are of all degrees of difficulty. In many cases, the only answer that can be given ("I want a five-room apartment in a city housing project, and my income is ten thousand a year") is "Sorry, nothing can be done." In other cases—for example, when an aged couple, seeking a city housing-project apartment, is perplexed by a one-year delay after due application—the answer may be "We'll see what's wrong and what can be done."

Very rarely indeed can the district leader say "Yes, it will be done." Perhaps in only one-third of the cases can anything be done—and for those cases months may be needed. And yet the district leader and his associates, who frequently take on responsibility for following through on problems, must make friends while doing no more than "their best," with no better than a one-third record of success except in purely routine matters. Dealing with constituents soon develops in the leader both a broad knowledge of government and considerable tact and diplomatic skill.

And when a local issue erupts that places the local community in conflict with city or state government—such as the proposal for the Lower Manhattan Expressway, which Robert Moses and various labor unions supported and which the local residents opposed; the destruction of a local hospital, which the hospital commissioner proposed and the local residents opposed; the closing of Washington Square Park to traffic, which was generally opposed by the city but violently supported by local residents; and so on—the party leader must be prepared to be the community spokesman, especially if he has an opponent or potential opponent for the leadership, who will be delighted to become the spokesman if the leader is silent.

Basically the leader cushions the impact of government upon his constituents and provides a pipeline for his constituents to the bureaucracy at the heart of every urban center.

Instead of the tenant calling a telephone number for the nth time to make a complaint about the absence of heat on a freezing day in January, the leader calls or goes to see a deputy clerk he knows—and that impossible temperature and the freezing tenants become a far more human problem, and far more likely to receive attention than if they were merely one address on a long list of telephoned complaints.

The political rewards for effective handling of such problems are simple: votes for the leader and his club's candidates when, every two years, they run for re-election to party office, and, it is hoped, votes for the party's candidates for public office on every election day.

The first reward is far surer. When someone has been helped—or even treated decently—he doesn't forget the man or the club that helped him. Translating that memory into a vote for a President or governor or mayor or even an assemblyman is a far chancier business. But chancy or not, this is an essential part of the duty of a district leader. And his willingness to devote his time to this kind of activity is one of the credentials he must possess if he wishes to be accepted as a political leader who is entitled to be heard by other leaders when candidates are being nominated and policies being decided.

This description of tasks undertaken for constituents is not a careful distillation of the legitimate from the illegitimate ones. The percent of illegitimate requests to which the author was subjected was minuscule. True, other leaders might attract more illicit requests and might accept the assignments. I can issue no guarantees of probity for all politicians. But my experience tells me that the percentage of misconduct among political leaders in this area is relatively insignificant. For example, as pointed out in Chapter 26, the locus of corruption (to the extent that there is corruption) has shifted. The politician is no longer the middleman. Public officials amenable to corruption can be approached directly, and with less exposure. Why use an unnecessary middleman?

Moreover, most of the problems that concern constituents do not require illicit intervention. So why do it?

Indeed, the myth of the corruptibility of the political leaders is, I am convinced, to a large extent and in a substantial majority of cases a relic from ancient history and a carefully exploited legend designed to immobilize and minimize the significance of political leaders.

After all, many a civic leader and many a public official makes his reputation by periodically denouncing "the politician," "the bosses," and "the political hacks." Yet the evidence of graft and misconduct in recent years has in almost all cases involved civil servants and public officeholders—not political leaders—who have gone wrong.

The Campaign

The final area of the leader's principal local activity is the management of the party's general election campaign in his area.

He has thirty election districts? He *must* have thirty captains—

one for each district. If there are thirty captains but six are no good, he must find six new ones and ease the old ones out without too much of a fuss.

Every year one or two captains retire. They must be replaced— by trained people.

Does Captain A have enough help? How can we get him or her a couple of assistants? The Fourteenth E.D. has two good co-captains sharing the district. They've developed to the point that either one can handle it alone—if he or she will. Can we move one over to the Sixteenth E.D.?

Last year's campaign chairman, who deals directly with the captains and handles the execution of the campaign, has gotten too busy in his law practice, or has gotten married, or has moved. Whom shall we put in his place?

We will want to send out two mailings the week before election day—one to Democratic registrants and one to Republicans. Can we put X in charge of getting the 25,000 envelopes (or 50,000, or 75,000) addressed during the summer?

Who will write our local literature? What should it say?

How about a telephone campaign the last two weeks? Can we get so-and-so to organize that?

We need a mailing to new residents to tell them where to register, so we'll need someone to canvass all the new buildings before September 1 to get the names of new tenants.

And so on and on. By September 1, the campaign machinery must be set up. By September 30, it must be rolling. After that it's too late to start concocting new campaign plans, or even to do much more than feed the machinery that has been set up, to oil it, and to make minor adjustments and replacements.

All year round, therefore, as the leader meets new members, as he deals with constituents, he notes those who might be helpful in a campaign and passes on the names to the campaign chairman. The campaign chairman looks about too. The club president, the secretary, vice-president, ex-leaders, ex-presidents —they all look, and suggest. The campaign chairman assigns people to specific tasks or areas. One out of three delivers. Those who don't are forgiven, but then are forgotten as campaigners.

The campaign chairman keeps a chart; it shows captains and

workers in each election district. Regularly the leader checks it. "We're light in the Eleventh. There's a fellow named so-and-so who was in to get some help who might work out. Why don't you try him?" And so the list grows. By election day there is, besides the captain, a list of five or six workers per election district. Two to four of them, moreover, are really prepared to work all day getting Democratic voters to the polls. The district is "manned"!

On election day, while voters sleep, the leaders and the campaign chairman and the lawyers and the captains and workers rise at 5:00 A.M. By 6:00 A.M. the leaders—male and female— are on the way around the polls to see they are open, manned by captains, functioning, peaceful, and happy.

All day long, the leaders check the polls—the voter turnout, the captains' attitudes, the morale. Where a district is light when it shouldn't be, the leaders or the campaign chairman find the captain and jack him up.

When there are legal problems at the polls, a lawyer is sent. When a machine breaks, the leader or the law chairman calls the Board of Elections again and again—until it's fixed. If a voter is denied the right to vote, one of the lawyers gets him a cab, and soon he's on his way to the Supreme Court to apply for a legal order authorizing him to cast his ballot.

When night falls, the leader gives his captains a last push to get out the Democrats, and then awaits the closing of the polls and the reports of the results.

The first four election districts often give the experienced leader a clue to the results—win, lose, or too close to tell. By 1:00 A.M. the results are finally in—good or bad.

The next morning—bright, early, and perhaps groggily—the leader and the campaign chairman and the captains are at work earning their livings, while their nonpolitical co-workers comment how nice it was to have had a day off. That night the leader may very well be at his headquarters—especially after a licking—surveying the wreckage, putting the election figures in the desk drawer so that they'll be available for later analysis, cleaning up the headquarters.

The week after election day, the leaders and the campaign

managers go over the results and compare them with those of
prior years. There was a new captain in the Fifteenth E.D. and
that district went Democratic for the first time in ten years
("That guy looks good—I hope we can keep him interested");
the margin keeps going up in the Eighteenth; according to the
captain in the Nineteenth, Y was a great help—maybe Y could
take on a district.

And so the planning starts for the next year's campaign. More
people, new people, different people. But the machinery is permanent, although the people who man it change and change and
change.

There are "promotions"—a captain becomes assistant campaign
manager, and then campaign manager, and then club president—
and then perhaps district leader. Or a captain, after two or three
or four (or ten) years grows tired of the drudgery, the stairs to
climb, the doorbells to ring, and retires.

Out of the shifting but steady process grows a small, semi-
permanent, semiautonomous political institution—the leader's
political home, and usually his successor's political home. The
club is the symbol of his district. It is his headquarters, his
meeting place, his responsibility, his ticket of admission to the
meetings where candidates are selected and political policy
made.

Part Three

The Role
of the
Political Leader
in Designating Candidates
to be Nominated in
Primary Elections

Introduction to Part Three

A major part of the function of the political leader is to find and then successfully promote the nomination of candidates for public office.

Reform attitudes resist granting the leader this power, and prefer a town-meeting type of convention. But this alternative has proved so unsatisfactory that even reformers are moving slowly back to the notion that their leaders—under proper safeguards, of course—should play a major role in this process.

This is how the process works.

7 ✻ How the Designating Process Works

✻✻✻

Once a political leader has earned his spurs—by organizing a club and securing the votes of a majority of the Democrats in his area—his counterparts in other areas are willing to accept him as their *de facto* equivalent, at least to the extent of permitting him to participate in some of the political decisions.

The less important the office, the greater the power of the local leader. The higher the office, the greater the power of the county leader. Of late, however, the whole fabric of party-leader designation of candidates on the county and city levels— for mayor and borough presidents (county leader designation of a candidate was once equivalent to nomination)—has been all but destroyed.

The process is simple, in theory. Democratic Party candidates are nominated by the enrolled Democrats in a primary election held for that purpose. The enrolled Republicans nominate the Republican candidates. The candidate in the Democratic primary who gets the most votes is on the ballot in November as the Democratic candidate, and the same is true for every other party. No party funds can be spent in a primary, because the results are supposed to establish the will of the members of the party, and the official party machinery is supposed to be used only in general elections.

Accepting this La Follette-Wisconsin-Progressive notion of pure democracy rarely troubled political leaders. They could get a majority of the party members who bothered to vote in a primary to support the candidate the leaders designated—without using party funds or "official party machinery." This was possible because only 10 to 20 percent of the eligible voters

99

bothered to vote in primaries, and they were the ones the organization made sure got to the polls, confident that this 10 to 20 percent was "loyal" to its benefactors—the local captains and the district leader. On such terms, once the five New York county leaders agreed upon a candidate, and their district leaders followed suit, and the 4,500 or so captains in the 4,500 election districts plus the three or four workers in each district followed suit, the primary was a formality.

In the period from 1946 to 1965, however, this old simplicity disappeared.

First, the five county leaders frequently couldn't agree. Then their district leaders divided. And when county leaders and district leaders "jumped the fence," why shouldn't the captains? With such disagreement within the party organization, why shouldn't the voter exercise his own judgment?

Under such conditions, the number of party members who vote in mayoralty primaries climbed and climbed. From 546,000 in a hotly contested 1953 primary, it went to about 769,000 in 1961.

The district leaders and the county leader do little more today than choose up sides when a mayoralty primary takes place—as it has with increasing frequency. The decision as to who shall be the candidate is made by the party members.

I have no direct knowledge as to the reasons why in 1953 the New York County and Bronx County leaders supported Robert F. Wagner in a primary against the incumbent, Mayor Vincent Impellitteri, who had the support of the other three county leaders. I suspect, however, that they based their support upon accurate predictions as to voter reaction in the primary and general election which ensued.

In 1961 a far more basic and yet more complicated situation arose when the five county leaders opposed Mayor Wagner because they accurately appraised his intentions as being directed at the destruction of the power of the county leaders. Many district leaders followed suit because they were aware of great voter dissatisfaction with the mayor, but were unaware of the even greater latent animosity directed against the incumbent New York County leader, Carmine De Sapio.

Making their decisions in June, they were unable to predict accurately that by the end of August the voters would choose Wagner over De Sapio. And yet in this area, where a primary is likely, the key to successful political leadership is the capacity to predict voter turnout and voter attitudes *at the time people vote.*

Polls sometimes help, but even polls are useless unless the leader has a capacity to listen, a desire to hear, an ability to understand exactly what the voter is saying (or isn't saying), and unless he has the capacity to predict what the voter reaction in June will mean in terms of votes in November.

At one time I obtained my estimates of voter reaction myself by ringing doorbells. Later, however, I came to rely on certain of my good captains, who knew how to listen and to report. When I saw them, as I did once every week or two during the year, and two or three times a week during a campaign (if they weren't around the club, I would call them), I would ask, "What do you hear? What's the reaction? How do the people feel? What are they saying? How does it look? What's with Wagner?" and the like. And they would report—specifics as well as conclusions. Later, as county leader, I did this in addition with key district leaders who, my instincts told me, had the feel of their districts, as well as with the captains in my own district.

The information thus obtained must be digested and analyzed. Indeed, in June of 1961, for example, every one of my captains told me Wagner couldn't win. But the information they brought did not support the conclusion. They reported voter dissatisfaction with Wagner; but there was always an unspoken—or occasionally a spoken—"but." The "but" was the even greater voter resistance to De Sapio.

I firmly believed that by late August the voters would see the issue as one of choosing between Wagner and De Sapio—and they would choose Wagner. Not many other leaders saw it this way, though a few did.

An instinct to distinguish unsound estimates of voter reaction from sound ones requires some years of experience, judgment, and some understanding of the political behavior of voters. If a leader believes that candidate X is a jerk, he may be right.

Being right is nice, but meaningless unless voters agree with you. Candidate X's reputation for wisdom may be so strong that his essential stupidity cannot be adequately demonstrated to enough people before the election with the political tools available. And temporary voter reactions to immediate situations must be distinguished from the likely behavior of voters three months later. Voter resistance to Wagner in a vacuum in June does not mean votes for his opponent in November.

Indeed, I remember a major reason why West Side reformers opposed John F. Kennedy at the national convention in 1960 was the oft-repeated prediction, "We'll never carry the West Side!" In November, the West Side was one of Kennedy's banner areas, as it was bound to be. The leaders confused voter preference for Stevenson in June—when he was a possible candidate for the nomination against Kennedy—with voter attitudes, after a campaign, in a Kennedy-Nixon contest.

Perhaps the most important qualification for performing this predictive function is that the political leader must be disinterested. His likes and dislikes are unimportant and must be eliminated from the equation—to the extent they can be—or they will destroy his capacity to judge electoral attitudes.

Of course, where there is no threat of a primary election to resolve competing candidacies, other considerations may dominate the thinking of the political leaders, but I have no experience in this area. Throughout my period of political activity, primary elections determined every mayoralty nomination and every borough-president nomination except one, where the incumbents were all designated for a second term. I suspect, however, that the process is not substantially different from that involved in selecting candidates for nomination for other office.

At the other end of the political scale—nominations for the lowest political office, member of the assembly, New York State's lower house—the power and function of the local leader is far greater, and that of the county leader far less significant. If the assembly district is not divided for political leadership purposes, and one male and one female leader (and one club) cover the whole district, the decision is normally reached within that single assembly-district club.

The procedures and the considerations vary, depending upon the strength and influence of the leader and the nature of the club. In some clubs the leaders by choice or necessity leave the decision to the democratic vote of the club members. In others, the club members in effect ratify a leadership decision. If the leaders' judgment (and that of their close associates, usually the club officers) is highly valued (or is law), the leaders' estimate on the best possible candidate will in many cases be conclusive. Generally, however, whatever the procedure, club members, captains, club officers, and leaders together reach a consensus on the candidate based on a variety of factors—such as past service and performance, personality, friendship, loyalty, capacity to campaign, judgment and intelligence, capacity to finance a campaign (and perhaps to finance the local clubs after the campaign).

Once a candidate is thus selected, his actual nomination, of course, comes from the enrolled Democrats at a primary election. But even if there is a contested primary, the initial selection is of major and usually conclusive import, and it carries with it the support of the existing leaders and their club. (In New York County in 1964 there were four assembly primaries in our sixteen assembly districts, and the "regular"—the district leader's—candidate, won in all but one.) If there is no contest, the primary is not even held and the single nominee is chosen by default. In most cases this is what happens.

Where the district is a consistently losing one, the task is rarely one of choosing among competing candidates (although there may be competing individuals who would like to be candidates), but finding and persuading a personable candidate to make the race—for the honor of the club and the party and the hope of future appointment to executive or judicial office or nomination to a winnable office. In such districts primaries are rare indeed, and frequently club-membership endorsements are a formality.

The selection process in such a one-club district almost never involves higher party officials such as the county leader, except when it falls to the county leader to help find a candidate in a losing district.

But where the assembly district is divided into two or three leadership areas, with two or three clubs, two or three sets of leaders, and two or three candidates vying for designation, the county leader participates—as he does when state senators (representing two or three assembly districts with six to nine sets of leaders) or congressional candidates (involving as many as seven or eight assembly districts and as many as twelve or more sets of leaders) are to be designated. The county leader is an arbiter, a mediator, a font of party wisdom, a disciplinarian who insists that the quarreling leaders meet and talk and seek a peaceful (no primary contest) solution.

It is in this context that the internal political process functions at its best for analytical purposes. Ideally it resolves all the competing claims of co-equal leaders in such a way as to produce a unified party after only one claim is honored and all the others rejected.

Occasionally, especially in retrospect, the problem seems so simple and the solution seems so obvious, that it is hard to believe that the problem, prospectively, seemed difficult. All that was required was the acquisition of an understanding of the political problem, the discovery of a solution, and the persuasive explanation of that solution to the leaders involved.

The nomination of State Senator Jerome L. Wilson in the Twenty-second Senate District in 1962 is a simple example of the retrospectively easy solution of what was a potentially explosive problem.

Until 1962, the Twenty-second District had been represented by an elderly anti-Wagner district leader who, in 1961, was defeated as a candidate for re-election as leader by a reformer in the Wagner landslide. He obviously had to be replaced as state senator in 1962 (when he was seventy-three years old).

The political problem arose out of the political complexion of the district. It was about 50 percent white and 50 percent Negro and Puerto Rican—an equilibrium of relatively recent origin, due to increases in the Negro and Puerto Rican population. Until

1962, most of the senate district had been part of a congressional district represented by a white congressman. But in 1962 that congressional district was abolished, and almost all its inhabitants were now part of Adam Clayton Powell's district.

This presented problems. The Executive Committee of the New York Democratic Party has been integrated for years in the sense that Negroes and whites—and, earlier, Irishmen and Jews—have worked together as co-equal members of the same organization, resolving disputes and claims internally. But tensions among the voters have existed, especially in a district such as this—principally lower-middle- and lower-income neighborhoods with deteriorating housing and an expanding Negro and Puerto Rican population.

Party leaders reflect these tensions, although party leaders of all colors, backgrounds, and religions (even Armenian-Swiss Unitarians) were accustomed to working together on an equal basis to resolve problems within the party.

But in 1962 the Negro and Puerto Rican leaders, reflecting local sentiment, were pushing for a Negro or Puerto Rican candidate. The other leaders, reflecting their local sentiment, were pressing for a white candidate, especially since Adam Powell was concededly to be renominated for congressman and to run in the part of his new congressional district formerly represented by a white.

A second divisive factor was the regular-reform division in the district. Regulars held two-thirds of the district, and two-thirds of the leaders' votes for nomination. But reformers with one-third of each had districts that cast almost half the total vote in elections. Middle- and upper-middle-income white districts, which the reformers represented, register and vote in far higher numbers than their lower-income counterparts.

Accordingly, a regular-reform split might have led to a close and bruising primary fight. And so the fourteen leaders involved, seven men and seven women, were convened in a preliminary meeting at county headquarters to explore the situation. It was a polyglot group. One leader was of Irish extraction, one was a WASP, there were 5 Negroes, 3 Puerto Ricans, 2 of Italian ex-

traction, and 2 of Jewish background. (6 whites, 5 Negroes
and 3 Puerto Ricans; 6 reformers—four whites, one Negro, and
one Puerto Rican—and 8 regulars.)

Initially there were four serious candidates: one of the reform
district leaders, Harry Sedgwick; John Edmunds, the candidate
of Hulan Jack, from a heavily Negro district; Marie Lanzetta, a
state Democratic committeewoman from one of the regular districts; and Assemblyman Ramos-Lopez, incumbent assemblyman
from one of the assembly districts included in the senate district.

The meeting droned on. No one was inclined to give an inch.
The regulars resisted Sedgwick, the reformers resisted Edmunds,
and no one suggested alternatives or solutions.

Typical claims for the nomination were asserted. The retiring
incumbent came from Sedgwick's district and he should get it;
Lanzetta had years of party service; Edmunds represented the
increasingly important Harlem community; Ramos-Lopez represented the Puerto Rican population, which had no state
senator.

There was a growing division, which seemed to involve every
possible dispute (reform vs. regular; Negro vs. white; Puerto
Rican vs. both; old party members vs. newcomers; lower income
vs. upper and middle income). No decision was reached at the
initial meeting; everyone went home to think about it.

I thought hard. The party wanted no racial war, no white
backlash by the sudden selection of Negro candidates for both
state senate and congress in a district which was under such
tension, and was already for the first time assured of one Negro
candidate. A regular vs. reform battle, an old-timer vs. newcomer fight, or a Puerto Rican vs. white and Negro dispute could
be devastating.

What was needed was a candidate who crossed the various
lines. By good luck—and it was luck—he was found.

Jerome Wilson was an assistant to and highly regarded by
Borough President Edward R. Dudley, an important figure in
the Harlem community. Wilson was young (about thirty) and,
although a WASP, he had worked for some years as a full-time
staff member of the Urban League before joining Dudley. As

such, he had made many friends in the Negro community. He had also found time to befriend some important figures in the Puerto Rican community.

He was from a reform club, but his service to Dudley outweighed that blemish so far as the regulars were concerned. (Harlem leaders seemed to dislike and resent reformers more deeply than other regulars. Hence, Dudley's support should be of great importance in neutralizing such resistance.)

Beyond those qualifications, Wilson was an extremely bright and attractive young man. He wrote particularly well and had great imagination in discovering, and occasionally creating, public issues that were of concern to substantial numbers of people. He had a knack for dramatizing anything—from the need for more parks, to tearing down an unused armory and replacing it with new housing, to beautifying First Avenue, which ran through his district.

In short, but for one thing, he looked like a natural solution. The one thing was the relative brevity of his political experience. He had been involved in politics only two or three years. I worried about whether he might prove to be impetuous in times of pressure.* Nevertheless, I decided to try him out.

First, I spoke to Wilson. He was interested. There were reservations, principally relating to financing. Wilson was not a rich man. I assured him he would be able to manage, and I said I'd try to help. He agreed to take a crack at it.

So we went to work. The mechanics were simple. The first step was to sound out his boss, Borough President Dudley, for Dudley's help was essential. Dudley was enthusiastic and offered to help. He did. He spoke to some of the Harlem leaders, and persuaded them that Wilson was a good friend of Harlem's and an able man.

---

* Later he did. But he survived his impetuosities, although there were one or two close calls. I remember once, when he decided to "endorse" a candidate for the United States Senate, I called him, told him he had done it again, and suggested that if he was so damned anxious to be a political leader we could arrange to run him for district leader and someone else for state senate.

I spoke to some of the leaders, explaining Wilson's assets. Some of them were persuaded that Wilson's candidacy would solve most of the problems.

I spoke to Sedgwick, the reform leader who was a candidate, and urged him to forgo his candidacy for the senate—since he lacked Wilson's support in the Harlem end of the district—and try the assembly, where he would avoid some of the problems he would face in the larger senate district. He ultimately agreed and along with the rest of the reformers agreed to support Wilson.

Meanwhile, the Harlem leaders made a last effort. They persuaded Congressman Powell to come to New York to meet with me. As the "head" of the local ticket (he was running for Congress), I was told his views should be ascertained. They were, but they weren't too helpful in resolving disputes. He, like his community, was for a Negro! And then the leaders met again. By the time of the meeting, however, the decision had been reached. Enough of the leaders had privately advised me they were willing to support Wilson as the best solution to guarantee that he had a majority.

The meeting itself was a formality. There was a safe majority for Wilson over Edmunds. Lanzetta and Ramos-Lopez graciously withdrew, recognizing they lacked the votes.

But that did not end the matter. For the complicated ethnic problem in the district remained an invitation to a primary fight. And Congressman Adam Powell, moreover, let it be known that if the leaders nominated Wilson, he would promise a "racial war."

A primary fight did develop. John Edmunds decided to run, without the support of any of the leaders. For, once a majority of the leaders had selected Wilson, all the leaders agreed to support him. This is one of the ancient traditions of the party, still observed by the regulars, and recently by the reformers, too. Once the leaders resolve their internal disagreements, they unite. Later, on some subsequent nomination, the defeated leaders have a claim for support because of their willingness to "go along."

This tradition gives the party organization great strength. The organization alone has a functioning apparatus—leaders, headquarters, captains—in every part of the county and every possible variable subdivision in the county.

While all of this is true in theory, in practice the degree of enthusiasm of the support understandably varies. A club and captain who have seen their choice for the candidacy defeated are expected dutifully, but not necessarily enthusiastically, to support the winner.* This being the case, the first task of the winner is to go to the clubs that backed his opponent and make friends. Then he goes to the clubs that supported him for reasons other than deep personal attachment.

Wilson did this job well. Although a reformer, he was soon accepted by regular captains and leaders as a "decent guy," a "nice guy," "he's okay," and the like. Dudley helped a lot. So did Wilson's old friends from Urban League days.

But Edmunds remained in the race. As the regular clubs gathered signatures on designating petitions for Wilson,† Edmunds and a few of his friends did the same thing for Edmunds. The probable result of the primary was not a source of concern. Wilson would win. But the by-products of the primary—the "racial war" Powell had promised and which was developing (and the monetary cost of a primary to a candidate without financial resources)—was troublesome. Any time is a bad time for that kind of battle, but 1962 was a particularly dangerous one. New York's Democratic Party had up to then avoided such issues, and survived as the party in which white and Negro could and did work together.

To head off the needless clash, the help of another Harlem leader, J. Raymond Jones, was enlisted. His district was outside the senate district, but his influence among his fellow leaders was great. In addition, Edmunds had worked under Jones in the Wagner primary. Jones agreed to talk to Edmunds. Jones did his job. It developed that Edmunds was interested in a position with a city agency to which he had applied many months before,

---

* On occasion, the disagreement is too deep, and the issue is resolved in a primary fight. After the primary, everyone is expected to support the winner, who is now the official Democratic candidate.
† To get on the primary ballot, a candidate must file "designating petitions" containing the signatures of a certain number of enrolled Democrats. For a state senator the number is 750. Since many signatures may be disqualified on technicalities, four times that number must be filed.

but no appointment had come through. To avoid Adam Powell's "racial war," I was willing to give the administrative process a push, and I did. Edmunds withdrew. He got the job. There was no primary. The "racial war" never took place. Wilson was elected in the general election, and two years later re-nominated and re-elected without any serious opposition. It has been a peaceful district since.

All of the conflicts—racial, economic, regular vs. reform—were avoided. And in fact the leaders of this senate district, earlier than any others, overcame the regular-reform division which had so badly divided the party.

This is a simple example of the way the internal political process resolves competing demands of co-equals. It involved persuasion, compromise, willingness to abide by majority decision, and a receptiveness to the judgment of the county leader. But essentially it was simply matching the problem with a sensible solution.

While the Wilson case shows the process as it works at its simplest, it is rarely that easy. The process is usually far more complicated, involving many more factors and much more maneuvering. The nomination of Constance Baker Motley for the state senate in 1964 in the adjoining Twenty-first Senate District shows a more typically complicated example of the process at work.

8. How to Nominate a State Senator the Hard Way

✿✿✿ ✿✿✿ ✿✿✿ ✿✿✿ ✿✿✿ ✿✿✿ ✿✿✿ ✿✿✿ ✿✿✿ ✿✿✿ ✿✿✿ ✿✿✿ ✿✿✿ ✿✿✿ ✿✿✿ ✿✿✿ ✿✿✿ ✿✿✿

The Nomination of Constance Baker Motley

Politics has often been compared with the game of chess. There are gambits, feints, and protective actions, moves and counter-moves. There are many similarities, but politics is not limited to a grid of sixty-four squares; the possible moves of the participants are not so narrowly fixed. Unlike chess, the game doesn't always end when the king is checkmated. In politics there may even be a move after that usually decisive point that will reverse the whole result.

The Motley nomination is a case in point. Apparently lost, it was subsequently won by wholly unorthodox internal political moves.

I once made a speech on "The Non-Euclidian Logic of Politics," in which I attempted to demonstrate that in politics as in non-Euclidian geometry, a straight line is not the shortest distance between two points. What follows is the non-Euclidian game of political chess in all its complexity that produced the result of launching the political career of Constance Baker Motley.

The Political Grid

The Twenty-first Senate District on the West Side of Manhattan consisted of three assembly districts. The Eleventh was a wholly Negro district in the heart of Harlem. The Seventh was a predominantly white district, with 20 to 25 percent Negro and Puerto Rican voters on its periphery. The third, the Thirteenth Assembly District, was about 50 percent Negro and 50 percent white and Puerto Rican.

The senate district included Columbia University, the surrounding upper-middle- and lower-middle-class housing, recently built middle- and low-income housing, and some of the worst slums left in New York City. Running from approximately 100th Street to approximately 160th Street, it included the heart of Harlem. It was predominantly a Negro district and had been represented in the state senate by Negroes for many years.

Its senator, until January 1964, was James Watson, the son of the first Negro judge in New York City, who followed his father to the bench by election in November 1963. His resignation as of December 31, 1963, had created the vacancy.

A nominee to succeed Watson was to be selected by the Democratic County Committee members from the Twenty-first Senate District.* The nominee would run for office at a special election called by Governor Rockefeller for the fourth day of February.

The Players

Edward R. Dudley, borough president of Manhattan (and chairman of the Democratic County Committee, a titular post), had by common consent of the mayor and myself assumed the responsibility of guiding the destinies of the Democratic Party in Harlem. Early in January he reported to me and to the mayor

---

* The enrolled voters of every election district in the county, an area which includes on the average about 500 voters, elect two or three county committeemen every two years. Years ago the county committeemen elected the district leaders; although district leaders are now elected directly by the voters in the party, the committeemen continue to be elected, meet every two years to organize the party and re-enact the rules, and theoretically remain the repository of all party power. In fact, almost all power is delegated to the Executive Committee, which consists of the sixty-six leaders. County committeemen, however, still retain vestigial powers; one is nominating candidates to run in special elections where no primary is held.

the existence of three nominees: Andrew Tyler, president of the Harlem Lawyers Association; Noel Ellison, a dry-cleaning store operator; and Constance Baker Motley, general counsel of the Legal Defense Fund, an arm of the NAACP, who had been the attorney for James H. Meredith in his efforts to secure entrance to the University of Mississippi.

Tyler had the backing of Lloyd Dickens, a regular district leader from the Eleventh Assembly District, which had 133 members on the County Committee. Of these, all but about 20 were Tyler supporters. That would give Tyler about 113 votes on the first ballot.

Ellison had the backing of the Ryan group, which consisted of the "reform" group in the senate district; Congressman William Fitts Ryan, and Franz Leichter and Eugenia Flatow, district leaders of the Seventh Assembly District, and Margaret Cox, female district leader of the Thirteenth Assembly District West. The Seventh Assembly District had 176 county committeemen, of whom all but a few were controlled by Ryan, and Cox had 34, for a total of 210 votes for Ellison.

Motley had no one's avowed support. This fact was the tip-off and it correctly led me to believe that J. Raymond Jones, a regular district leader of the Thirteenth East known as "the Fox," was her unavowed sponsor, with 97 county committeemen behind him.

The remainder of the county committeemen came from Angelo Simonetti's club in the Thirteenth West (51 county committee-men). Simonetti (a regular) and Jones (a regular) were feuding —something they had done every few years for some twenty years during which they had shared the district. Simonetti was for no one—but obviously *not* for Ellison, the reformer supported by Simonetti's opponent in his district, Margie Cox, and by Ryan's Riverside Democrats, likewise bitter opponents.

In this situation, Dudley advised us he thought the nomination should go to Andy Tyler—largely because Tyler, a decent and attractive fellow, had been active in politics for some years, and Motley was a newcomer.

Dudley discounted Ellison completely. First, although a Negro (as all the candidates were), he came from the predominantly white and, more important, reform Seventh Assembly District. The rest of the district, the Eleventh and Thirteenth, had authentic roots in the Negro community and its voters were not attuned to the reform ideology or mentality.

Second, Ellison apparently had a police record and he did not even seem to be a serious candidate. Rather, it seemed the Riverside Democrats had put forward Ellison for bargaining purposes of some sort.

And then, with the mayor's blessing (and mine), Dudley took over. The meeting was arranged and called for January 13, and the chess game started.

Preliminary Maneuvers

It soon developed that the reform forces were serious about Ellison. They pressed J. Raymond Jones, now the county leader but then a city councilman and district leader, for support.

Jones, it developed, had agreed a half year earlier to support the nominee of the reform forces for the senate vacancy, in exchange for support for Jones from the reform forces for Jones's 1963 City Council candidacy.

But, it seemed, Ray Jones had hedged his commitment: he had agreed to support any *qualified* candidate of the reform forces.

While such a condition opened the door to Jones to assert captious refusals to come through on his commitment, it is really hard to quarrel with his refusal to support Ellison, who, it now developed, did have an honest-to-God police record that included four convictions for policy—a form of gambling banned by the law but widely practiced in lower-income areas. It is known locally as "the numbers game," and to the press as "the numbers racket."

Ellison's reform supporters were prepared to overlook these derelictions and did. The "reasons" were a strange mixture of old-fashioned clubhouse politics, reform ideology, and liberal condescension to the Negro community:

1. Ellison was the president of the Ryan-Leichter-Flatow assembly-district club.

2. Ellison was a Negro and the candidate, in light of the Negro composition of the district, had to be a Negro.

3. The reform group had disqualified its only other possible Negro candidate for political heresy. He was a college graduate, a law-school graduate, a practicing lawyer, who had had the bad judgment to accept the first appointment ever tendered to a Negro as a referee of the Appellate Division of the Supreme Court of the State of New York. The sin in this act was that the position is classified by the reform ideology as "judicial patronage" and therefore evil. Ellison, in contrast, held a so-called "no-show" job as clerk to the retired state senator, which required no work but paid $1,800 a year, and which the club had gotten for him. Even though Ellison did no work for his $1,800 a year and his lawyer counterpart worked quite hard indeed, Ellison's "job" was no bar to his candidacy but the "judicial patronage" job held by the lawyer was.

4. Finally, the representatives of the white reform community were, in their own patronizing way, prepared to believe that "playing the numbers" in Harlem was acceptable to its inhabitants, and therefore to be forgotten and forgiven.

And so Jones had the option of supporting Tyler, the president of the Harlem Lawyers Association. But Tyler was supported by and beholden to Dickens, Jones's old enemy, and probably by Simonetti (in a choice between Tyler and Ellison, certainly).

Accordingly Jones had to find a new candidate. Lo and behold, Constance Baker Motley!

As the contestants went to the meeting of county committeemen from their senate district on January 13 (a majority of those present was necessary to win), any rational prediction would have been that on the first ballot Ellison would lead, Tyler trail, and Motley come in behind, with the latter two subject to adjustment, depending upon what Simonetti decided to do with his 51 votes.

At that point, the regular opponents of Ellison, the reformer and the convicted policy figure, would unite on Tyler or Motley under Dudley's gentle prodding.

The Moves

Everything went wrong.

First of all, it was a terribly snowy night. The meeting, organized and chaired by Borough President Dudley, was being held at a school at 155th Street in the northern end of Harlem. My guess was that the white, liberal reformers from the Seventh Assembly District—from Morningside Heights and southward, at the southern end of the district—would attend in far fewer numbers than the committeemen from the Eleventh and Thirteenth, who would be meeting close to home.

The guess was wrong. For, to compensate for the weather, the Ryan group applied techniques that would have done credit to the Tammany of a hundred years ago. Indeed, they overcompensated, and in this lay their undoing.

Late that night, the incredible result was announced. Noel Ellison, the "convicted gambling figure," as the *Amsterdam News*, an influential Harlem weekly, described him that week in a banner headline, had been nominated! The Seventh Assembly District forces, combined with those of Margie Cox from the Thirteenth, had eked out a majority of 3 votes: 179 for Ellison to 72 for Tyler and 104 for Motley. (Jones and Simonetti, who made up for the umpteenth time, supported Motley.)

At this point the chess game should have been over. The candidate was selected. There was no primary. The election was three weeks off.

In fact, the game was just starting.

On Tuesday, January 14, there was a stunned silence around Manhattan's Democratic County Headquarters. Both Justin Feldman, who was chairman of the Law Committee and the counsel to the Democratic Party of New York County, and Nelson Kantor, Feldman's vice-chairman, attested to the magnificent organization the reform forces had demonstrated in producing 179 of their committeemen, or about 85 percent, while the other leaders hit as low as 60 percent of their attendance.

Feldman started to tell me about a technique the reform forces had used to elect substitute county committeemen for those who could not attend. I did not pay too much attention, because I was too stunned. How, I thought, does the Democratic Party look in Harlem when predominantly white "reformers" select a four-times-convicted policy figure to represent Harlem? What will happen to the attitude of that community toward the party? For I already knew via telephone calls and telegrams that the community was boiling.

Dudley had been in charge of Harlem till then, but I decided I would have to step in.

First, on Tuesday, January 14, I called a meeting for Wednesday afternoon of Simonetti, Jones, and Dickens to bawl them out for letting this happen and to tell them they had to get together. No sooner had they been notified than I received a call from Dudley. What was the meeting for? What was I trying to do? Didn't I realize the decision had been reached? Bad as it was, it was only for one term, and we were all stuck with Ellison.

I told Dudley I intended to tell the leaders involved they had goofed badly, and I told him no more. I suppose he was concerned lest there be any criticism of the meeting over which he had presided. I said nothing.

Late that afternoon I called Feldman and got a more detailed report on the meeting. I asked him to check on how long we had, before the legal deadline, to get Ellison to decline.

I tried to reach the mayor, in the hope that I could get him to persuade Ellison to withdraw. I was very lucky—it only took twenty-four hours and about ten phone calls at strategic times and places to get through to him.

By Wednesday afternoon, when I reached him, the press had reported the news of Ellison's nomination and editorialized on it. The news and editorials were bad. Even the New York *Post*, whose chief political writer had a love affair with the Ryan club (his wife was a member of it and a county committeewoman, and through the club she had obtained a job with the city after the 1961 Wagner campaign), was hard put to justify the reform judgment.

On Wednesday afternoon Feldman had gotten back with the

bad news that we had only until midnight to get Ellison's declination.

So we went to work.

When I got the mayor on the phone, I told him that I was convinced the Ellison candidacy would seriously injure the party in Harlem and that we had to get Ellison out. Wagner agreed. Despite the fact that his wife was then in the hospital and, as many of us knew, seriously ill, he agreed to meet us at his official residence, Gracie Mansion, at 11:00 P.M., after his nightly visit to see Mrs. Wagner.

I was to get Ellison there.

I was to get a commissioner of the Board of Elections, with whom we could file a declination before midnight.

Justin Feldman suggested we get the Liberal Party candidate to file a declination too, so that we could both get together on a single replacement. That was done.

Ellison was at first hard to reach, and when we finally found him he was reluctant to meet the mayor. Did he have to come? I said yes. Could he bring someone with him? Reluctantly, I finally said yes.

And so at 11:00 P.M. we gathered. In one room was Ellison and the two district leaders who had engineered the nomination, Franz Leichter and Genie Flatow, the "someone" he had brought with him. In the other room Justin Feldman, Commissioner Maurice O'Rourke of the Board of Elections, a Liberal Party representative, J. Raymond Jones, and I waited for the mayor.

He arrived, and we gave him a quick briefing. Initially he was distracted. He had just left the hospital. Someone asked how his wife was, and his answer left no doubt as to what lay ahead. But he pulled himself together, gathered the facts, and he and I joined the reformers across the hall.

The talk went on until we lost track of time. We were getting nowhere. At about 3:30 A.M., long past the deadline, the mayor eyed Ellison rather coldly and said something like this: "I'm sure you are a nice fellow. I have nothing against you personally. But I don't think you are qualified to be a state senator, even without regard to the policy convictions. If you persist in running, I will not support you. I will, if I can find an opponent of yours running on another ticket whom I can support, support your opponent. In any event, I will denounce your candidacy."

And then he bade us good night and left us in his living room.

At times during the evening Ellison had seemed prepared to get out of the race, but there were always conditions. One example I remember was, "I know this sounds a little silly, but if Noel got out could the mayor say he wasn't guilty of . . . what he was found guilty of?" I said I doubted it.

Soon it became clear that Leichter and Flatow wanted, as the price of his withdrawal, the right to name his replacement, either by agreement or possibly via another county committee meeting.

In light of the judgment they had demonstrated in selecting Ellison, I was not prepared to agree to give them such power. And it was awfully late and probably illegal to have a second county committee meeting—under state law the last day for such a meeting was January 14, one day earlier. The best solution was to have his replacement—if he withdrew—named by the Committee on Vacancies, a five-member committee which had been elected at the nominating meeting to fill any vacancy on the ticket caused by death, withdrawal, or disqualification. The reform forces, although they had had a majority at the meeting, by oversight had elected only two of that committee against a majority of three others (Jones, Simonetti, and Dickens).

We broke up after 4:00 A.M.

The next day, after Feldman and I attended to our respective private jobs as lawyers, we met. We agreed that there were two ways out. One, if we couldn't get Ellison out of the race by some method, we could get Constance Baker Motley to run on the Liberal Party line (Liberal Party leaders had indicated to me that the Liberals would nominate Motley if she would run as their candidate), with the mayor's support, my support, and, we hoped, the support of Simonetti, Jones, and Dickens. At our Wednesday meeting all three had demonstrated appropriate contrition, and I felt with the mayor's lead they would go along.

Second, we could bring a lawsuit challenging the Ellison nomination. I was convinced there was something phony about that 85-percent attendance from the Seventh.

Feldman agreed to look into the lawsuit angle. I called a couple of newspapermen and issued a statement that we were looking into the possibilities of a lawsuit based upon "irregularities" in Ellison's nomination. (Little did we suspect we would develop a documented case of old-fashioned Tammany tactics—used by, of all people, "reformers.")

Then I decided to talk to Connie Motley, and I arranged to drop up to see her.

There were a number of people present. The meeting ran late, and I got nowhere. Connie, then a neophyte in politics, took the wholly logical and unassailable position that she was a Democrat and would love to run on the Democratic ticket, but the Democrats would have to nominate her—not the Liberals.

I couldn't shake her. (Nor could the mayor, at a meeting arranged a day or two later at Gracie Mansion.)

The next morning the papers reported my statement about the possibility of a lawsuit. As yet, however, we had nothing to go on, except that Justin Feldman now had some of the papers filed by the reform people when they purportedly had filled vacancies on the County Committee, but he could not find any record of resignations from those who were replaced.

And then the phone rang. It was someone whose name was wholly unfamiliar, but I took the call (as I usually did). It was an outraged county committeeman from the Seventh, a Motley supporter, and he had read the *Times* story.

"How did you find out?" he asked. And then, without waiting for an answer, he went on to say that the whole resignation and replacement procedure, which had resulted in over thirty replacements of county committeemen, was a fake.

Therein lay the difference between the 60-percent turnout of the other districts and the 85-percent turnout in the Seventh.

"I haven't got the material here at the office. It's at home. Can I call you tomorrow?" he asked.

I said, "Don't call me; I'll call you." And I did. The next morning, Saturday, he told me the whole story over the phone. He had documents, he said, and he agreed to bring them down the next morning.

And so on Sunday morning, with a court reporter to take down the details and four of five members of the county organization's law committee, Feldman and I got the story—orally and with documents.

We drafted an order to show cause why the nomination should not be set aside. We drafted a petition to support it. While Nelson Kantor, our vice chairman, checked the law, Feldman and I and two or three law-committee members listened to a tale that would have made Honest John Kelly proud of his "reformer" descendants.

On January 8 there had been a meeting of the county committeemen of the Seventh Assembly District to fill vacancies among them which the meeting had the right to do. There were five such alleged vacancies reported to the meeting, though resignations for the five were never produced. Five replacements, plus three "alternates"—apparently to fill unknown or future vacancies—were then elected!

The minutes of the meeting so stated. But Leichter a few days later had certified in writing to the secretary of the County Headquarters that *ten vacancies had been filled*—and the ten replacements were among those who were part of the 85-percent turnout.

The January 8 meeting of the county committeemen of the Seventh Assembly District was adjourned.

On January 13, the day of the meeting of the county committeemen from the entire senate district, with the snow falling, Leichter called Justin Feldman and asked whether vacancies that might exist that night among the committeemen from the Seventh could be filled by calling a meeting of them just before the full meeting. Feldman said no, because under the rules a five-day notice of such a meeting would have to be given, and it was then too late—unless, of course, he added, in his unfortunately thorough, lawyerlike way, the January 8 meeting of the committee had been *recessed* to January 13, instead of *adjourned*.

Taking the unintended hint, Leichter said that, by golly, that is just what had happened.

And so that night, while the meeting of all the county committeemen from the entire senate district was in progress, "substitutions" of new county committeemen for "vacancies" caused by absences of committeemen in the Seventh Assembly District were being made by a "meeting" of the committeemen from the Seventh, "held" at the same time and place as the larger senate-district committee meeting.

The resignations of absent members were never filed with County Headquarters or anyone else, so far as we were able to discover. But the secretary of the County Committee had been conveniently present at the meeting, and he accepted notices of election of new members to fill vacancies.

All of this was theoretically permissible on the assumption that the January 8 meeting had recessed to January 13, instead of adjourning, and that the recessed meeting was actually going on at the same time and place as the full committee meeting on January 13.

But the minutes of the January 8 meeting showed that the meeting had in fact been *adjourned*, not recessed; and thus on January 13 there had been no meeting of the Seventh Assembly District committeemen at all!

There was more, but this was enough. Our legal papers were completed and ready to go.

Then the question arose of who would bring the action. Justin Feldman said he was ready to do so if I told him to, but pointed out that I would be severely criticized, at least, and would certainly be in serious trouble if I directed the law chairman and law committee to bring an action to remove a candidate who had been duly nominated at a meeting of the county committeemen that had been organized and called by County Headquarters and at which Borough President Dudley had presided.

Especially if we lost.

I didn't want to call a meeting of the Executive Committee to get authorization for a lawsuit, for a lot of reasons. We argued, and he prevailed. Late Sunday afternoon telegrams were sent out to all sixty-six leaders calling a meeting for Monday at 6:00 P.M.

The Executive Committee Meeting

I was in Philadelphia all that wet, snowy Monday, closing a corporate merger for my best client (by then, almost the only one left).

I got to the meeting at 6:30 P.M. and found, for the first time, with a few exceptions, a unified Executive Committee—unified against me.

The West Side reformers—supporters of Ryan—did not want to vote against him or his club. East Side and downtown reformers, although not inclined to support the Ellison nomination, saw in the proposed lawsuit a dangerous precedent which, they feared, might be used against them. (It would have been, as far as I was concerned, if they ever nominated a four-times convicted "policy figure.")

One reformer, famed for his ability to find a middle-of-the-road hair to split, disapproved both positions and suggested negotiation.

Most regulars viewed the proposal with suspicion and did not want to be asked to vote for it. They agreed with the reformers that the county organization should keep its nose out of local matters.

A few Harlem leaders, outraged by the audacity of white reformers in selecting a convicted numbers-operator over the president of the Harlem Lawyers Association and the general counsel of the Legal Defense Fund, were prepared to back me. But they, with my co-leader, Freda Barlow, and I, amounted to only 3 out of 16 votes.

But the big surprise came from J. Raymond Jones, Motley's original sponsor. He wanted no lawsuit. He no longer wanted Motley. He wanted Ellison, so he could use Ellison and his record to beat reform, Ryan, and the Seventh Assembly District over the head for the next nine months. Then, in November, he was sure *both* Ellison *and* Ryan, along with reform, could be demolished.

So he made the best speech of the evening.

It culminated in an appeal I remember: "We should not be

asked to vote on this. It is something which the County Executive Committee should never do—to bring a lawsuit to remove a duly nominated candidate. I move we adjourn."

He had the leaders, and I knew it. They would adjourn.

Given the problems I had had with some of the reformers, and the incredible stupidity and indefensibility of the Ellison nomination, Jones's tactics were appealing to me and to others. But I had previously concluded that the damage to the party was too great to justify any internal political benefit one or another faction might obtain by allowing the Ellison nomination to stand.

So, disregarding every rule of parliamentary procedure, I seized the floor and said, "I won't let you get away with that. We are not going to have this mess swept under the rug."

I reargued my case as to the damage Ellison's election would do to the party, and ended, "If you adjourn without taking action, I want you to know I will bring this lawsuit myself, and I won't listen to any complaints from any of you later."

That did it. The best of all possible worlds was now available to reformers and regulars alike: no vote, no precedent, no responsibility for what might happen.

Only Wilhemina Adams, a Harlem leader, bless her soul, objected: "You mean you're going to leave Eddie out there all by himself?" she asked. "I wouldn't do that to a dog!"

But do it they did, and I counted it a great victory!

The motion to adjourn was passed, but it amounted to an authorization to bring the lawsuit—not, as Jones wanted it, a refusal to authorize it.

And the lawsuit was brought.

The Lawsuit

The problems that came with the lawsuit—other than the basic one of proving our case, which, although it took Feldman's time and ingenuity, was not difficult—were two:

First: the reform forces and their attorneys drove us crazy with proposed settlements: settlements they proposed that we accepted and they then withdrew; settlements they proposed that were so fantastic as to defy credulity; settlements proposed by one or two of them and vetoed by others; settlements, settlements, settlements—all day, all night, settlements—even at four o'clock in the morning before the trial.

When the case was actually on trial, one of Ellison's lawyers begged Feldman to go out in the hall for a brief conference. Feldman reluctantly went. He heard a new and incredible proposal, and rejected it. Said the Ellison man: "If you aren't willing to negotiate in good faith, why did you come out here?" To this day, Feldman doesn't know the answer to that one!

The second problem was: Who fills the vacancy?

The meeting had elected, unanimously, a five-man committee to fill vacancies. Under the election law, if Ellison died or was disqualified between nomination and election, the committee would fill the vacancy. But if the meeting that had elected both Ellison and the Committee on Vacancies was illegal or improper, then both were improperly selected.

That would require a new meeting of the county committeemen to select a candidate.

The trouble with this alternative was that the election law required the committee to select a nominee by January 14, and it was now January 22; that the election was scheduled for February 4; and that no one knew who was and who was not a county committeeman in the Seventh Assembly District, what with wholesale "oral resignations," and so forth.

For these reasons, I didn't want a new committee meeting. Moreover, the reform forces, who had had a majority of the committeemen when they selected Ellison, had by carelessness not elected a majority of the Committee on Vacancies. It consisted of Flatow and Cox (Ryan supporters) and Simonetti, Jones, and Dickens.

And so I went to work on Simonetti and Dickens. Simonetti was no problem. He felt, especially after the Ellison fiasco, that we needed the very best, and he agreed that that was Motley. Dickens was more difficult. The mayor had not been friendly to Dickens, and Dickens wanted an understanding with the mayor before saying yea on Motley.

Feldman and I decided that, however Dickens might vote, the

only practical answer was to have the Committee on Vacancies fill the vacancy—if we got Ellison out.

On Wednesday, January 23, Justin went to Court.

I arranged a hurried meeting between Dickens and Wagner and, while the case was on trial that morning, they met. Before noon, Dickens called me to say his discussion with Wagner had been satisfactory and he was for Motley.

By one o'clock Justin called with the result of the lawsuit. When his first witness was called, the reform forces collapsed, conceded "irregularities," avoided the inevitable finding of misconduct, and fought for a couple of hours for a new county committeemen's meeting.

They lost.

We won. I was authorized to convene the Committee on Vacancies.

That night I sent Justin a bottle of champagne.

On Thursday, January 24, at 12:30 P.M., the Committee on Vacancies convened in my office. All appeared, but only Simonetti, Jones, and Dickens voted. They selected Motley.

She arrived at one o'clock to sign her acceptance and meet the political writers. She dazzled them.

The political decision itself—the formal selection of Motley—was the big news, but in fact it was an anticlimax to all that had gone before.

But it was a satisfying anticlimax. That night I told Frances, my wife, "Well, for once something worked out right."

The fact is that the Motley nomination was one of the few such operations that worked out perfectly, step-by-step and move-by-move. It was, in this regard, a rarity.

But it illustrates very well the complexity of the internal political process at work, and the multitude of considerations that play a role in formulating the attitude of each participant and in bringing about a result.

9 * Factors, Maneuvers, and Deals in Candidate Selection

✻✻✻

In both the Wilson and Motley cases, and in almost every one I can think of, the candidate has a "rabbi"—a leader who makes it his business to plug for the particular candidate. What leads a leader to adopt a protégé depends on the leader. There are undoubtedly a handful now, and in the past there were many, to whom a financial contribution was the primary consideration. Indeed, I am told that there were periods of very poor party leadership when the party and its leaders had little to offer to justify public support, when nominations—particularly in the judicial area—were all but auctioned off.

I have no factual data on the basis of which to disprove these reports, since they relate to an earlier era. In my time, however, if there were auctions, they were mighty private. During the thirty-two months when I was county leader, I know there were no auctions for the nominations I had the power to control.

A candidate coming out of left field might justifiably arouse suspicions that his sudden sponsorship was the product of money. But in local politics such candidacies are rare indeed, and normally there are adequate political reasons to justify the result without searching for illicit causes. Both the Wilson and Motley nominations illustrate what I mean. In Wilson's case, the major consideration in the support he received was the fact that he apparently could bridge a gap and prevent a deep party schism, and so was backed by Dudley and me. In Motley's case, she was needed to erase a bad party blunder.

Since I was the principal, if not the only, contact between the candidates and the leaders in these cases, I know that in neither one did money play a role in the decision of the leaders. On the contrary, in both cases, I had to help the candidates raise necessary funds.

Well, then, why did Wilson and Motley get support? In both cases the sense of obligation of a majority of leaders to "the party" produced the result. The suggestion from any of them that there be a financial *quid pro quo* would have been out of character, out of place, and out of order. At the same time, I must acknowledge that, especially with rising campaign costs, the financial ability of the candidate is a factor. But it is not great enough to overcome obvious liabilities. "Can he make a speech?" "Can he campaign?" "Does he get along with people?" "Has he any sense?" "What's his political background?" "How long have you known him?" "Is he known in the district?" "How long has he lived there?" "What's his private life like?" "Can he win?" "Who will be happy if he's nominated, besides him?" These are among the common questions.

Generally, "financing a campaign" is not a euphemism for buying the nomination by a private pay-off to a key leader. In some cases, however, it does involve the ability of the candidate to defray club expenses in a campaign—sometimes expenses not directly attributable to the campaign, such as headquarters rent, telephone, heat, and light. Club budgets in New York County probably average better than $10,000 a year. Some are closer to $20,000 or $30,000, depending upon the size of the club and the size of the district. For the thirty-three clubs in New York City, the total is probably well over $300,000 a year. Given the citizens' dependable disinclination to help meet the cost—whatever kind of club is involved, reform or regular—the leaders expect the candidate *in a winning district,* where nomination is but a prelude to election, to contribute something to the cost of the campaign and to keeping alive the club which produced his nomination.

In some cases the amount is in terms of a dollar amount—usually ten or twenty dollars—per election district, which is supposed to go to the captain for his election-day expenses and, perhaps, for his time. In regular clubs it usually does. In reform clubs it generally pays for mailings, signs, and other campaign aids—including rent. In other cases, a contribution may take the form of a flat amount to the club to defray the cost of the large street sign outside headquarters listing the names of the candidates, or for the rent, or the campaign mailings, or the telephones, or what have you. (In losing districts—where the Democrats are a minority—no such contributions are expected or, usually, received. In some situations, the candidate is so wholly the club's candidate that the club itself manages to raise the candidate's funds.) This is a usual, but not inevitable, concomitant of a candidacy. It is not the essential determinant of it. Money helps, but it only answers one of many questions.

Concededly, this practice does not find approval in theories of pure democracy. But it exists and it is understandable. It is not a rigid rule, and it would be most misleading to suggest that every district leader is a saintly man, devoting himself altruistically to the good of his neighbors in his unpaid job, paying the local headquarters and campaign expenses out of his own pocket, with nary a thought that part of the load ought to be carried by a candidate who could not have been nominated without the existence of the local club and the leader.

It is equally misleading, however, to suggest that the general rule among leaders is that money comes first and that without it a man is out of the running. If that were true, Al Smith would have been born and died a resident of the Lower East Side, Robert F. Wagner, Sr., would never have gone to Washington, William Randolph Hearst would have spent his life in elective office, and every rich young man with a political ambition would see it promptly satisfied.

But the facts are otherwise. One of the wealthiest young men I know has been an as-yet-unsuccessful candidate for a legislative nomination for several years. He neither flaunts his resources nor even alludes to them, although it is generally known that he is wealthy. But he still hasn't been nominated.

Others, who have flaunted their wealth, have been repeatedly rejected by the leaders as candidates and have abandoned politics or moved elsewhere. Indeed, the ranks of unemployed, wealthy, would-be candidates are filled with men who missed what chances they might have had because they believed that one asset—money—could hide a dozen liabilities.

I suppose in a way this is a vain exercise. Logic cannot establish the rarity of purchased candidacies. Only experience can teach that the myth is a myth, and that the pathway to political advancement is not the purchase of political leaders. But the willingness to help a leader meet his annual club overhead, preferably *before* a candidate even suggests he is interested in running, is something else, far *different* from buying a nomination.

If money is only one of a number of factors, and is not the key,* what are the principal factors?

They defy classification, because the variety of principal factors is too great. In only four of eighteen new candidacies in New York County, in a thirty-two-month period, was the candidate's capacity to finance a campaign a principal factor, and in two of the four cases the districts were losing ones, and were duly—although in one case surprisingly closely—lost. In exactly half of the eighteen, the candidates did not have any real financial capacity but were nominated nevertheless, and in four out of the nine cases they won.

Then what were the considerations? Past political association of a candidate with a key leader or leaders (three cases—two reform, one regular), a leader's ambition to take the nomination himself (four cases—two reform, two regular), a squabble between two leaders over pre-eminence in a shared district, which produced a compromise dark horse (one case), political promise based upon past capacity to campaign for others or past public service (four cases), and so on.

In each case there was one leader who was "high" on the

* There are still a few leaders to whom "making a score," i.e., a pay-off, is a major factor in giving their support. But leaders of this sort have short political lives in New York these days and, unless they happen to possess unusual political prestige, their support is almost useless, because there are usually too many other leaders involved in the process, the originating sponsorship of such a leader is regarded as indicating some hanky-panky is involved, and the overwhelming majority are more interested in their political futures than in a fast buck.

candidate and pushed him through. But the varieties of considerations that result in political support are as broad as the considerations that lead any human being to do anything with or about another.

It is a fact, however, that political leaders are hesitant to sponsor someone they haven't known and worked with for some time. Those who have had the experience of finding a bright newcomer and rushing him into a candidacy have usually lived to regret it. The very qualities which are so attractive always seem to lead the candidate into situations where he may blow a winnable race, from lack of experience or judgment. Or having won or lost, his subsequent behavior may belie his initial good impression.

There seems to be at times a thin line between the psychopathic personality and the magnificent, young, energetic, driving campaigner. And so political leaders understandably tend to turn to tested potential candidates who, on the basis of past association, they trust are on the rational side of the psychopathic line and who are not low in energy. For example, if my campaign manager in my first campaign ten years ago called me today and announced his interest in a nomination or appointment, I would help him, although I have seen him only once or twice a year in the last six or seven years, since he moved outside the state. But I *know* him. We went through a rough campaign together. We learned together. We won together. I know he can be trusted. I know he gets along with people. I know he has good judgment. I know he works like a demon. And I am grateful to him for all his help.

Who would not favor such an old associate over someone he had known but briefly, who was untested, uncertain?

This attitude sometimes makes political leaders appear to be unduly cautious or inexplicably hostile to newcomers. But appearances are deceptive. There is nothing worse for a political leader to have to do than to apologize to his fellow leaders because a candidate he sponsored, advanced, and vouched for six months earlier suddenly endorses a Republican or in the middle of an international crisis and halfway through the campaign, calls, say, for the admission of Red China to the UN, or is so psychologically messed up that his private life threatens to become a public scandal. These examples are not hypothetical. There have been recent examples of all of them.

Finally, what is the role of the back-room maneuvering, of the "deal," in selecting candidates? The story of the Motley nomination certainly demonstrates that maneuvering behind closed doors plays a major role in candidate selection. The Wilson nomination demonstrates that the selection can be almost devoid of any really devious activity.

But certainly in the Motley case, if Jones had prevailed in his attempt to adjourn the county Executive Committee meeting —and this was a maneuver, directed at achieving other legitimate political objectives—and if the adjournment had *not* been construed as an authorization to bring a lawsuit to remove Ellison as a candidate, she would not have been nominated.

I have sat in on many meetings which were all maneuver— every leader, for example, urging a candidate he didn't want, so that, after that candidate was knocked down by the other leaders, he could come forward with a "second choice" who was his real first choice. I once engaged in a five-month maneuver to get the leader with whom I shared the Eighth Assembly District to offer the candidacy of a resident of his end of the district who I believed would solve a lot of reform-regular disagreements. After those five months of work, my opposite number actually offered the man's name to me as one of three possibilities, and I was privately (I thought) elated. Maybe my elation showed, or maybe my opposite number got suspicious of this newcomer on general principles. Anyway, three days later the name was withdrawn. Five months of (I thought—and I still think) untraceable maneuvering went down the drain!

When a split among leaders seems irreconcilable and a primary fight is threatened, the maneuvering goes on in earnest. Somehow a "deal" ought to be possible, but it rarely is—although the effort is almost always made. The reason why the effort usually fails is that the most frequent cause of irreconcilable disagreement among leaders is not a difference in evaluation of the quality of candidates. Indeed, in all my years of activity, I have seen only one, and possibly two primary fights that were the result of genuine disagreements as to the quality of a candidate. The primary always has involved a fight for party power.

Even the two exceptions, where the merits of the candidates seemed to have been deeply involved, had heavy overtones of struggle for party power. These were the Wagner-Impellitteri primary in 1953 and the 1956 primary between Alfred E. Santangelo and James G. Donovan for Congress. By the time the die is cast in such cases and the leaders have split, they have all analyzed their collective local strength and both sides believe they can win. Of course, where the primary campaign soon demonstrates the *absence* of real power on one side or another, settlement is easy. A face-saving device to camouflage a rout on the battlefield is sufficient.

And once the primary has started, even when the participants would like to forget it, the heat of battle, the making of alliances, and the mere progression of the campaign has a way of generating new obstacles to settlement faster than they can be removed.

The Ryan-Zelenko primary fight in 1962, in the Twentieth Congressional District, was a perfect example of this snowballing effect. Until 1962, Ryan and Zelenko had represented separate congressional districts. William Fitts Ryan was a reformer from the Morningside Heights area, and his district was roughly from Fourteenth Street to 116th Street on Manhattan's West Side. Herbert Zelenko was a regular from Washington Heights, whose district ran from 116th Street to 231st Street, roughly—all the way to the north end of Manhattan.

In 1962, congressional redistricting cut Ryan's district in half and joined the area north of Eighty-sixth Street with the Zelenko district. Hopeful of avoiding a reform-regular donnybrook on the whole West Side, in early spring I managed to get a public opinion poll taken. It confirmed what I suspected; even with many "undecideds," Ryan was running far ahead among the decided vote.

I spent weeks talking privately to the Zelenko leaders involved (about two-thirds of the leaders in the congressional district). I pointed out the likelihood that they would spend time and money in a futile effort to defeat Ryan, thereby merely making him an enemy and building him up for the future. Meanwhile,

Ryan was busy consolidating his support by setting up new reform clubs in districts controlled by Zelenko supporters. Within three or four weeks, a substantial majority of the Zelenko leaders were willing to forgo support of Zelenko, provided Zelenko would agree to withdraw (which would have meant some commitment to Zelenko to appoint him to some position in the future, so that his political career would not end), and provided Ryan would stay out of any *other* primary fights in the district for subordinate offices, such as state senate, assembly, and delegates to the state and judicial conventions.

I then spoke to Ryan. By that time, in order to get support for himself, Ryan had made an alliance with a group in one of the assembly districts and had agreed to support that group's candidate for assembly against the incumbent in the primary election. A commitment is a serious thing in politics—at least it was to me—and so, rather than try to get Ryan to break his commitment, which he probably would have refused to do, I went back to Ryan's opponents.

They were willing to agree to make one exception, recognize Ryan's commitment, and let him support the insurgent in the one assembly primary only (which they correctly believed they could win).

Back to Ryan, and we reached apparent agreement.

I was patting myself on the back for a great peacemaking effort. But before our agreement could be confirmed by Ryan and me in the presence of Ryan's and one of my principal supporters, Senator Herbert H. Lehman, it evaporated. (I had felt such oral confirmation by all of us was essential to guarantee performance by all of us.) The meeting with Lehman ended almost before it started, because the one assembly race in which Ryan was committed to give his help to the insurgent had now expanded to that plus twenty-eight delegate and twenty-eight alternate-delegate contests, and two other party position contests. Instead of a contest for one office, we were talking of contests for fifty-nine offices!

This could hardly be viewed as "peace" in the district.

And so the "deal" never was made.

It should have been. Ryan and his supporters and Zelenko

and his supporters probably spent, between them, about a hundred thousand dollars in the primary. The result was exactly what Ryan could have had, by agreement, without all of the trouble, expense, and torn thin-skins of the primary. (It took Ryan and his supporters a couple of years to pay off the debt they had to run up in the campaign.) For Ryan, and Ryan alone, won. Neither his assembly candidate nor any of his fifty-six delegates nor any of his other candidates for party office won.

But we never could catch up with the dynamics of the developing primary campaign. When the contesting forces are as sharply divided as were the Ryan-Zelenko forces, the candidates do not control their forces, nor is it feasible to eliminate the party battle.

There is one reason why political "deals" in such situations are rare, and why, when they are made, they are not usually of much significance—for they usually eliminate only nuisance disputes, not genuine struggles of competing party forces. The fact is that the roles of "deals" in the candidate selection process are grossly overrated—especially if by "deal" one means "I support you now for position A and you support me later for position B."

The variables are too great, the situation changes, the future is unpredictable, and a wise leader neither seeks nor gives such a commitment, except in the clearest and most essential circumstances. Far more common is the situation where a candidate (who probably can't win) steps aside for a stronger candidate, and he and his leader are "owed one," i.e., sometime in the future, when another nomination or an appointment is available, this act will be a plus, an argument, a persuader for him and his leader—and perhaps a clincher.

At a convention, where the candidates are actually nominated by the leaders and the delegates they control, and where there are no primary elections in which the enrolled voters in the party can veto the leaders' selection, deals *can* play a large role— if only because of the number of positions to be filled *at one time*, the anonymity of the delegates, and their subservience to a handful of powerful county and state leaders. But the significance of deals in the process of designating primary candidates, it must be said, is greatly overrated.

Part Four

The

Convention

System

Introduction to Part Four

One of the unique creations of the American political system is the party convention.

Once every four years, every respectable newspaper carries an editorial (egghead papers carry two—one before and one after) about how something must be done about the convention system for selecting Presidential candidates.

The fact that the system works is, it seems, less important than the impact upon television viewers of its vulgarity and apparent disorder. Suggestions that the solution may be found in reducing television coverage regularly meet a deaf editorial ear.

What is lost sight of in this appeal for a more dignified, more genteel nominating process is that the whole panoply of the convention system is in fact a cover—perhaps an unsatisfactory video cover, but a cover nonetheless—for significant political action and political decisions.

The national convention system, I believe, works well. The New York State convention system, on the other hand, is far less successful.

Why does it work well on the national level but not so well on the state level? And how does it work, anyway?

10.∗ The National Convention System at Work

✽✽✽ ✽✽✽ ✽✽✽ ✽✽✽ ✽✽✽ ✽✽✽ ✽✽✽ ✽✽✽ ✽✽✽ ✽✽✽ ✽✽✽ ✽✽✽ ✽✽✽ ✽✽✽ ✽✽✽ ✽✽✽ ✽

The Seating of the Mississippi Delegation, 1964

The best example I know of the effectiveness of the national convention system took place at the 1964 Democratic Convention and involved the problem of seating the Mississippi delegation.

This is the story as far as I knew it. It constitutes no more than one spoke on the wheel. But it is the spoke I know.

The Saturday before the convention opened on Monday, August 24, was supposed to be a nonpolitical day for those of us who had gone to Atlantic City early: a swim in the morning, lunch with a friend in television, chats with old friends, strolls down the boardwalk. But that afternoon the Credentials Committee was hearing the Mississippi delegation case.

We all knew something about the case.

Mississippi was one of the Southern states that denied the right to register and vote to Negroes. By every stratagem, including violence and terror, Mississippi had maintained an almost all-white electorate and an all-white Democratic party organization.

Negroes, denied the right to participate in the regular Democratic Party, had organized their own "Freedom Democratic Party," and had sent a delegation to the Democratic National Convention. Even though many, if not most, of the many thousands of Mississippians who participated in selecting the FDP delegates were not registered as voters (because they *could not* register), this delegation came to Atlantic City demanding that the Freedom Democrats and not the regular delegation be seated as representing Mississippi.

Every delegate (at least every New York delegate), had been deluged with mail pleading the cause of the Mississippi Freedom Democrats.

And most of us, I believe, had concluded that the case for refusing to seat the regular Democratic delegation from Mississippi was very strong, but that the case for seating the Freedom Democrats was about equally weak.

Because we were accustomed to regular procedures and recognized the importance of compliance with local requirements in qualifying as representatives of local groupings of Democrats, both factions seemed vulnerable in their own defense, although strong in their condemnation of their opponents' qualifications.

A few of us went to the hearings. As at most conventions, getting in—with or without tickets—is the first and greatest art. This time we did it as unpaid, unofficial, but duly accredited representatives of a major TV network—our credentials as mere delegates were useless.

And we heard the case.

Both sides argued and produced their witnesses. And we watched while a white minister, with half of his face destroyed, told the terrible tale of life in Mississippi for men who attempted to practice the gospel of Christ.

We heard Fannie Lou Hamer tell, in her quiet, tired voice, of the indignities and brutalities she had suffered because she simply wanted to register and vote.

And we heard the well-groomed and well-trained Southern-gentlemen lawyers try to explain how all of this testimony was, within the context of the legal dispute, a total, albeit disturbing, irrelevancy.

The case was argued for almost two hours. And then the members of the Freedom delegation—these obviously legally unauthenticated delegates who risked their lives and exhibited their noble spirits simply because they wanted to register and vote—were asked to rise in the full light and exposure of television.

And they did so.

The room erupted in prolonged applause—and many of the spectators had tears in their eyes.

Just then I saw one of the top officials of the National Committee leaving the platform and heading for an exit near me. I intercepted him. "John," I asked, "is this going to be settled?"

He didn't know. So far there was no solution.

"If it goes to the floor, and this is on television coast to coast," I suggested, "there'll be hell to pay."

The official agreed. But he also pointed out a new notion.

"Suppose," he said, "a group of Puerto Ricans from your Nineteenth Congressional District in New York show up here and point out that they couldn't vote because of the New York State literacy-test requirement. Suppose they claim they represent fifty thousand other Puerto Ricans who live in the district, who were similarly disenfranchised by your local laws. Suppose they claim that those literacy laws are unconstitutional, which they may very well be, and that but for the laws fifty thousand Puerto Ricans would have voted and elected different delegates. What do we do then, if we accept the Freedom Democratic Party's argument now?"

"We don't beat up people in New York just because they want to vote," I replied, although I recognized the validity of the analogy.

The official accepted the distinction, but still looked unhappy.

"What will the delegates from your state do if it comes to the floor?" I asked.

"Hell, most of them are running for office, most of them are liberals, and most of them don't think it's right to treat people like this. They'll probably vote to seat the Freedom Democrats."

We chatted about the impact of such a decision in the South—Texas, Arkansas, Louisiana, Georgia, Florida, South Carolina, etc.

"The President and all our friends in the South think it will mean losing all the Southern states—right up to and including Virginia," he said.

That was certainly not an unreasonable forecast.

"What are we going to do?" I asked.

He shrugged his shoulders. "Try to work it out," he said—and he left.

The Credentials Committee heard the rest of the challenges and disposed of everything but Mississippi in due course.

But all day Sunday, while delegates continued to arrive, one subject ran around every hotel lobby, over every bar, up and down the boardwalk, and over everyone of the many, many drinks: What's going to happen about Mississippi?

New York had, like every other state, two members on the Credentials Committee—one man and one woman. Jack English, Nassau county chairman, was the man. Joyce Phillips Austin from New York County was the woman.

Mrs. Austin, a Negro, was an assistant to Mayor Wagner. Bill McKeon, our state chairman, had worked with her and was impressed with her. Weeks before the convention he had told me that he would like to designate her as one of New York's two members of the Platform Committee.

I had then seen a chance to get two New York County Democrats appointed. Since I was unconcerned with being appointed myself, and since I felt a debt of gratitude to Eleanor Clark French, who had agreed to run for Congress against John Lindsay, an almost unbeatable congressional candidate, I suggested that he put Ellie French on Platform and Joyce on Credentials. Bill agreed: New York County got two out of the six major committee appointments.

Because of this well-meant maneuver Joyce was in the middle of a maelstrom, for it soon became clear that great pressure was being exerted, direct from the White House, for a compromise. The compromise would have seated only those Mississippi regulars who pledged to support the nominees of the convention and would have denied seats to the Mississippi Freedom delegates while making them "honorary convention guests."

The Credentials Committee met on and off most of Sunday. And the word was that they were divided. A minority report, which required eleven votes, was likely. The minority would urge seating the Freedom Democrats.

With a minority report, the issue would have to go to the floor. On the floor, before national television, the Freedom Democrats would put their moving case. And if they won, the pros who knew the South (I didn't) said we would lose the South.

Joyce Austin was one of the putative minority. Indeed, as we heard it, she was the eleventh vote!

On Monday, the convention officially commenced. I suppose lots of people watched the formalities. But by then the formalities were important to the convention only because they were consuming time, permitting the facts on the Mississippi problem to sink into the minds of the delegates, and providing time to continue efforts to work out the problem.

On Monday morning I became sufficiently concerned to call a caucus of the New York County delegates for that evening on the whole issue. The purpose was to ascertain, if I could, what *our* delegates (who were notoriously independent) would do if faced with the issue of seating the Mississippi Freedom delegates in a floor fight. I also hoped to give some guidance, and perhaps support, to Joyce Austin.

And so the word went out via the county's executive secretary, Lil Halloran (through a communications network which she developed and only she understands): "New York County caucuses at 5:00 P.M. in County Headquarters suite, Room 1021."

Our announcement was followed by another one that the whole state delegation would caucus an hour later.

At 5:00 P.M., we put the vanishing supply of liquor in the closet, closed the doors to all but delegates and alternates, and opened discussion among the fifty-odd delegates, delegates-at-large, and alternates in the largest of our three rooms.

I called the caucus to order and stated that the principal purpose of the meeting was to ascertain the views of the delegates on the Mississippi delegation contest. I reported on the Saturday hearings I had witnessed and commented on the impact I believed a repetition during prime TV time would have on the public and upon the delegates.

I pointed out the views of the Administration as to the impact of the seating of the Freedom delegation upon the rest of the South. (At the time of the convention, it should be remembered, no one expected a Republican campaign that would gain Johnson votes: the election didn't yet look like the landslide it soon became because of Senator Goldwater's incredible campaign.)

Then I asked the delegates to talk. Impassioned pleas were interspersed with calm appraisals.

At the end I stated that, on the basis of the discussion, in my view a substantial majority of the delegates, knowing what they then knew and barring further developments, would be inclined to vote to seat the Freedom delegates, should the issue come to the floor.

I asked if this seemed to be a fair report, and whether anyone desired an informal count of heads. No one questioned my appraisal of the sentiment and no one asked for a vote.

I then stated I would so report on behalf of New York County at the coming state caucus. We adjourned to attend that caucus.

At the state caucus, held at about 6:30 P.M., Jack English and Joyce Austin reported on the Credentials Committee deliberations. As yet, no decision had been reached, although there was apparently general agreement in the committee that no regular Mississippi Democrats would be seated unless they agreed to support the nominees of the convention and to use their best efforts to see that the convention's nominees appeared on the Mississippi ballot under the Democratic designation.

The disagreement was on what to do with the Freedom Democrats. Jack English reported that he was inclined to accept the Administration's view that the Freedom Democrats be seated as honored guests at the convention, but not as delegates from Mississippi. But, he indicated, he would honor and carry out the decision of the caucus.

Joyce Austin, in a moving and compelling speech, said that she had already agreed to sign a minority report—indeed, she was the eleventh of eleven necessary minority signers—calling for the seating of the Freedom Democrats. She said she had done so without awaiting the views of the caucus because it was a matter of conscience, and she had now given her word. She hoped the caucus would not feel she had acted improperly; in any event, her conscience and her commitment bound her to support the minority report.

There was further discussion, including some more impassioned oratory from some of my New York County delegates.

I reported on the results of the New York County caucus and Joyce Austin flashed me a big and happy smile from the platform.

A vote of thanks to and confidence in Joyce Austin and

Jack English, coupled with hopes that some solution could be found, brought the meeting to an end.

Most of the delegates rushed to the convention, and after a leisurely dinner I followed.

At the convention, nothing was happening except the usual speeches that consume time and give the delegates time to meet, converse, argue, and settle problems.

The Credentials Committee had reported on everything but Mississippi, which was to be reported "later"—presumably on Tuesday. This left another twenty-four hours to work out something.

The next twenty-four hours were hectic ones. I am sure many, many delegates played a role in bringing about a solution. What follows is what I know about the discussions during those twenty-four hours. I am sure many other delegates had similar experiences.

When I got to the floor, there were few if any seats and fewer delegates left in the New York State section. It was filled with visitors, friends of officials, alternates, and a miscellany of hangers-on.

I spotted a nondelegate friend sitting next to Bill McKeon, our state chairman, and appropriated the chair. I went to work on Bill. For thirty minutes, while the speeches droned on, I told him of the great danger I saw of New York—New York County especially—rejecting any majority report that did not recognize the Freedom Democrats as spokesmen for the State of Mississippi in some ways.

Billy listened, agreed it could be bad, and then former Governor Averell Harriman arrived. He sat next to me, and he raised the Mississippi question almost immediately.

He told me of the consequences the Administration feared if the Freedom delegates were seated. Mississippi and Alabama were already written off. But Texas, Louisiana, Georgia, South Carolina, North Carolina, and other Southern states, which should otherwise go for Johnson, would, it was feared, rebel if an insurgent group, predominantly Negroes, with no legal claim to represent the predominantly white (and bigoted) regular Democrats of Mississippi, were recognized.

I acknowledged the problem but pointed out that, whatever these risks might be, Northern Democrats, outraged by the brutality of whites in Mississippi, sickened by the murder of three idealistic youngsters engaged in attempting to register people who were entitled to register and vote, would be as moved as were the spectators at Saturday's Credentials Committee meeting.

The convention went on and on while the speakers droned on. And Harriman gave me a private—and unintended, I am sure—demonstration of the remarkable ability he has to run a problem to ground. How many New York delegates did I think would bolt? the Governor asked. A substantial majority—including every candidate for public office, I told him.

What impact would an appeal from the White House have? After an hour of Joe Rauh's production (Mr. Rauh was the attorney for the Freedom Democrats), none.

And many other questions. The more we talked, the more convinced I became that my prediction was valid.

And then Mayor Wagner arrived, and he became a party to the continuing discussion. He recognized the great risk I had forecast. He acidly commented that such a reaction would not be limited to New York but would include every Northern, liberal, urban state.

His solution struck me as genius—albeit typical Wagnerian genius: postpone the report from Tuesday to Wednesday, then from Wednesday to Thursday—then adjourn the convention, whose business would end on Thursday.

Altogether, between McKeon, Harriman, and Wagner, the discussion had gone on for almost two and a half hours. Finally, the convention recessed, and I went back to my motel room. There I found a typical convention "party" in progress (in which we rehashed the problem for another two hours), had "a few drinks," and went to bed at 4:00 A.M.

The phone rang early the next morning. Justin Feldman, a born conventioneer who can stay up late talking and rise at the crack of dawn, answered it. There was to be a meeting at 9:00 A.M. in the suite of our new national committeeman—Ed

Weisl, Sr., a close friend of the President's—on the Mississippi situation. Would I be there?

Knowing my disinclination to rise early, let alone to attend a meeting of politicians in the morning, Justin didn't mention the subject until I staggered into our jointly occupied sitting room, in pajamas, at 9:10 A.M.

When he did mention the subject, he added that apparently Governor Harriman had been up all night trying to persuade Weisl and others of the seriousness of the problem. Hence the meeting.

I muttered that everyone would be late anyway, and was drinking some coffee unhurriedly when the phone rang.

Where the hell was I?

I was, it was reported, on my way. The statement became true within five minutes.

Ed Weisl, Bill McKeon, Governor Harriman, about six other county leaders and a few other members were seated in a large circle when I arrived.

"We understand," I was told in what sounded to me at that hour like a somewhat disapproving tone, "that New York County won't back the majority proposal on Mississippi. What's wrong?"

And then, for two hours, we talked.

It wasn't just New York County, I said. I named other counties, whose leaders were present, which, I said, would do the same thing.

And, without any basis at all except my assumption that we New Yorkers weren't so different from other decent people, I threw in New Jersey, Connecticut, Michigan, Massachusetts, Rhode Island, Illinois, and California.

The argument raged.

Ed Dudley, borough president of Manhattan, a Negro, was called to add his views. People went in and out of the room.

Every political argument that is properly directed to developing a consensus has one or two points where, in retrospect, it can be seen that the argument was won.

Ed Dudley provided the first point. After carefully listening, analyzing, agreeing, and commenting, it seemed he accepted the arguments for the White House view. They were, he said, reasonable and understandable.

And then he was asked, "Ed, when your name is reached on the roll call, how will you vote?"

"Oh," he said, "I'll vote to seat the Freedom Democrats. You fellows may be right that we'll lose the South as a result, but I don't think so. And if you are right, we'll win the election anyway."

"And how," I asked the people in the room, "do you think the mayor will vote when his name is reached?"

There was silence. Someone muttered, "He'll vote the same as Dudley."

"And so will everyone else," I added.

"Well," said one of the county leaders, "I still think my county will go the other way."

The speaker was also a candidate for public office that fall. He was asked, "And after Wagner, and Dudley, and ninety percent of New York County vote for the Freedom Democrats, how will you personally vote when your name is called?"

Silence.

"Well, I personally would vote the same way, I guess," was the reply.

There was silence.

"Excuse me," said Weisl, "I want to make a phone call." We waited. New York County was no longer a pariah. The conversation turned to ways to resolve the issue short of a floor fight.

A few minutes later Weisl returned. He was on his way to see Senator Humphrey. Would we meet again at two-thirty? We would. And at about 12:15 he left.

We killed the whole afternoon waiting. Meanwhile, the wheel of consensus, its hub in Washington, its spokes all over Atlantic City, continued to roll through the fifty state delegations.

Repeated phone calls asked us to wait—Weisl was on his way. Shortly after 5:00 he returned.

There had been an acceptable compromise. There would be no minority report. Two Freedom Democrats would be seated "at large" from Mississippi. A committee of the National Committee would be charged with democratizing the party. In 1968 any state that denied the right to register to Negroes would be outside the party.

There would be no floor fight.

"Whose idea," we asked, "was the seating of two delegates?" Weisl changed the subject. But I believe to this day it was his idea.

And so the dreaded and damaging confrontation was avoided. The principle of an open Democratic Party was written into the rules of our national party for the first time. And the intensely emotional desire of most delegates to recognize the valor and magnificence of the Freedom Democrats was given tangible recognition, without the consequences upon the South which the Administration feared.

But that was not the end of the story. The New York caucus was yet to meet. And the Freedom Democrats had not agreed and would not agree to the compromise.

New York State caucused an hour later, and again Ed Dudley —plus Joyce Austin—saved the day.

First Joyce announced her willingness to accept the compromise. That meant no minority report. Joyce made another moving speech and was cheered to the rafters.

Dudley's role was different and, as matters turned out, silent.

As the meeting was starting, a few white reform-liberals had made it clear *they* would not care, *they* would not fold, *they* would not accept the compromise.

Standing in the aisle at the head of the room, Dudley had asked them why. He listened to the reply, then shook his head.

"You're asking more than anyone has a right to ask," he said. "This means more to me than it does to you. If you try to destroy this agreement, I'll get on my feet and fight you every inch of the way." And he turned and walked to a seat in the rear of the room.

I had overheard the conversation. "Will you talk?" I asked Ed.

He was visibly moved and tense by reason of the encounter. But he winked, and said, "If I'm needed, but I don't think I will be because I don't think those characters will go through with it."

And he was right. The caucus voted unanimously to back the majority report.

Four days had now been consumed by the problem. Countless man-hours had been spent discussing the problem and seeking a resolution.

And when the resolution was reached and enacted, but for one flaw no one would have distinguished this boring business from any other.

On Tuesday night, at the convention, Governor David Lawrence of Pennsylvania gave his report as chairman of the Credentials Committee. It was adopted by the convention as a routine matter without any apparent thought. Like most political decisions, when the time came for it to be made, it was an anticlimax.

The only flaw was that after all the high-level thinking no one had thought to translate the decision into the practical problem of arranging the seating.

And so, to the delight of the TV audience (and the TV networks and many of the delegates), one by one the Freedom Democrats from Mississippi infiltrated the hall and found their way to the Mississippi delegation's seats.

The next day a prominent columnist congratulated the convention for a good and sensible decision.

"But why," he asked, "wasn't this solution forthcoming on Saturday?"

I read it and laughed. My wife commented, "I wonder if there's any way to get across the fact that it took four days to think up the answer that seems so simple now, in retrospect."

The answer to that I do not know. But I do know that those four days—which the editorialists and the TV networks regarded as a waste of time and which were for the TV viewers, I am sure, a bore—were the most important four days of the convention.

For in those four days the only major issue that faced the 1964 convention was resolved.

The compromise represented the greatest step forward in building a national, liberal Democratic Party taken in this century. For years, the shame of the Northern Democrats has been the conduct of the Southern branch of the party. Indeed, the national Democratic Party for years has been an unstable mixture of Northern liberals and Southern conservatives, Northern integrationists and Southern racists, with Northern and Southern moderates sandwiched between their more vocal and vituperative brethren.

The Mississippi Freedom Party contest forced a long-delayed sectional showdown between the members of the party who rejected racism and its members who rejected the integrationist doctrines of the overwhelming majority of the party. The resolution of that contest marks the end of a long internal battle, the opening of the Democratic Party organizations in the South to new life, the probable liberalization of the Southern Democratic Party, and the ultimate release of Southern Democrats from sectional dogmas that have isolated Southern Democrats and Southerners generally from the mainstream of American life.

If the compromise is carried forward, and integrated Democratic organizations in the South are created, it will surely be possible to restore the force of the familiar belief that any child (including a white Southern child) has the chance to grow up to be President of the United States in his own right.

11. The Conditions under which New York State Conventions Meet

✳✲✳

No New York State convention makes any sense unless one understands what is convening. It is the New York State Democratic Party, a nonexistent entity comprised of independent local organizations which assembles every two or four years in the hope that it can get through its business without doing too much damage.

It rarely does. Normally, the mistakes of the convention take about three years to clear up, by which time the party is ready for another crack at it.*

Why does this happen? What makes the convention such a problem in New York State?

First, the party is far too big.

New York State has 62 counties, stretching over an area of 49,576 square miles, almost 600 miles from one end of the state to another. It has almost 18 million people. Each of its harassed county chairmen must deal with his local problems. These conditions create, by necessity, a loose-knit, locally oriented collection of county and district organizations, all of which regard their local interests as far more important and their local loyalties as far more compelling than any abstract interest in or loyalty to an amorphous state party.

Kings County alone is larger in population than twenty-six of the fifty states. Its population is larger than that of Alaska, Delaware, Hawaii, Idaho, Nevada, and Wyoming combined.

---

* The senatorial conventions have not been too bad. But every fourth or gubernatorial year has been a mess.

Imagine the chaos that would result in getting these six—or any six states—to act as one unit, with one Democratic Party organization.

New York City is larger in population than all but seven states. It has more population than the combined populations of Alaska, Delaware, Hawaii, Idaho, Nevada, Wyoming, Montana, Utah, New Mexico, North Dakota, New Hampshire, and Rhode Island. Again, imagine the problems if all of these twelve states, even if they were contiguous, were asked to regard themselves as one subdivision of a larger state entity.

New York State has more people than the above states plus Maine, Vermont, Oregon, Nebraska, Colorado, and Arkansas combined.

So New York's Democratic Party must merge the equivalent of eighteen states into one organization. Since the problems of New York are as varied as those of any combination of states, small wonder that the state Democratic Party rarely seems to exhibit unity.

No county leader has a foreign minister or secretary of state, but every county leader has a host of district leaders or committeemen demanding attention. So over 95 percent of a leader's time is spent trying to maintain a semblance of local order.

The other 5 percent is spent reporting to whoever is regarded as the political "leader" of the state and asking what the other similarly beset county leaders think.

Such a set-up gives "the state leader"—or, more usually, "leaders," whoever he or they may be—a great opportunity to formulate and report state sentiment to the local leaders as *he* or *they* see it and want it. Or, at least, to guide sentiment in such a direction.

A party organization this large is about as manageable as the national Democratic Party, which as an effective political organization is also nonexistent. It is, rather, a loose affiliation of sovereign state parties, which meets as infrequently as possible, decides as little as possible, establishes no public policy whatsoever, but does manage to hold a convention every four years. The national party raises fantastic sums of money and provides a place for state chairmen, national committeemen and women, and significant county chairmen to visit when they travel to Washington.

New York State's Democratic Party functions much the same way, except for two important differences: first, it finds it difficult to raise funds; second, unlike the national party organization, it is expected to function as a single political entity. But New York's sixty-two county chairmen probably know each other a little less well than do our more than one hundred national committeemen and women, and meet each other less frequently.

Small wonder that when the representatives of this disoriented collection of separate feifdoms arrive at a convention, there is a great risk of confusion and disunity.

The second significant condition that often contributes to the failure of the convention to perform its function is the composition of the party. For the 1937 New York City mayoralty campaign, Franklin Delano Roosevelt saw fit to encourage the creation of a third party, the American Labor Party, to help re-elect a Republican, Fiorello H. La Guardia, as mayor of New York City. (Where but in New York City could this happen?) In 1944 that party, consisting largely of anti-Tammany liberals who supported all Democrats except the candidates for city office, split. The Communist-dominated wing remained as the American Labor Party (the party died within ten years). The non-Communist and anti-Communist wing departed and formed the Liberal Party, which has survived. It now accounts for about 350,000 votes out of over 7,000,000 in a state-wide election. But it attracts a not insignificant number of liberal New Yorkers—especially the activists—who would otherwise all be Democrats. As a result, the New York Democratic Party, unlike any other state Democratic Party, operates without a good part of what ought to be its liberal wing.

The absence puts liberal New York City * Democrats at a double disadvantage: first, they lack the influence and votes they should have at state conventions (since Liberal Party involvement, by absorbing much normal liberal Democratic strength, substantially decreases liberal strength in the conven-

---

* There is some Liberal Party activity outside the city, but it is insignificant.

tions of the Democratic Party); second, they are on the defensive at the conventions, especially when the Liberal Party decides to adopt a liberal Democrat as its choice for nomination ("Who do those Liberals think they are, telling us Democrats what to do?").

The Democratic Party, as a result, suffers from a conservative imbalance, which is inevitable when a large part of what ought to be the liberal wing is elsewhere. And so, instead of a true liberal-conservative consensus within the party, and party unity after resolution of disputes, the battles are fought outside the party. Indeed, what few fights the party manages to avoid within its ranks are made for it outside—after a party decision is reached.

The third cause of convention problems is found in a blind willingness among delegates to "follow the leader," whoever he may be. This disease persists even after the leader's blindness, or self-interest, or stupidity, or loss of effectiveness, is established. Thus the party often looks like the pack of animals in James Thurber's *Fables for Our Time* which followed the allegedly wise but totally blind owl (who answered "Who" to every well-selected question) down a highway in broad daylight, shouting, "He's God, he's God," until all were laid low by a speeding truck.

In 1956, most New York Democrats followed Carmine De Sapio to Chicago pretending that New York's fine Governor Averell Harriman was really a serious candidate for President. That time the Democratic convention mowed the New Yorkers down.

In 1958, most of the party stuck with De Sapio at the state convention in support of Frank Hogan for United States Senate. In so doing, the party humiliated its standard-bearer, Governor Harriman, who was backing Thomas Murray, and as a direct result Harriman lost his bid for re-election. A further result was to permit Frank Hogan to be labeled as the "candidate of the bosses"—a disservice to him—so he lost, too! That time the voters drove the truck and the party was laid low.

Then, in 1960, the New York County organization, after losing several important primaries, learned that Carmine De Sapio was an albatross around the neck of every candidate. One congressman, one state senator, one assemblyman, and two state committeemen bit the dust—all beaten because their opponents labeled them as "De Sapio's choice."

De Sapio was rewarded for the quality of his leadership by an almost unanimous vote two weeks later at a state committee meeting that denied Senator Herbert H. Lehman a place as a delegate-at-large to the 1960 Democratic Convention. That decision was so atrocious that, after a huge public outcry, it was corrected a week or two later. Notwithstanding, the hard core of the party went to the national convention and under De Sapio's guidance "sat tight"—waiting for Kennedy to fall short of a majority on the first ballot so that New York's power could "go to work." That time it was the Kennedy bandwagon that laid the New York Democrats low.

Undismayed by that failure, a majority of the party office-holders—still shouting, "He's God"—loyally followed De Sapio down the main highway of the 1961 primary, and were extinguished by the Wagner bulldozer. Thereafter the party had a new chance—and pretty soon a new leader. Mayor Robert F. Wagner, who had defeated De Sapio in 1961, finally took over De Sapio's empty chair—after some hesitation—and, regularly excoriating the bosses, led his flock down a new (but "unbossed") highway. And he watched his followers all over the state get rolled over in 1962 when they vainly fought for the ticket he had dictated against the better, but unspoken, judgment of a majority of the party: Morgenthau for governor—Donovan for senator.

The probable causes for this willingness to supinely "follow the leader" are discussed in Chapter 13. Whatever the causes, the convention seems inevitably to operate on such a basis. Indeed, the "follow the leader" mentality seems to be the dominant feature of every state convention.

A final contributing factor to the usual ineptitude of the convention may be found in the shift of political power from the political officeholder to the public officeholder. As on the national level, so in New York political power is vested more and more in elected officials. The President, the Senate, the House—these, not the national committee or the national chairman, are the sources of internal party political leadership on the national level. In New York it is the governor and the mayor of New York City who, more and more, are the bosses.

This is a mixed blessing at best.

Fifty years ago the political leadership was vested in men like Charlie Murphy, the last real leader of Tammany Hall. It was his function to find and develop candidates concerned with public issues and with good government. And Murphy found them: Al Smith and Robert F. Wagner, Sr., were two. There were many others.

In return for running the party and finding the candidates, Murphy merely expected that, when government privileges were given away, he would be first in line and that he would have something to say as to where those he didn't take himself would go. This self-interest did not interfere with his finding, supporting, and developing good candidates.

But now the political leader is also himself a public official, eager for renomination or promotion. The valuable government privileges that are given away, such as urban renewal project sponsorships, are now given—without the protection of public bidding—in exchange for political support for the giver of the gift.

And the last thing such a leader is anxious to foster is the creation and development of a new, young political person—a potential opponent for *the leader's* public office.

And so, today, the public officeholder who now possesses the political power—himself a candidate for public office—is not out beating the bushes to look for potential opponents.

A Democratic district leader who wants to run for the assembly is not out searching his district for a candidate for the assembly when he himself wants the nomination. A Democratic district leader who is also a congressman is not working to develop potential opponents for the congressional nomination.

Of course, if the demise of the Murphys had meant the end of the giving away of valuable government privileges, one might approve the shift to public-officeholder political leadership. But it has not. The privileges are still being given away—and the dollars involved are vaster than ever before—but the party and the government do not get the valuable by-product of an Al Smith or a Robert F. Wagner, Sr.

Instead, the party gets a dearth of new possibilities for public office.

And so, if party members hesitate to stop the game of "follow the leader," there may be good judgment displayed. For in so many cases there is really no other leader to follow.

And if the candidates nominated by the convention seem to fall far short of appropriate standards, the reason may well be that the candidates were the best of a not-too-impressive lot, or that the better material was blocked by "the leader" or "leaders" who did not welcome the competition of other public office-holders for political power.

What better way to avoid such competition than to see to it that the candidates nominated are those who for one reason or another are unlikely to be elected?

These are the conditions under which New York's Democrats attempt to meet in convention assembled.

Considering the conditions under which the attempts are made, perhaps the results are not as bad as they could be. Indeed, most large urban states have majority parties that exhibit similar idiosyncracies, although no other state Democratic Party has managed so consistently to impair its own political chances by its own behavior.

Two examples stand out in our recent history—the 1958 "bossed" Buffalo convention and the 1962 "unbossed" Syracuse convention. "Bossed" or "unbossed," they were remarkably similar in every way. For different reasons, each made it inevitable that the party candidates would lose.

12.* A Tale of Two Conventions

Buffalo, 1958

At Buffalo in 1958, 1,100-odd Democratic delegates assembled to renominate Governor Averell Harriman. Re-election was freely predicted for Harriman and victory for whoever his running mates might be. By car, by train, by bus, conventioneers arrived, certain of their support for Harriman, and awaiting "the word" on the rest of the ticket.

Most of these delegates had never met any other delegates except their fellow district or county delegates, knew no party officials other than their leaders, and were looking forward to visiting Niagara Falls and having a few days of fun.

Rumors abounded in the jammed lobbies. Harriman was thinking of a new running mate for lieutenant governor to replace George De Luca; replacement of Arthur Levitt as state comptroller was possible; everyone and his brother was a candidate for attorney general; but the focus of major attention was upon the nomination for United States senator to replace the retiring Republican, Irving Ives.

Three candidates occupied the stage, and one hovered above all three. The three were Thomas K. Finletter, egghead, liberal, former United States secretary of air, and the favorite of the small band of liberal Democrats and the larger Liberal Party; Thomas Murray, former member of the AEC, then in his late sixties, apparent favorite of Governor Harriman; and Frank S. Hogan, district attorney of New York County, a pleasant, attractive, amiable, generally liberal man, with a substantial nonpartisan, nominally Democratic record, apparent favorite of New York County Leader De Sapio.

Above the three hovered the brooding omnipresence of Robert F. Wagner, mayor of New York City, who had run for the Senate unsuccessfully in 1956. In 1958, few doubted that Wagner would be the strongest candidate. But in a fit of something-or-other in running for re-election for mayor the year before, he had pledged himself not to run for anything else if he were re-elected mayor. This unnecessary gesture (he won anyway, by almost a million votes) left Wagner unwilling to seek the Senate nomination, and his family adamantly opposed his doing so.

In this set of circumstances the delegates sort of assembled. Harriman was dutifully renominated for governor. Rumors surged about the lobbies about the lieutenant-governor nomination.

De Luca was renominated for lieutenant governor.

Now there were rumors in the lobbies about the nomination for comptroller.

Arthur Levitt was renominated for comptroller.

Still no answer on the Senate, and Finletter supporters dragooned delegates from the lobby to Finletter's suite to meet the candidate, as if (as we reformers devoutly believed) the delegates were in fact free agents exercising judgment.

On Tuesday afternoon, while speakers filled time and air, things came to a halt. Delegates visited Niagara Falls. They chatted. Tension was building. The word was that Wagner was weakening. But almost all delegates were convinced that "they"— that is, the party leaders—would work it out: there was no cause for concern.

And then on Wednesday, the third convention day, the roof fell in. In a startling eighteen-hour day, "they" managed to make sure the ticket they nominated would be defeated.

How was it done?

The popular version is that Carmine De Sapio, in a brazen demonstration of brutal bossism, rammed through the nomination of Frank S. Hogan over the opposition of Ave Harriman, the party's standard-bearer for governor.

The fact is that a stumbling group of delegates, each delegate following his stumbling leader, who was in turn following *his* stumbling leader, followed the leader into a chaotic fight that no one anticipated, wanted, or understood.

First of all, Wagner was *almost* everyone's first choice. While he could not *become* a candidate, he could never have said no to a real draft—and by Wednesday night a real draft was wholly feasible, and probably the only sane solution. For no one would have held Wagner accountable or charged him with duplicity if, despite his 1957 pledge, he had merely not refused a nomination after the convention in desperation had turned to him.

But it never turned. It never created the conditions which would have enabled it to select the candidate it wanted.

Why?

First, the dominant county leaders—De Sapio from New York, Buckley from the Bronx, Sharkey from Brooklyn, Koehler from Queens, Crotty from Erie, and Prendergast, the state party chairman—didn't *want* Wagner. Some wanted Hogan, and others Murray.

Second, the strategists advising Harriman apparently were in basic agreement with the party leaders, and never sought the simple solution of a vote for Wagner which, after the event, Wagner could not have declined, although before the event he could never have agreed to accept. Indeed, Harriman's advisers advised him that Finletter ought to be the candidate.

Third, the governor, beset by conflicting advice, never made up his mind or declared it until too late. Instead, heeding advice from the political leaders that Finletter "couldn't get it," he finally shifted to Thomas Murray.

This alienated Finletter's liberal supporters, who remembered Murray's authoritarian and somewhat nasty treatment of J. Robert Oppenheimer in the AEC proceedings against him.

The pot boiled all Wednesday. Convention sessions scheduled for early afternoon were postponed hour by hour while delegates waited for the word from their leaders, who together waited for the word from *their* leaders, who were in turn meeting with the governor and mayor on the sixth or seventh floor of the hotel.

All day long everyone waited and waited and waited.

And no word came. Leaders, delegates, and the press haunted the corridors. Angry voices were heard behind closed doors.

Finally, at 10:00 P.M., the word was out: a floor fight. Except for a handful of New York County delegates (I think there were twenty-one of us) who supported Finletter, and Mayor Wagner (who supported Murray), and one or two other exceptions, almost every delegate was voted by his county leader.

The New York City counties and Erie County went for Hogan, who had been De Sapio's candidate all along. The rest of the state went for Murray. Eight people, essentially, cast the votes. The five New York City county leaders and the Erie county leader cast the votes for Hogan; the state chairman and the governor cast the rest of the votes for Murray.

Hogan won. Murray lost.

The unwholesome spectacle of a wild convention, "bossism," and the humiliation of Governor Harriman defeated the entire ticket in November except for lonely comptroller Arthur Levitt. He had been almost denied renomination and had stayed away from and outside it all.

The aftermaths of the convention were incredible. The day spent in the hotel seeking agreement off the convention floor became known as "bossism."

De Sapio's meteoric career was nearing its end. Governor Harriman was defeated, and the Democratic Party finally fell out of the control of the pre–World War II leaders, mostly non-veterans, who had dominated the party's affairs since the days of Roosevelt and Lehman.

But the convention reflected the party as it was—composed of delegates who "followed the leader," to whom the exercise of independent judgment was about as permissible an act as murdering one's grandmother.

And so the party plunged down the rocky road to reform. In 1958, no more than eight principals had voted over 1,100 delegate votes at the convention. In 1962, after the supposed defeat of autocracy in the party, the number of people who voted the over-1,100 delegates at the Syracuse convention was successfully cut to at most five.

This excursion through the 1958 bossed Buffalo convention complete, let us turn to the unbossed 1962 Syracuse convention.

Syracuse, 1962

At Syracuse in 1962, "bossism" having been defeated, the party had *all* its arguments, not just the denouement, on the convention floor in the full light of television.

The result was no better.

Mayor Wagner, with an assist from Washington, could and did direct the casting of all but a relative handful of votes from the five New York City counties and Albany County and its satellites for United States Attorney Robert M. Morgenthau for governor. Wagner's then ally, State Chairman McKeon, was in charge of upstate New York, and under his direction a dozen upstate counties followed suit. Two principal county leaders, English of Nassau and Crotty of Erie, spearheaded the Morgenthau opposition—unsuccessfully.

How did Wagner get the votes?

Why did New York County cast 80 out of 116 votes for Morgenthau, while Brooklyn and the Bronx were solidly for him, and Queens ultimately threw enough votes on the second ballot to nominate him, when Morgenthau, as he himself would willingly concede, was certainly not the popular choice of the convention?

The technique in New York County was simple: Wagner announced that he endorsed Morgenthau, and 80 of the 116 delegates followed suit! A week before the Wagner endorsement, it had not been possible to muster ten firm votes for Morgenthau.

Simply follow the leader, again? Yes and no. For some, being with the mayor came first—as if it were magic of some sort. For some it was merely loyalty to him. But followership produced more than a wholesome sense of righteousness. It meant continued access to jobs, no firing of supporters, and a degree of unity within the party that might in the long run result in its rebuilding its strength.

The Bronx came along because its leader received a phone call from Washington asking him to support Morgenthau. Brooklyn (Kings County) came along because Wagner, in exchange, agreed not to oppose the holding of an election by Brooklyn district leaders to elect their own county leader. (This concession permitted the quiet disappearance of a triumvirate, selected some months before by Wagner in his capacity as chief party leader, which had conspicuously failed to perform the functions of Kings County leader.*)

Queens came for the same reason as New York.

Albany came because its leader and the mayor were old friends. So did a handful of upstate counties.

And all came—to some extent—because Mayor Wagner was then rated to be a political genius. He had—singlehandedly—defeated the five New York county leaders in the previous year's mayoralty primary. By God, if Wagner could do that, maybe he was right and Morgenthau could win.

This act of faith and loyalty to the leader was a vain one, and sowed the seeds of resistance to Wagner's leadership which bore fruit in 1964 and 1965.

The ingredients were simple: trust, confidence, awe, respect, self-protection, and an unwillingness to repeat the experience of 1958, when defiance of the public officeholder's views led to party defeat. But the end result was no different.

Both conventions were fiascoes. Both were controlled by a handful of men. Both were vain attempts to create the image of a state-wide party when none in fact existed.

In both, promises were made in order to obtain votes. In 1958, Erie County's support of Hogan was rewarded by the nomination of its leader, Peter Crotty, for attorney general. In 1962, Brooklyn's support of Morgenthau was rewarded by the removal of mayoral objections to its organizing itself.

---

* No one was happy with the triumvirate—not the men who served in it, not other Brooklyn Wagner men on the Kings County Executive Committee who had given it support, not Brooklyn's few lonely reformers, and certainly not Stanley Steingut, the Brooklyn leader with whom Wagner was feuding and against whose leadership the triumvirate was supposed to offer an attractive alternative.

In 1958, leaders sat around a hotel room and argued all day in an effort to complete the ticket. In 1962, they sat around a hotel room and argued most of the day in an effort to complete the ticket.

In 1958, the political leaders fought the public officeholders, Governor Harriman and Mayor Wagner. In 1962, the same fight was fought on the convention floor, but this time against Wagner alone.

In 1958, the public had been shocked by the spectacle on television of the bitterly divided convention. In 1962, the same public was shocked by a similar spectacle on television as the convention was racked by bitter division, disputes as to methods of counting the ballots, threats, shouts, and, for almost thirty minutes, an angry demonstration that sought an adjournment and prevented the conduct of business.

Was there a difference?

Well, there were many—principally, that different people were playing different roles. The spokesmen for democracy this time were political leaders (fighting other political leaders, in name, but actually the public officeholders) "Buckley, free the Bronx," shouted Jack English's Nassau delegate, over and over and over again, to the embarrassed Bronx delegates sitting behind them.

The public officeholder Wagner, who had had only his one vote in his home county in 1958, now had 80 out of 116 of them, plus all the Bronx, Brooklyn, Staten Island, and ultimately half of Queens.

The power had shifted. "Bossism" was dead.

But the convention wasn't much different. True, there was no Niagara Falls to visit. But the delegates were, with a few more exceptions perhaps, voted by an even smaller leadership than in 1958.

How were these results accomplished? What were the techniques that transformed a disunited group of delegates into majorities for Hogan in 1958 and Morgenthau in 1962?

13. What Produces a Majority Vote at a Convention

✿✿✿✿✿✿✿✿✿✿✿✿✿✿✿✿✿✿✿✿✿✿✿✿✿✿✿✿✿✿✿✿✿✿✿✿✿✿

The first thing a candidate who wants a nomination from a convention should realize is that the delegates themselves are not free agents, nor are they individuals subject to persuasion. They are slightly more independent than the members of the Electoral College, who in most states are not legally bound to cast their ballots for any particular candidate. Like the members of the Electoral College, most delegates regard their designation as an honor, as recognition of some kind of their importance. As in the case of members of the Electoral College, who are selected by the key party leaders, delegates are selected by a particular political leader, or by the political leader's club. They then run in the primary election, if there is a contest. If there is, the result is almost inevitably decided on the basis of which slate they are on—that is, under which leader's banner, the regular or the insurgent, are they running?

In these circumstances, the delegate is an honored and flattered designee of one or another leader, and naturally he is interested in proper behavior toward the man or men responsible for giving him the opportunity to spend his money, listen to awful speeches, and cast a vote for freedom. When that leader suggests that the delegate "go along" with candidate X, the natural reaction is to say "yes." Even if the delegate has every intention of exercising his own judgment and reaching a rational decision on the merits of the candidates, the odds are against him. There he is, one man out of 1,100 or 1,200. He sits in a gigantic barn of a building filled with brute sound, parades, bands, orators, and 1,099 other delegates, most of whom are shouting at one another at the top of their voices.

Noise, movement, heat, unheard speeches, hundreds of people —the delegate looks for the other five or six delegates he knows. They huddle together, eat together, drink together—and ultimately vote together. Finally, if the mythical independent delegate sticks to his independence, by the time a vote is to be taken he is exhausted. Perhaps he has left; if he hasn't, the long, long hours of waiting, the speeches drowned out by the floor commotion, the dozens of unauthorized nondelegates with "credentials" who mill around him on the floor, will leave him bereft of energy.

In short, the delegate is the property of his leader, for even if all the obstacles outlined above are overcome, the delegate can't find out what is going on. Inevitably he turns to his leader who, since he is the leader, must supply an answer. The answer can usually determine the vote the delegate will cast.

And so the ambitious candidate courts the leaders—the people who are in control of the delegates.

In New York State, there are sixty-two county leaders. There are perhaps twenty significant district leaders from New York City (depending upon how strong the particular county leader is, and how strong his leadership is; the stronger it is, the fewer significant district leaders there are).

These eighty-two leaders, however, have made alliances. Five to twenty of the upstate counties are associated together in separate informal groupings, informally presided over by one of the county leaders—Crotty in Buffalo, Van Lengen in Onondaga, O'Connell in Albany, and so on.

There are anywhere from ten to fifteen key leaders—including the mayor and the governor—whose support would mean 90 percent of the votes at the convention. But the support of these ten to fifteen leaders is not obtained that easily. For not even they are that independent. Each in turn has allies, who are consulted, and joint action is agreed upon.

The winnowing process continues until three or four or five or eight or ten leaders end up with the joint power to cast an overwhelming majority of the votes nominally cast by over 1,100 delegates.

This hierarchal set-up leads to the "follow-the-leader" phenomenon. Indeed, the major factor in any such convention, where over a thousand individual delegates from different and basically isolated localities are thrust into this environment, is a willingness—a desire—on the part of most delegates to "follow the leader."

In addition to the political and environmental factors which are conducive to going along with one's immediate leader, there are others, especially in a state like New York. For one leader it may be a fear of economic reprisals on himself, or more likely his supporters, that leads to conformity with the desires of a potent superior. This fear persists, although a firing of a Democrat by a Democrat for political reasons in a city or state like New York is as rare as a budget surplus. The examples are few. Indeed, most examples are ambiguous at best.

Thus: In 1960, a De Sapio district leader suddenly became a reformer and attacked De Sapio with vigor (after too many De Sapio men had lost in the primary). He was promptly fired from his post as law secretary to a New York Supreme Court judge. Since that judge was one of De Sapio's closest personal friends, and given the close relationship that must exist between a judge and his secretary, the action was probably to be expected, and was not wholly in the nature of a political reprisal.

In 1956, the day after the author's local club voted to support Stevenson for President instead of Harriman, one of our few members on the public payroll was dropped. De Sapio was then the county leader; when the matter was brought to his attention (rather forcefully), the man was put back to work within a week.

In 1961, a city employee who opposed the mayor in the primary was fired during the campaign, but the reason given was that he had an awfully large unexplained and unexplainable cash accumulation.

Such firings happen very rarely, if at all, and then only when a good *governmental* excuse exists. This is so because public officials are afraid to fire people for political reasons. The press will scream, and the public official fears the voters will resent it; after all, they have been educated to believe that politics is evil and what is more "politics" than firing a man for political disloyalty?

What happens in the rare instance where it is done is that a previously unknown or overlooked defect in a public employee is brought to the attention of a senior public official who, lisping the litany of political purity, uses it as the basis for an act of political revenge. The thing to remember is that it almost never happens. Where there is no cause at law, it never does. An act of political revenge without such cause smacks too much of political jeopardy for the average public officeholder.

But still the fear of loss of a job inhibits the delegates—especially those in some appointive political position. No one really believes "the leader" will use the power of patronage by firing people in order to enforce discipline, but everyone suspects that maybe he will. ("Maybe in my case he'll make an exception.")

More productive of silence and conformity is the number of just expectations for appointment or promotion which are outstanding. Everyone and his brother in the party is waiting for a promised something and wants to do nothing to jeopardize the expectation.

Neither the fear of firing nor the promises which a promising leader can make, however, are enough to explain the general unwillingness of party members to take issue with the boss, whoever he may be. Perhaps the great size of a state such as New York and the relative paucity of political positions available to aspiring young politicians makes most of them turn elsewhere —to business, or law, or other states—for their rewards; this leaves in New York politics only those who are content to wait in line for their turn. Having waited for years, they are not about to lose their places near the front of the line over some silly issue of principle. This is especially true when they hear a deafening silence from the party seniors—who are being "smart" and keeping silent until the "right time" comes. Should not the young men in the party learn by this example, and likewise keep their peace?

Moreover, loyalty to a leader as an individual and a willingness to go "down the line" for him and to abdicate the exercise of personal judgment so as to "follow the leader" may be the result of the absence of any other cohesive force holding a polyglot party together. When one's only contact with other leaders and other parts of a gigantic and loose organization is through one person, the renunciation of loyalty to that person seems like a renunciation of any relationship to, or affiliation with, the state Democratic Party.

Independent political leadership within the party—requiring as it does the renouncing of such personal loyalty to "the leader"—is a lonely and self-isolating act. Few political leaders in the party can see within its disorganized structure enough hope of success, or of striking a responsive chord, or of breaking a majority away from "the leader," to justify such acts of independence. Of course, delegates and subordinate party workers are also encouraged to believe that any dereliction on their part will not be forgiven—and some potential dissidents guide themselves accordingly.

After all, why should a leader push delegate A for appointment, nomination, promotion or a pay raise after delegate A has refused to go along with the leader's views? And if the leader does so anyway, won't the governor or the mayor remember that delegate A wouldn't accept the proper guidance at the last convention?

But overt "arm-twisting" is rare. Indeed, in some organizations the subject of how the delegates will vote is hardly discussed. In 1958 and 1962, I doubt that before Charles Buckley of the Bronx cast his county's vote he even polled the 108 delegates. It would have been a total waste of time to bother with that process. They were "his" votes.

In 1962, the only example of arm-twisting in New York County came when the author's wife was sworn in as a delegate to fill a vacancy. She promptly announced she was for one of Morgenthau's opponents and bounced off to join her candidate's demonstration. When she was notified to cease and desist, she said, "I thought you said New York County was unbossed." The response was, "The county is unbossed, but the family isn't." And that was the extent of the pressure exerted.

Well, then, how does one get the support of the five or ten leaders who cast the 1,100 delegate votes?

The answer to that question depends upon the convention, who the leaders are, what they are interested in, and what makes political sense at that time and place. The techniques and persuaders used by Stevenson supporters in 1952 and 1956, by

Kennedy in 1960, by De Sapio in 1958, and by Wagner in 1962 were all different—just as the candidates and key leaders and situations were.*

Undoubtedly, in every case there are some *quid pro quos*, although frequently unspoken. The "For Roosevelt Before Chicago" club members in 1932, and the "For Kennedy Before West-Virginia" club members in 1960 fared far better after victory than their late-joining comrades in arms.

And no doubt those who stuck with De Sapio in 1958, or with Wagner in 1961 and 1962, fared far better with De Sapio and Wagner thereafter than those who joined later or never joined at all.

But the basic question—So how do you get the support of those five to ten leaders?—goes to the heart of the political art. For the causative factors in the giving of support vary as people do. And the people involved in politics are as different, one from another, as most people are.

Like a great organ with multiple keyboards and hundreds of stops, each voice in the political choir is moved by a specific impulse. The master politician is the man who can find the key and the stop that activates each note and each vote, and with them produce harmony rather than dissonance.

---

* The 1966 Democratic state convention was doubly unique. First, it was the final state convention to be held. A statewide primary bill had been enacted to apply to all future statewide nominations. Second, the delegates, although docile enough to have been controlled by the six or eight leaders who cast their votes on the gubernatorial nomination, were inadvertently left to their own devices on the lieutenant-governorship nomination. The leaders allowed the convention to be convened, but remained at the hotel wrangling over the identity of the nominee for lieutenant governor. They ultimately decided on Orin Lehman, a nephew of the late senator, while the leaderless delegates on the floor were deciding that the nominee would be a popular, but unsuccessful, candidate for governor, Howard J. Samuels.

By the time the leaders arrived at the convention floor, the delegates had seized control. They rejected a leadership effort to reverse the order of nomination—which would have helped Lehman—by organizing a noisy, impromptu demonstration that prevented the conduct of any business. That demonstration was abated only by the leadership agreeing to a roll-call vote on the order of nomination. The roll call was never finished. After eight counties voted, it became clear that the leadership was licked. Samuels was nominated by the delegates—not by the leaders—by acclamation.

Part Five

The

Judiciary

Introduction to Part Five

Nowhere is the mythology of politics more firmly entrenched than in the area of judicial selection. The mythology is clear:

The elective system of judicial selection is bad because the "politicians" use the bench to pay off past political obligations owed to incompetents. They balance tickets, not qualifications, for judicial office.

The appointive system is better, because "politics" and "politicians" play a lesser role, and the quality of the judges thus selected is higher.

A blue-ribbon selection panel, in which the power to originate candidacies is vested in a nonpolitical group, is best.

Every law student is taught these propositions as if they were facts. Every editorialist accepts them as basic truths. What is worse, all efforts to improve the processes of judicial selection start from these assumptions.

I held these beliefs when I started in politics. I no longer do. For my experience has indicated the assumptions are at best half-truths, and that the ultimate solution they propose—blue-ribbon panel organization of whatever form—is a smokescreen and no more.

No system of judicial selection with which I am familiar is satisfactory.

Many of the criticisms of the elective system are valid. But the cure—blue-ribbon origination—seems to me no cure at all. Moreover, the remedies that have been suggested seem to me all to lead to a less perfect method of selecting judges rather than a better one.

What follows is the experience that led the author to reject the myths and to propose some recommendations for what I believe to be genuine reform in this area.

14.* The Nomination of Judges

✳✳✳

Plus: An Excursion on the Balanced Ticket

The selection of judicial candidates is a process that differs from the selection of candidates for other office. There are rarely one or two or three logical candidates from whom to choose, but usually anywhere from ten to twenty equally logical aspirants whose qualifications do not differ markedly (although on occasion there may be one or two very highly qualified candidates) and whose claims for the nomination are equally compelling.*

The political result is that the dominant leader or leaders have broad discretion which they do not have in other areas. Accordingly, the selection of judicial candidates has been the area where it has been most frequently charged that money—licit and illicit—plays a major role in candidate selection. Given the nature of the situation, however, this should be the area in which political leaders have the greatest opportunity for creative political leadership. Putting a candidate in "out of left field" over the heads of two or three logical aspirants in the legislative or executive fields can breed political revolt. But almost all judicial candidates are in a sense "out of left field," for the reasons stated above.

Prior to 1962, the process of judicial selection was one to which I was not privy, and I have no information on the standards of choice that were utilized. Between 1962 and 1964, however, while I was county leader, nine judicial candidates

---

* In New York, judges for the following courts are elected: Court of Appeals, Supreme Court (the court of general jurisdiction), and Civil Court (a court of inferior jurisdiction).

were nominated to run on a countywide basis, and four on local district bases.

Before analyzing this experience, I must note that I recognize the danger of generalizing from relatively little data. I know there may have been factors involved of which I was unaware. I know that all methods of selecting judges have their defects. And I recognize that no system promises perfection.

But theoretical solutions to social problems should have some relationship to experience.

This was my experience.

In *no* case where the decision was made by the New York County political leaders was money a principal factor. The principal considerations, in each case, were as shown in the table opposite.

The results demonstrate the following:

In six out of thirteen nominations (46 percent) high qualifications were a principal consideration, but in each case such qualifications were coupled with one major political factor.

In five out of thirteen nominations (39 percent) ethnic considerations played a principal role and in each case political support of one or another political leader was the other principal factor. (In almost as many cases, ethnic considerations were disregarded.)

In only two cases out of thirteen (15 percent) was the sole principal factor purely political.

(It should be noted that, although high qualifications were not a principal factor in seven nominations, this does not mean that those designees were poorly qualified. On the contrary, I believe that might be suggested in only one case. On the basis of reports to me from practicing lawyers who have appeared before five of these seven judges, three of them have been consistently reported to be "a good judge." As to the other two, I have as yet received no reports, although the Bar Association found both to be qualified before they were elected.)

What do these figures mean, and what do they reveal about the nominating process?

First of all, it is clear that support of one significant leader is of great importance. In eight out of the thirteen nominations (61

PRINCIPAL FACTORS IN NOMINATION

Factors	Candidate									Candidate				Total
	COUNTY LEVEL									DISTRICT LEVEL				
	A	B	C	D	E	F	G	H	I	J	K	L	M	
Outstanding qualifications	x													1
High qualifications				x				x		x	x		x	5
Ethnic considerations		x	x		x		x	x						5
(Ethnic considerations disregarded)				x		x			x	x				4
Support of a single leader who for various reasons controlled nomination	x	x	x		x	x	x					x	x	8
Repayment of past political obligations			x			x		x						3
Unclassified political considerations				x					x	x	x			4

percent) this was *a* principal factor (six out of nine [66 percent] of the county-wide nominations). Accordingly, it would follow that the motivation of the leader would have more to do with the quality of the judiciary than anything else in over 60 percent of the nominations.

In four nominations (30 percent) "other political considerations" were principal factors. They ranged from:

. . . a disagreement among political leaders on a somewhat personal level (for which I, for what then seemed and still seem to be excellent reasons, was responsible), to

. . . a desire to reaffirm that district leaders were significant and decent people by nominating a district leader, to

. . . ambition for a change of position by a strong political figure with a number of years of outstanding legislative service which was acknowledged by the local leaders to be valid and entitled to recognition, to

. . . the desires of a number of reformers to launch a new "nonpolitical" system for political leaders to exercise their power to select judicial candidates.

Three of the four candidates (75 percent) nominated by reason of these miscellaneous political considerations must be described as highly qualified. (In each of these three cases, support by a single key political leader was also a factor, but not a principal consideration.)

Where the support of a single key leader was a principal consideration, in only two of eight cases (25 percent) was that support coupled with apparent "high" or "outstanding" qualifications of the candidate.

Of the six candidates selected in substantial part because of their high qualifications, the political support of four came from a group of leaders (66 percent), and of two from a single key leader (33 percent). This suggests that multiple responsibility and sponsorship tend to produce more highly qualified candidates than single leader sponsorship. And it has grave implications for the notion that an appointive system is better than an elective one.

A major factor is ethnic background; in five out of thirteen nominations (38 percent) this played a major role.

Why? Is such a consideration a valid one?

I believe it is. And since this aspect of judicial nomination raises the whole question of the balanced ticket, it is appropriate to explore that subject in depth.

The favorite and most popular illustration used to prove the evil of politics and of the behavior of politicians is the concept of the balanced ticket. It results, say the critics, in the selection of candidates on the basis of race, religion, and national origin. These, say the critics, are invalid considerations; the *best-qualified man* should be selected, regardless of such considerations!

I have looked for this mythical "best-qualified man" for years. Very, very, very occasionally he appeared—his qualifications were outstanding. But in nine cases out of ten there is no such person.

Every candidate has different qualities and qualifications. The wisest lawyer may not have been in a courtroom in twenty years; the best trial lawyer may never have been in a political club-house or met people with small but galling and, to themselves, seemingly insurmountable problems; he may have no sympathy with or understanding of people he will deal with on the bench. He may have no judicial temperament. The legal scholar may live in a world of abstractions, or be arrogant, or have doubts about (or be shy of) the calculated tumult of the adversary system. The man with a deep understanding of human motivations may be a poor lawyer. And so on.

Beyond this, the theoretically "best-qualified" candidates rarely appear on the political scene. To the leaders in the legal community, it is considered beneath one's dignity to *seek* nomination to the bench or to legislative office. One must wait until sought out—preferably on a bipartisan basis! In the rare cases where such a candidate seeks judicial office, his fear or suspicion of politicians, or his attitude about politics and politicians, frequently destroys his chances. This is needless, for politics is not a dirty business unless there is a will to make it so, and most politicians are not thieves. A candidate's attitude that politicians are presumptive crooks does little to generate political support. Thus, as a practical matter, the problem is not one of choosing a man who is clearly best qualified, but rather one of measuring and balancing assets and liabilities of candidates who do not differ substantially one from another (although the difference between top and bottom may well be appreciable).

In such circumstances, is ethnic background a valid consideration? (As noted, in five of thirteen court nominations [39 percent], it was a principal consideration, and in four [30 percent] it was disregarded and an unbalanced ticket was nominated.)

Of course it is. New York City—and every American city of any size—is a heterogeneous community.

A *representative* representation on the bench and in the legislature and in executive office is of tremendous importance in preserving the fabric of democratic government, in preserving the confidence of all elements in the community, in sustaining the willingness of minority groups to accept the status of minority *participants* in government, and in stimulating the confidence of minorities that they are in fact *part* of the community and *part* of a greater majority.

Imagine, if you will, the kind of community we would have and the attitude of minorities

. . . if all the judges in the criminal courts were graduates of Wall Street law firms, which rarely, if ever, manage to find qualified Negro or Puerto Rican lawyers to join their staffs? (50 percent or more of the defendants who appear in the criminal courts are members of these minority groups.)

. . . if all the police were Irish?

. . . if all the legislators were WASPS?

. . . and if, surveying the government, minority group members found no one of *their* background, *their* tradition, *their* community in office?

Theoretically valid or no, the balanced ticket is on occasion the price American citizens pay in order to make social mobility —another term for "the promise of American life"—a reality. They do so in order to create one community instead of fifteen or twenty separated and antagonistic ones. They do so in order to give the *next* generation a less separated, segmented, and divided community in which to live. They do so to give all the members of our society tangible hope that they can succeed.

The "balanced ticket" concept is not wholly confined to politics. Any university, it might be added (say Harvard, Columbia, Stanford, or Brandeis), whose admissions policy is to any extent geared to the concept of a "national student body," or whose admissions officers make a special effort to admit qualified members of the more disadvantaged minorities, or who provide special preadmission programs (whether formal or informal) to improve the qualifications of the disadvantaged, has embraced its own version of the balanced ticket.

Of course, the desire to balance the ticket has at times led to mischief, usually where the desire for balance has overridden evaluation of qualifications. But, the whole subject is grossly misunderstood by politicians and public alike.

In the first place, tickets are not always balanced. Nor is it important—or for that matter possible—that every ticket contain representation of every important group. What is important is that *from reasonable time to reasonable time* every group secure some form of participation.

In fact, tickets are rarely put together on a purely ethnic basis. It is not so much: "We *must* have an Irishman." The thought is rather that "We ought to have an Irishman." "Can we find an Irishman?" "An Irishman would make sense."

Frequently there is no one of a particular ethnic group who is in the same class, as far as qualifications go, with other aspirants. If the decision in those circumstances is made wholly on an ethnic basis, it is bad and *unnecessary* politics.

Furthermore, ethnic balance is important only where the constituency is heterogeneous. For example, on Manhattan's West Side, which until very recently was almost exclusively a Jewish area, no one ever suggested it was desirable to run a Negro or a WASP. Indeed, an observer once commented on a West Side ticket, "That's real balance: one reform Jew, one orthodox Jew, and one agnostic Jew."

We have frequently run unbalanced tickets without difficulty and with no substantial adverse results at the polls. But where one group finds itself *consistently* unrepresented on the ticket, then there is trouble. And there ought to be.

In short, balancing a ticket doesn't mean more votes for the ticket. But consistent unbalancing means trouble. Whatever the theoretical rights or wrongs, in the end good politicians will instinctively seek balance in tickets. They may articulate no theories to justify balance, they will be willing to forgo it from time to time, but deep feeling tells them good government and good politics call for representation of all significant ethnic and religious groups on the ticket, in the party, and in the government.

Of course, no ticket is ever really balanced, and it all depends on how you look at it. In 1962 and 1964, in the Tenth Assembly District, the local legislative slate included a Negro for Congress (Powell), a white for state senate (Wilson), and a Puerto Rican for assembly (Rios). Real balance, you say? I thought so too, until a disgruntled candidate muttered, "Powell—a Protestant, and a minister at that; Wilson—a Protestant; Rios—a Protestant, and another minister. You Protestants are taking over the party!"

You can't please everyone.

So much for ethnic considerations. What other factors were involved?

Money? In eleven cases of the thirteen cited in the preceding chart on judicial nominees, money played no significant role. In two cases of which I had detailed knowledge, money could have played a part, but I have no evidence that it did. Score: 85 percent clean—15 percent possible but not, I think, likely.

No one bought his nomination from the county organization, and absence of funds to run a campaign did not bar a nomination. Indeed, in only five cases out of the nine county-wide candidacies (55 percent) did the candidates raise or cause the contribution of the amount that, on my figuring, constituted their share of the out-of-pocket costs to the county organization of their campaigns.

And what of the results? I have rated the successful candidates according to their performance, to the extent that I have a basis to make judgment. I have assigned a numerical value of 3 to outstanding judges, 2 to highly competent ones, 1 to merely adequate ones, and −2 to inadequate ones.

Of course, this is a subjective judgment, as any judgment of competence must be. But it is based upon published ratings by civic groups, on my own knowledge of the character and legal ability of the candidates, and on my own background of fourteen years of active trial practice.

The box score:

Outstandingly qualified (3)	Highly qualified (2)	Adequate (1)	No rating*	Inadequate (−2)
1	5	4	2	1

On a numerical basis, the total is 15. But 15 out of a possible what? I believe the fair measure is 15 out of 22—on the assumption that highly qualified judges should in all cases be nominated (11 judges are being rated—if all were highly qualified the total would be 22).

I do not believe that one can ask for outstandingly qualified judges in all cases, or indeed in more than a handful of cases. There simply do not exist that many potentials. How many potential Cardozos or Holmeses or Blacks or Hands or Shientags are there? We nominated one—and perhaps a second—in the 1962–64 period, and I suspect that is par for the course. On this scale, therefore, the judicial batting average was 15 out of 22, or approximately 70 percent, with two judges who are as yet unknown qualities.

Let us go on to compare this result with the results of the appointive system in New York from 1962 to 1964—a system that embodied the claimed use of a blue-ribbon selection system. After such a comparison, perhaps some answers to the problem of a better way of selecting judges may reveal themselves.

* Although the Bar Association rated these two candidates as qualified, I have no information to confirm that judgment and I suspect it was one of those typical Bar Association judgments—a courtesy, not an appraisal of quality.

15 ✻ The Appointment of Judges

What of the judges appointed in the period 1962–64? I have omitted federal judges since I was not privy to the selection process that resulted in their appointment. In the table on page 185, I have included all those from New York County or from other counties where I had information concerning the considerations leading to their appointment.✻

Using the box score rating system to rate the qualifications of the appointive judges, who serve on the criminal and family courts, may be a little unfair, because there is little opportunity to demonstrate high qualifications or outstanding qualifications in those courts. What follows, therefore, is a somewhat less precise and specific evaluation than in the case of the elected judges, where high qualifications—because of the offices they hold and the nature of the cases tried before them—are more apparent.

Outstanding qualifications (3)	High (2)	Adequate (1)	Not rated 0	Unqualified
1	1	5	1	—
Total 3	2	5	0	—

The total is 10 points out of 14 (71 percent), with no "unqualified" judges (although one was declared unqualified by the Association of the Bar of the City of New York. Since I have

✻ In New York City, judges for the Criminal and Family Courts are appointed by the mayor.

PRINCIPAL FACTORS IN JUDICIAL APPOINTMENTS

Factors	Candidates								Total
	A	B	C	D	E	F	G	H	
Outstanding qualifications								x	1
High qualifications						x			1
Ethnic considerations									—
Support of a single key subordinate leader	x	x		x				x	4
Repayment of past political obligations by top leader	x	x	x	x		x	x		6
Support of top leader for other reasons					x		x		2
Party originated	x	x		x				x	4

little confidence in the appraisals of that organization, for reasons set forth in Chapter 16, I have disregarded that evaluation). I have, I think, given the benefit of many doubts to the appointees.

A comparison of the results of the two systems (eliminating the judges of whom there is inadequate knowledge) indicates the following competence level:

ELECTIVE 70%
(15 out of 22)

APPOINTIVE 71%
(10 out of 14)

Of course this is only a rough calculation, and the judgments may be regarded as arbitrary. But it is a measure. Certainly it shows no appreciably *higher* results obtained via the appointive system—even though a blue-ribbon selection panel theoretically originated the appointments.

Another comparison is appropriate. The appointive judges are on the same judicial level as Civil Court judges, who are elected. Taking these judges and comparing their appointive counterparts produces the following:

Competence Levels

CIVIL COURT	78%	CRIMINAL AND FAMILY COURTS	71%
(*Elective*)	(11 out of 14, 1 not rated)	(*Appointive*)	(10 out of 14)

More meaningful, perhaps, is another analysis—the extent to which past political service to the top leader was rewarded by appointment. In six out of the eight cases of appointment (75 percent), this was a principal factor. A seventh involved the appointment of a Republican, in part because of complaints that there were no Republicans on the bench, and in part as a consideration to Republicans to forgo forcing the passage of a rather gerrymandered court districting bill.

In only two cases of appointment (25 percent) was the political obligation of the appointing authority to the recipient for past political service not directly involved. These were the two judges originated by and appointed on the recommendation of the Democratic and Republican political organizations.

Support of a single key party leader was a key factor in half the appointments. In two of the eight (25 percent), the recommending authority was the head of the Liberal Party, who had a substantial claim for recognition from the mayor by reason of that party's willingness to support the mayor when the leaders of his own party turned upon him. Of the other two cases (25 percent) where support of a single party leader was significant, one involved the Republican Party leader and the other involved the Democratic Party leader. These figures strongly indicate that past political service is a greater factor when the judge is appointive rather than elective. This is so because, when a number of political leaders are involved, it is always easier for the other leaders to veto such a consideration. There may be past political service to *one* leader, but the other leaders are not required to recognize and honor that debt. When the power is vested in one man, it is far harder for him to duck such an obligation.

Moreover, in two of the three cases (out of thirteen) where this was a principal factor in the *nomination* of judges, the obligation was *also* that of the mayor. Because of his standing, it was honored by the district leaders. In only one case out of thirteen nominations was the past political obligation of a leader other than the mayor, or of the party, a principal factor. In that case it was coupled with high qualifications and ethnic consideration. In the six out of eight cases (75 percent) where it was a principal factor in appointment, it was coupled only once with high qualifications.

A statistical summary of the results of this analysis shows the following:

Principal considerations	Elective	Appointive
Past political obligations	23%	75%
coupled with high qualifications	[33%]	[16%]
High qualifications	49%	25%
Ethnic considerations	39%	0%
Solely political	15%	75%
Support of only one political leader not		
coupled with other considerations	8%	37%

This experience convinces me of the following propositions:

1. The more politicians involved in the selection process, the less likely it is that past political service will be rewarded by judicial nomination or appointment.

2. The more politicians involved, the more likely it is that qualifications will be a principal consideration.

3. The nominating system, involving more people, tends to produce better judges.

4. The nominating system makes it difficult for private political deals to include a judicial nomination or appointment as one of its terms.

5. The nominating system makes it less possible for political leaders to control the nomination without regard to apparent qualification (6 out of 13 in nominations; 6 out of 8 in appointments).

6. Assuming that the control of a nomination by a single person creates more of a possibility of bribery, the nominating system is safer than the appointive, since in the latter *all* of the appointments flow from the sole support of the one man who makes the appointment.

I am sure that other inferences can be drawn. I have drawn those my experience indicates are appropriate. Others may draw their own, or, indeed, quarrel with my evaluations.

There are, of course, those who will find both systems inadequate; 15 out of 22, or 10 out of 14, they say, is not good enough.

I agree.

But what is the way to a better result?

The theorists have increasingly called for the use of blue-ribbon selection systems, such as the Missouri plan and its New York counterpart, the Mayor's Committee on the Judiciary.

Let us see what light experience can cast upon these efforts.

16. Blue-Ribbon Panel and Bar Association Selection

Blue-ribbon panel selection implies some form of nonpolitical origination of judicial selectees. Either a civic group, or a Bar group, or a combination of the two is to have some kind of power to limit the appointing authority to a choice among a small, select, "well-qualified" group of aspirants.

Since these committees will be composed of human beings expressing judgment, it is fair initially to inquire what kind of judgment such groups have demonstrated in the past in appraising candidates originated by the politicians. In New York, we have two principal groups of this type in operation—the Citizens Union and the Judiciary Committee of the Association of the Bar of the City of New York (hereafter referred to as the "Bar Association"). Neither has exhibited the kind of judgment in the past that would lead me to entrust any more authority to either of them.

First of all, they frequently disagree. Thus, in 1964, the Bar Association rated Judge Darwin Telesford as "unqualified," the Citizens Union as "highly qualified and preferred." The Bar Association was unable to express an opinion as to Judge James Watson. The Citizens Union found him "highly qualified." There are many other examples, and they seem to occur every year. If such disagreement is possible and frequent, one wonders just what standards of judgment are being applied. Clearly either the standards differ, or the applications of them do.

Secondly, both groups operate under tremendous disadvantages of time. Brief interviews and hasty reviews of written dossiers lead to superficial judgments based upon quick impressions. For example, in 1962, the Citizens Union rated the ten candidates for five Supreme Court positions (5 Democrats, 3 Republicans, 2 Liberals) in order, placing the one since universally acknowledged as the man with the highest qualifications as number four on the list. Above him the Citizens Union rated a political leader who had served for some eight or nine months by appointment to fill a vacancy—whose background, though adequate, was hardly outstanding—apparently on the ground that he was a sitting judge!

Again, there are many other examples.

And what of the Bar Association's record?

It is hardly more reassuring.

First, it must be understood that we do not have in this country the kind of bar, and hence the kind of bar association, that plays such a significant role in judicial selection in England. Eighty percent or better of our bar rarely sees the inside of a courtroom. Of the remaining 20 percent, well over 10 percent have an occasional fling at trying a case or arguing a motion, but have sparse experience or training at the trial bar. Only the remaining 5 to 7 or 8 percent of the lawyers are really competent trial lawyers. While their views as to judicial qualifications might be most helpful, it is very difficult to identify these lawyers since they are not organized as a group. Moreover, the active practitioners at the bar are probably less well represented in Bar Association activities than the less time-pressed office lawyers who can plan to attend meeting after meeting. Accordingly, the judgment of the Bar Association is *not* the judgment of active trial lawyers, but of an organization, itself the forum for a different brand of politics, which is concerned with *itself* as much as it is with the realities of trying cases before a particular judge.

And what of that judgment?

First of all, let us disregard the Bar Association's judgment on sitting judges. Every time a sitting judge comes up for renomination—with rare exceptions—he is dutifully found to be "qualified" and therefore entitled to renomination.

The Bar Association once rated as "highly qualified" one judge before whom I had tried several cases. For fun, I checked with every other lawyer I knew who had tried a case before that judge. The decision was unanimous: the Bar Association didn't know what it was talking about.

The reason is simple—disinclination to offend a sitting judge who will probably be renominated anyway. It is true that in recent years there have been examples of more courage, but the over-all record does not commend itself for independence of judgment or capacity to make disinterested judgments.

On four occasions I have had direct experience as a member of the Bar Association in regard to judicial candidacies when I was politically involved, where I had had more than a thirty-minute exposure to the candidates and where the committee involved had made recommendations with which I disagreed. On three such occasions, at Bar Association membership meetings, I was successful in persuading the membership to reverse the committee. I am convinced that on all three occasions the judgment shown by the committee was simply no good.*

In the first case, the committee recommended that we renominate a judge who had served one ten-year term. Prior to the recommendation, over a three-month period, I had met with the committee repeatedly and set forth the reasons why I and my club did not believe the judge should be renominated.

On the day the recommendation was made, the committee chairman was in my office for several hours. He heard the arguments again. I finally asked him, "In light of these facts, would you *really* renominate him if you were in my shoes—putting aside any political considerations—solely on the basis of what you, as a lawyer, believe should be proper?"

"No," he said, "I wouldn't. But our committee is like a committee of expert plumbers called in to review the work of the town plumber who is up for reappointment. How he was selected in the first place is beyond our scope. All we report on is whether he's done okay as a plumber."

Stunned, I said, "Let me get this straight. Tonight you will recommend that he be renominated. But if you were me, you wouldn't take that advice?"

"Right," he said.

The second case involved the same judge, who was denied

* Then the rules were changed. See next page.

renomination by the Democrats but was running on the Republican line. The same committee now said he was "outstandingly qualified."

I was satisfied to get the "outstandingly" removed at the membership meeting. Afterwards the chairman said to me, "I expected you'd win. But you only knocked him down to 'qualified.' If we had said he was simply 'qualified' you'd have knocked him out. And that's why we did it."

It happened that he was wrong. I would have paid no attention to a "qualified" rating. But certainly he was not exercising good judgment. He was merely playing inferior politics.

The third case was even more incredible. On the recommendation of the political leaders, the mayor appointed a 35-year-old law secretary to a Supreme Court judge to an interim Municipal Court vacancy. The Bar Association advised the mayor, before the appointment, that the candidate was "qualified." Three months later, when the same judge was running for election to a full term, the same committee found him unqualified because of his age, now three months greater than when they had found the same man qualified!

That result was likewise reversed by the membership. Nettled, the Bar Association establishment soon thereafter terminated the process of requiring membership approval of such recommendations, so that now there is no longer any opportunity to review and reverse such recommendations!

My final experience with the Bar Association's capacity to review qualifications left me even more doubtful of its capacity to function as an originator of nominations. In 1963, the city's commissioner of investigations was Louis Kaplan, a former Criminal Court judge, whom the mayor some four years earlier had persuaded to leave the bench in order to take over the difficult and politically dangerous post of commissioner of investigations. A return to the bench must have been promised to Kaplan, who liked the bench and was not too anxious to enter the rough and tumble of city affairs. As commissioner of investigations he did an outstanding job. The petty scandals that had afflicted the second term of Wagner's administration disappeared, and throughout Kaplan's administration there were no major scandals and almost no petty ones—indeed, I cannot remember any.

After four years, in 1963, Kaplan wanted to return to the bench. There was a civil-court vacancy. The mayor had the interim appointive power, but Kaplan would have to run for a full term. The mayor submitted Kaplan's name to the Bar Association, which reported back to the mayor that Kaplan was not qualified. Why, it did not say.

The mayor in early June announced his intention to appoint Kaplan anyway—this at my suggestion, since it was clear to me that the district leaders would not nominate Kaplan unless Wagner's support was unequivocal. The Bar Association immediately and publicly announced its vigorous disapproval of the proposed appointment. (The Mayor's Committee on the Judiciary and the New York County Lawyers Association found Kaplan qualified.)

In these circumstances, I worked out an agreement with representatives of all factions in the County Executive Committee—reform, regular, Harlem, etc., as follows:

We would ask the Bar Association for the reasons why any of our prospective candidates were found to be unqualified (there were three judges to be nominated and about ten names were submitted to the Bar Association before our final meeting to select the three candidates).

If the Bar Association refused to give its reasons, we would nominate Kaplan.

If the reasons were trifling, we would go ahead anyway.

If the reasons were troublesome, they would be referred to the full Executive Committee for its decision.

If the reasons were convincing, we would drop Kaplan and select one of the other candidates.

And so a letter was written to the Bar Association requesting reasons for the rejection of any candidate. I postponed an Executive Committee meeting one day to give the Bar Association committee time to meet.

It met.

No response.

I called and called, and finally the executive secretary of the Bar Association read to me over the telephone a message that went something like this:

"The committee will advise the mayor of its views. If Mr. Costikyan wishes to know those views and the mayor desires to let Mr. Costikyan know those views, the mayor is free to do so."

This in response to a letter from me concerning a nomination, not an appointment, which was to be made by the district leaders, not the mayor! And the mayor was in Japan and would not be back until a week after the meeting at which the nomination was to be made.

Publicly the Bar Association announced that if we *did* nominate Kaplan, *then* they would release their reasons for disapproving him.

The next day the Executive Committee met, nominated Kaplan (although some of the reformers reneged on their agreement to support Kaplan if the Bar Association gave no reasons for disapproving him), and rejected the Bar Association's unexplained disapproval as a species of political blackmail.

When the Bar Association's "reasons" for disapproving Kaplan were released, they amounted to nothing of any substance. As investigations commissioner, the Bar Association said, Kaplan had not demonstrated "judicial temperament." Kaplan was elected.

For years I suspected that Republican political considerations played a role in the conclusions reached. But upon reflection, I am persuaded that it was not anti-Democratic sentiment, but anti-political-leader attitudes and preconceptions that brought about these curious results.

So much for the record of the Bar Association and Citizens Union in passing upon qualifications of candidates originated by others. Now let us turn to the examples of blue-ribbon panel origination that have been tried in the recent past.

The Mayor's Committee on the Judiciary

In the last weeks of the 1961 primary campaign, Mayor Wagner issued a statement committing himself to a new method of origination of judicial appointees. He promised, if he was re-nominated and re-elected, to appoint a committee on the judiciary, which would originate and submit to him five names for each judicial vacancy, from which he would choose his appointee. On nominations, he promised to use his influence to see that the party leaders selected candidates similarly rec-ommended by the committee; if the party leaders did not, the mayor pledged himself to support his committee's recommenda-tions as independent candidates, in a primary or general election.

The statement was hailed as a great step forward, as a "Little Missouri Plan," and as going a long way towards getting politics out of the judiciary and improving its quality.

These are valid objectives. Judges should not be involved in politics, and of course they should be better. On the basis of my experience, however, and on the basis of what I have heard about similar plans elsewhere—including the Missouri plan—I am convinced that the proponents of such plans are either deluding themselves or the public.

For the Mayor's Committee has not gotten the problem of selecting judges out of politics—it has merely added a new and additional political arena to the political arenas that already exist, and provided a further political obstacle for a potential candidate to surmount. For the fact is that, with one possible exception referred to below, the Mayor's Committee has not originated a single appointment. Every successful appointee or nominee was politically sponsored by one political leader or another—usually the mayor—and the political sponsorship was in each case one of two, or at most three, principal considerations in his election or appointment.

The reason is simple. Among those submitting names to the originating committee is the mayor, and it is he who has the appointive power.

Except where the candidates thus submitted are plainly im-

possible, the inevitable result is that among the five names submitted to the mayor will be the one originally submitted by the
mayor or the political leaders to the committee. And so the
committee becomes a screening committee, not an originating
committee.

The record is quite clear on this. The first appointee named
to the bench under this system was a former district leader, an
old friend of the mayor's, who had been publicly promised
appointment by the mayor months before the committee was
even appointed.

He was recommended both by the Mayor's Committee and by
the Judiciary Committee of the New York County Democratic
Party. His qualifications were high, and the occasion of his
appointment was used to extol the "nonpolitical" system of
judicial selection which the Mayor's Committee was supposed to
inaugurate. Indeed, in order to preserve this fiction, it was
gently suggested that the county leader not appear at the swear-
ing in, lest the "nonpolitical" aura of the appointment be disturbed. I stayed away.

Thereafter, each of the mayor's intended recipients of appointment was regularly included in the committee's list of proposed
appointees. In two cases, at least, the Mayor's Committee recommended individuals (their names had been originally submitted
by the mayor to the committee) whom the Bar Association
thereupon found to be unqualified. This fact suggests that the
standards used by the two groups varied.

In one case, a candidate who believed he had a political
claim on the appointment recognized that he would never be
approved by the Mayor's Committee and abandoned his judicial
aspirations. On two other occasions, the committee refused to
recommend the candidates submitted by the mayor and successfully blocked their appointment.

In one of these two cases, however, political considerations
played a major role in the committee's refusal. By that time, over
forty recommendations had been made to the mayor in groups
of four or five. In each case, he had selected one of the four or
five—the one he had originated—and the remaining three or four
languished there, unbenched. With about forty unbenched candidates, the committee began to understand what was happening,

and rebelled. It would make no more recommendations until at least one of the unbenched forty was appointed, and accordingly it refused to approve a candidate submitted to it by the party through the mayor.

I was advised that our candidate would be approved for "the next vacancy" but not for the one that then existed. Ultimately the candidate thus "rejected" was nominated to an elective judgeship, and was duly found to be qualified by all bar associations and the Citizens Union! *

For five months the deadlock continued, but finally the committee gave way and started making recommendations again. I have since heard that the committee's *quid pro quo* for resuming recommendations was the appointment of one judge in Queens.

This is not to say that the committee served no useful function. As a screening committee it tended to raise the level of judicial candidates—by an occasional rejection and by the possibility of rejection which its existence created, both of which had an inhibiting effect on the political leaders. For practical purposes, however, it was *not* the originating committee it was intended to be. Moreover, as long as the appointing or nominating authority exists in politics, it strikes me as highly unlikely that the candidates supported by the appointing authority from the start will not be selected from the four or five names submitted to the appointing authority by the committee.

While the operation of the Missouri plan and variants thereof has been beyond the scope of my direct experience, attorneys from Missouri with whom I have discussed this aspect of the problem have told me that Missourians are no different from New Yorkers in this respect. One, a participant in the process, commented, "The guy the governor wants is almost always on the list." Another summed it up, "The people who get on the bench by our system are pretty much the same people who would get on it under a straight political system." A third lawyer, from another state, which uses a variant system, commented, "When you know X is the appointing authority's candidate, it's pretty hard to turn him down. And the appointing authority always has a candidate. I've never seen him turned down."

* The other was appointed by the mayor on the last day he was in office.

All of this makes great sense, provided one has some understanding of the dynamics of politics. It is confirmed by our brief experience in New York.

This experience leads me to suggest that it is time for proponents of such programs to analyze them in order to ascertain whether they are any more than public relations screens to give superficial respectability to the political activities they hide. Our democracy is not well served by the use of public relations gimmicks, which mislead the public into believing that public relations gimmicks are the reality. Nor do I believe anything is served by the myth-bound reformist mentality that insists on demeaning politics and politicians and finds self-righteous gratification in the creation of self-deceptive and public-deceptive devices to shield the reality of what is really happening.

Indeed, such attitudes twice led to experiments in which well-meaning political leaders, confused by the barrage of publicity accorded to "nonpolitical" selection systems, actually reversed the theory of the Missouri plan, and instead of turning over to a nonpolitical group the task of *originating* the candidates, turned over the deciding power. Once this had been done, it took a mountain of political maneuvering to rescue the situation—but the candidates were able, in effect, to run on anti-political platforms (which the voters loved), a situation in which they ran against the very political leaders who selected them in the first place.

I think this is bad government, because it demeans the political process by insulting politicians, and because it is a form of deception of the voters.

The best example of this variant of the Missouri plan took place on New York's upper East Side. Twelve leaders from six leadership districts, six male and six female, were involved. Bemused by the editorial adulation the Mayor's Committee had received, and obsessed by traditional reform attitudes about political leaders, they agreed to appoint a committee of three distinguished lawyers, and to submit to this committee all candidates supported by the political leaders. The committee would select "the most highly qualified candidates." (Originally it was contemplated that the committee select one such candidate, but the mandate to the committee was expanded to authorize—indeed, to invite—a finding that more than one candidate was "most highly qualified." Any conceptual or other problems involved in requesting such contradictory findings were quietly suppressed.)

The committee selected initially was perfectly adequate, except for the fact that, its members having been nominated by three different leaders, suspicions were aroused as to the relationships between the committee members and the candidates—in fact, it was charged that leader A had selected a committee member who was a law-school classmate of leader A's candidate. But ultimately a first-rate committee was selected—with my assistance, although I had doubts as to the wisdom of the whole operation.

The committee met, reviewed biographies, interviewed the candidates, and made a recommendation. It privately found that one candidate (whose political support came from one of the few regulars in the district) was "the most highly qualified." As an afterthought it added the name of a second candidate (whose political support came from reformers). It omitted the name of the husband of one of the district leaders, who was a candidate.

And then politics took over.

The committee never publicly indicated which candidate was its first choice, or how wide it regarded the gap between the two. But that information was available to me and, I presume, to any other leader who made inquiry.

Notwithstanding, after several weeks of meetings, threats of primary fights, attacks upon the integrity of the committee, demands that the committee be reconvened and directed to report one or two more "most highly qualified" candidates, bickering back and forth, and promises of financial support by supporters of the successful candidate, a final decision was forced by the use of time-honored political techniques such as repeated long meetings, repeated ballots, and recesses to "discuss." The leaders finally agreed to support the man who was Number 2 on the "most highly qualified" list.

It was a good decision. He was a good candidate. He has been a good judge. But it was as political a decision as I have ever seen.

Indeed, the use of the committee-selection system gave him a great issue in the campaign—he ran against "bossism"! And he won. If this is what the political leaders had in mind when they concocted this system, they were far more cynical than I can believe. The leaders, I know, thought they were taking a giant step forward by voluntarily passing on to a high-level committee the power they were elected to exercise. When they had done so, it took every political technique in the book to salvage the inevitably impractical result of the committee's deliberations.

There must be a better way to select judges.

17 ❖ A Suggested Program for Improving Judicial Selection

❖❖❖

The terms of the premise of all moves to replace the elective system of judicial selection are familiar enough. They are that the voters routinely vote the whole ticket, thereby refusing to exercise discrimination; that they are not qualified to pass upon judicial qualifications; and that nomination by the dominant party is equivalent to election. There are many defects in this premise. Highly qualified judges usually *do* run ahead of the ticket. Moreover, any theory that the voters are not qualified to decide is a highly undemocratic notion, and the same criticism might well be leveled at the capacity of the voters to judge the qualifications of congressional, state legislature, or mayoral candidates. Nevertheless, I will not quarrel with the premise. For, while it is true in regard to most candidates on the ticket (indeed, who *is* well qualified to judge the qualifications of a candidate for Congress whom he has never met?), it is also true that party affiliation, while it is theoretically a valid consideration in judging executive and legislative officeholders, has, generally, little to do with judicial qualification.

All well and good, but what are the alternatives?

The appointive system tends to place greater weight upon prior political service to the appointing authority, and is as political as the nominating process, as we have seen. See in this connection the attempted appointment by President Johnson of Judge Morrissey to the federal bench. What is most important about this attempt was not that it was an effort to pay a debt for personal political service to a man plainly unqualified for the federal bench; this is not unusual in the operation of the appointive system. Rather, it illustrates my point that the more people involved in the process, the less likely is it that the bench will be used for such purposes. For even with the pro forma backing of the President, the Vice-President, and the Senators Kennedy, the effort failed as a result of opposition engendered when a hundred senators were asked to approve the appointment.

No such independent arena, as the United States Senate can be, exists under any of the Missouri-plan, blue-ribbon panel selection systems.

Next, the use of blue-ribbon selection panels, in theory attractive, in practice, as we have seen, produces no substantial variation from what might otherwise be expected.

What, then, is the way to a better judiciary?

First, I think it should be recognized that the selection of judges is, by law and by custom, part of the political process. Even when the law is changed, apparently, as under the Missouri plan and its counterparts, custom controls and produces the same result. Efforts to change either the law or custom do not seem to offer any preferable alternative to the present system. Especially in light of the absence of any demonstrably better results obtained by these alternatives, I see no real benefit to be obtained by pursuing them.

Second, it seems clear that political leaders are capable, if encouraged and supported, of putting a premium upon qualifications in selecting nominees. So the figures indicate.

Third, experience indicates that the more individual politicians are involved in the selection process, the more likely it is that the selectee will have high qualifications.

Accordingly, it should be obvious that the quality of the political leaders has a great deal to do with the quality of the judicial candidates they support. But those avowedly concerned with the quality of the judiciary seemingly insist upon believing that the political leaders are pariahs, that they are merely people who must be dealt with, not people who ought to be involved.

On the basis of my experience, it became clear to me that those who ran the organized bar did not wish to co-operate with the existing political leadership in an effort to improve the quality of the bench, *so long as the basic power remained in political hands*. Indeed, at times it seemed as if they would rather have had the political leaders do badly, hoping that they would ultimately succeed in wresting the power of selection from the political arena.

Well, why not? Wouldn't the organized bar do better? I doubt it.

First, as pointed out above, the organized bar tends to be dominated by men who know little of the courts. It constitutes a political system unto itself, and its choices are as political, in the bad sense, as any emanating from the political parties.

Not long ago, for example, the organized bar succeeded in persuading someone in Washington that one of its own excellent internal politicians would make a fine federal judge. After the FBI commenced a check on him, which is the last prelude to appointment, the word got out that he was almost "in."

I was deluged with calls from practicing lawyers—not party politicians—begging me, for God's sake, to stop the appointment. The man was, I was repeatedly told, impossible!

It was stopped—not by the protests I reported, but by reason of many such protests to many people. But it left another real residue of doubt about the ability of the organized bar to exercise as good judgment as the political leaders who were the object of so much opprobrium.

Third, the legal establishment is wholly insensitive to the governmental importance of representation of all significant community elements on the bench. Negroes and Puerto Ricans with neighborhood law practices do *not* have the breadth of legal experience that Wall Street practice offers. But they have something else—which Wall Street practices fail to offer. The bar associations tend to look for legal as distinguished from community experience—"How many times have you argued in the Court of Appeals?"—and tend to discount character and judgment derived from practice and experience other than *law* practice and *law* experience. But political practice and experience can be as important as law in some courts, especially lower courts where human and not legal problems make up the bulk of the calendars.

A characteristic example of the Bar Association's myopia is found in its once-confessed inability to pass upon the qualifications of a Negro state senator who was running for judicial office. The senator involved had served for eight years as a member of the senate's Committee on the Judiciary, but because he lacked experience in the kind of law practice the Bar Association thought essential for the lower-court judgeship in question, he was not certified as fit.

With such experience to go on, minority groups who make up a large part of the electorate regard proposals for Bar Association origination of candidates as a device to eliminate Negroes and Puerto Ricans, who by reason of generations of prejudice and restrictions do not obtain access to the kind of experience the predominantly white Bar Association establishment values above all else. In this I believe Negroes and Puerto Ricans are substantially correct. It is myopia—not malice—on the part of the Bar Association that led to these exclusions, but I am afraid the Negro and Puerto Rican communities believe it is malice—not myopia. While this may well be seen by the excluded as a distinction without a difference, it is not *bias* per se on the part of the Bar Association so much as a narrowness of judgment largely based upon parochial professional experience.

What is involved is understandable enough. The leading men of the New York bar and its associations reflect the patterns of mind and milieu of their best clients, usually corporate clients. The latter have not made it a habit to hire Negro counsel. The law firms to whom the major corporations headquartered in New York turn for legal advice are not firms whose staffs ordinarily include Negro seniors or juniors.

Given this state of affairs, efforts by the leaders of the organized bar to seize control of the judicial selection system are likely to be unsuccessful because the resistance to their efforts is not confined to political leaders alone but is found as well among the minority groups themselves and among their not inconsiderable allies.

Finally, forms of window dressing, such as the Mayor's Committee on the Judiciary, may look like progress, but behind the façade political selection by a smaller group of politicians will remain entrenched.

What, then, is a better way? The elements that will make for authentic progress are not especially complicated.

First, the *quality* of political leaders is very important. It can be improved. The bar, *as a matter of policy*, can encourage rather than discourage efforts by lawyers of good repute to be elected to such positions.

Today twenty or thirty law firms between them dominate the Bar Association. This is not the result of accident. Young lawyers are encouraged, and in some firms directed, to be active in Bar Association activities. Usually, no similar encouragement is afforded to political participation by the young lawyer. On the contrary, his standing in the firm and his income may suffer if he devotes too much of his time to such endeavors. Small wonder that there is not now on the Executive Committee of the Democratic Party of New York County *a single leader from a major law firm.*

If the Bar discourages the good young men from political activity, has it the right to complain that the good young men are not *in* politics?

Moreover, this discouragement of able young men from political activity means that, when political leaders are looking for candidates for the bench, they will not have a reservoir of the able and talented. The bright young men have been taught by their elders to stay away. If, as a result, the ultimate choice does not meet the qualifications of the leaders of the Bar, who is to blame but the Bar leadership itself?

Recognizing these problems, I once urged responsible Bar Association leaders to co-operate in a program to consolidate the efforts of all those with different backgrounds who wanted to improve the quality of the judiciary. My notion was that the Bar Association as well as political leaders could submit recommendations to our County Judiciary Committee. The proposal was made after the County Executive Committee rejected a Bar Association proposal to make all judgeships appointive, and to require that they be appointed from lists originated by a blue-ribbon panel.

This is the text of the informal proposal:

November 7, 1963

Chairman
Special Committee on Judicial Selection and Tenure
Association of the Bar of the City of New York

DEAR MR. [CHAIRMAN]:

I have read with interest the proposal of the Special Committee on Judicial Selection and Tenure. As I am sure you know, this is an area in which I have had a very deep interest over a number of years, and I have long recognized that the method of selecting judges is certainly not perfect.

As I am sure you are aware, the substance of your committee's proposal was submitted to our Executive Committee and rejected by a two-thirds vote. Nevertheless, I still believe that your proposal reflects an attitude among the leaders of the Bar which, if it gave fair and appropriate consideration to the views and wholly legitimate interests of the rest of the community, including the leaders of the political parties, could be extremely helpful in improving the process of judicial selection.

The principal reasons why our Executive Committee rejected the proposal are, I believe, as follows:

(1) The selection committee which you suggest would not, in our judgment, be responsible or accountable to anyone. Nevertheless, it would tie the hands of the appointing authority. If its actions were improper or incorrect, there would be no redress of any kind, either by the people or by the appointing authority.

It seemed to a majority of our Executive Committee that this is highly undesirable in a democratic society. At least under the present system the political leaders themselves are subject to control and removal by the enrolled voters in their party, and the determinations of the leaders as to nominations are subject to approval or disapproval by the electorate. The same is true as to the actions of the mayor in that he, too, is accountable to the public. The electorate also has the right to choose between alternatives.

The right to an accounting and the right to choose are important even though the rights are not frequently exercised.

(2) There is a deep feeling among a substantial majority of the Executive Committee that the kind of a select committee you have

in mind would be insensitive to the needs and aspirations of minority groups whose members would find it extremely difficult to meet the kind of standards which committees of this kind have traditionally applied. This is a deeply felt community reaction and, if any effective progress is to be made, there must be sincere recognition of this aspect of the problem. Suggestions that this reaction is merely a cover or a screen for improper motives are unworthy and demagogic in the extreme and do a deep disservice to men and women who are conscientiously expressing deeply felt convictions of their own and of their constituents.

(3) Unfortunately, your committee's proposal has become a political football within the party in an entirely unrelated power struggle, which is really wholly irrelevant to your proposal, and I need not burden you with its details. This fact, however, colors the thinking of a majority of the Executive Committee.

In light of these problems it is clear to me that the basic radical change in the method of selecting judges which your committee suggests will encounter deep, sincere, and probably insurmountable opposition.

Nevertheless, if the objective of your proposal is, as I assume, to feed into the selection process names of people recommended by leaders of the Bar whose principal concern is the selection of outstanding judges, I believe that an avenue for co-operation exists which has not been adequately explored in the past, to wit:

As leader of the Democratic Party of New York County, I would be happy to receive and entertain recommendations from your association, the Harlem Bar Association, the New York County Lawyers Association, and any other professional group which is concerned with helping the Democratic Party select highly qualified candidates for the judiciary. Whether this would be done through the kind of select committee you have suggested or some other kind of mechanism is a detail which I am sure could be worked out.

I would suggest, however, that, if a new entity is to be created, it should be representative of the entire community—not just the legal community, and certainly not just the downtown legal community.

I could not, of course, guarantee that the candidates who might be suggested in this manner would be nominated, any more than any member of the Executive Committee can receive a guarantee that a candidate he might suggest would ultimately receive majority support. This is one of the risks to be taken in attempting to carry out such a program. I am perfectly willing to undertake those risks if the organized bar is prepared to attempt such a co-operative endeavor.

One major result of such a joint effort might be to demonstrate that a select committee of the kind you envisage would not result in disqualification of Negroes, Puerto Ricans, and members of other minority groups. If that alone is accomplished, the effort will have been worthwhile.

I am confident that co-operation such as I am suggesting between the leaders of the profession and the leaders of the political parties promises greater opportunities for the improvement of the judiciary than the suggestion that the locus of power to select be changed, and vested in a select committee responsible to nobody.

If you believe this suggestion is worth pursuing, I would be glad to discuss it with you, your committee, or anyone else whom you might suggest.

I am taking the liberty of sending a copy of this letter to the Chairman of the judiciary committees of your association and of the New York County Lawyers Association and to the president of the Harlem Bar Association.

Sincerely,

EDWARD N. COSTIKYAN
County Leader

That letter produced no response. A few of the members of the committee, however, recognized this as a promising possibility. But one of them told me a majority of the committee regarded this as a "Tammany trick." So I tried again:

I was discussing with Bill Chanler [former Corporation Counsel under Mayor La Guardia and a distinguished lawyer] the contents of my letter of November 7, and it struck me that perhaps there might have been some misunderstanding as to exactly what my position was.

The Executive Committee took no position whatsoever concerning so much of the proposal of your special committee as dealt with the subject of appointive judges. Indeed, it strikes me that what your committee proposed was merely institutionalizing the present system which the mayor has been pursuing voluntarily and, while I understand there are some questions as to the composition of the committee which you propose, this did not concern us and has not concerned us.

The thrust of my proposal related to assistance to the political leaders in the performance of their functions in relationship to all elective judges, including the State Supreme Court.

I hope the above will clarify what may have been a misunderstanding of my earlier communication.

I received a polite acknowledgement but no response to my suggestion.

This general scheme still seems to me to be the likeliest path toward a better judiciary. It would include the best of the old and the best of the new. It would recognize the power realities and what might be done within a context that cannot be changed without turning to alternatives that, as experience has shown, offer no better solutions than exist in the present system.

I suggest that it is time for those concerned with the quality of the judiciary to forget their theories about who ought to have the power, abandon their efforts to create artificial and mechanical restrictions upon the exercise of political power in the selection of candidates (which merely camouflages the political selection of judges), encourage and support the selection of the right kind of political leaders in both major parties, agree to submit the names of highly qualified candidates to those political leaders, and finally accept the political leaders on the basis of their own best myth—that they are responsible citizens rendering public service through party activity—and help them do their job.

I should add that screening committees to eliminate unqualified candidates are most helpful. The New York County Democratic Committee has had a Committee on the Judiciary charged with this duty since 1962. It has done a first-rate job. The Mayor's Committee on the Judiciary has done the same job.

Screening committees of this kind, *before nomination or appointment*, are essential to a better system of judicial selection. They not only eliminate the unqualified, but this in turn makes it easier for political leaders to do a good job. Moreover, they give the political leaders valid excuses to justify their failure to turn a legitimate political "due bill" into a nomination or appointment for an unqualified candidate.

The kind of co-operation I have suggested between the bar and the political leaders is not a utopian proposal. We should see considerable progress in the improvement of the judiciary, I believe,

. . . if those *outside* politics who are concerned with the quality of the judiciary would recognize that there are those *inside* politics who are similarly concerned;

. . . if those outside politics would forgo efforts to wrest the power of selection from politics, or to camouflage the political selection of judges by the creation of blue-ribbon selection systems, and make an effort: (a) to help the right kind of political leaders to get elected, and (b) to help the political leaders select highly qualified judicial candidates.

More than lawyers and their professional associations are involved in the selection of judges. The public's stake in the courts, in their quality and efficiency and in the protections they afford, is enormous. Is there any sound reason why good lawyers through their bar association and good politicians through their parties should not learn to help each other sustain, support, and improve the courts?

Part Six

Political

Tools

and Techniques

18* The Use and Abuse of Polls

✲✲✲✲✲✲✲✲✲✲✲✲✲✲✲✲✲✲✲✲✲✲✲✲✲✲✲✲✲✲✲✲✲✲✲✲✲✲

There is a popular suspicion that election results are pre-ordained. Pollsters comb the countryside, talk to twenty-two of the folks, and, presto chango, the outcome of the next Presidential election is decided.

Nothing could be farther from the truth. For a poll is no more than a projection based upon past experience; it assumes the use of every known political technique in the campaign; it presupposes that the result is in doubt and that voters who would normally show up on election day will continue to do so (notwithstanding the result of the poll). Indeed, it presupposes that the results of the poll—if made public—will not thereby alter expected voter behavior.

All these assumptions are invalid. There will be new political techniques. There will be new issues. The poll results, when publicized, do affect the result. These defects, however, do not diminish the fact that polls are a valuable political tool. When well used, they can win an otherwise lost election; when badly used, they can lose an otherwise winnable election. An example of the latter is the 1962 New York gubernatorial race.

In 1962, New York's Republican Governor Nelson Rockefeller was in serious political trouble. His personal life had taken a turn that alienated many voters. His arrogance had offended others. His Presidential ambitions were clear and their negative impact upon the state government was about equally so. And his fiscal policies—called by him "pay as you go"—had left many voters disenchanted.

The search for a candidate to beat him involved the use—and later the abuse—of polls. As early as April and May of 1962, polls were taken. They showed a weakened support for Rockefeller and a profound defection of 1958 supporters.

Many, if not most, of these 1958 supporters were liberal Democrats, who flourish in predominantly Jewish districts but exist everywhere. They had bolted the 1958 Democratic ticket in rebellion against De Sapio. Manifestly, if these normally Democratic voters could be returned to the fold in 1962, there would be a solid Democratic majority.

The problem was, how to get them back. Analysis of past performance indicated that Herbert H. Lehman was the last state-wide Democratic candidate to bring out the maximum vote from this part of the population. And so, why not find a candidate in the Lehman image? The search began. Initially the poll results were a well-guarded secret. Only a handful of leaders were aware of them and of the direction in which they pointed. While the poll results were still a secret, the candidacy of Bernard Botein, presiding justice of the Appellate Division of the First Judicial Department, was launched. He was, indeed, in the Lehman tradition. He had the qualities of decisiveness, forcefulness, physical attractiveness, and capacity to campaign, which could have resulted in a successful candidacy. But his candidacy aborted over his refusal to engage in political activity in any form however mild while still on the bench, and over the unwillingness of his initial supporters to stay with him and round up the votes while he remained in his chambers at his judicial duties. And so a new candidate was needed.

At that point the fatal mistake was made. A number of party leaders went to Washington for some occasion or other. At a party after the occasion, a New York *Times* reporter was welcomed by the leaders. Either deliberately or by accident—probably the former—the whole "Lehman tradition" theory was spilled. And the next day the front page of the *Times* announced, "New York Democrats Seek Jewish Candidate for Governor"—or words to that effect. The article went on to explain the "secret" strategy that would bring gubernatorial victory to the luckless New York Democrats. It explained that polls showed that in 1958 the major defecting Democratic group was the

"Jewish vote" and that party leaders expected to get it back by nominating a Jewish candidate.

If the damage done by this news article was not bad enough, it was followed up by a series of stories carefully detailing the search for and ultimate selection of the man who would be crowned as the "right" Jewish candidate.

Indeed, a major factor in selecting the candidate was the reputed existence of polls showing such a candidate could win.

I never saw those polls. The delegates never saw those polls. But the story of them succeeded in clinching the nomination. All that was left to do was to lose the election, as hundreds of thousands of offended voters of Jewish origin turned out en masse to vote for Rockefeller in order to prove they were not so narrow-minded as to vote for a Jew merely because he was a Jew, and that there was no "Jewish vote."

The election was lost the day some one man decided to "leak" the poll results in order to win the nomination, and to launch a public search for the "right Jewish candidate." Whatever non-Jews might do, it was clear that the ultimate designee faced a hostile and suspicious Jewish voter. For no voter likes to be told—in advance—that his vote will be had because of his religion.

This is the way polls, improperly used, can lose an election. But when they are properly used, they can win them.

An example of the effective use of a poll is the 1963 primary between Carmine De Sapio and Edward Koch for the district leadership of the First Assembly District South.

A word of explanation: the cornerstone of De Sapio's political empire was his leadership of the First Assembly District South. It covered roughly Greenwich Village and its environs. When De Sapio lost the leadership of that area in 1961 in the Wagner landslide, he became ineligible to serve as New York County leader and his political empire was destroyed.

In 1963, he was on the comeback trail. Starting at the bottom, he hoped to win a majority of the fifteen thousand Democrats of the First Assembly District South as a candidate for district leader, and then start back up the ladder.

The man who had defeated De Sapio for the district leadership in 1961, reformer James Lanigan, had fallen out with his reform supporters. He thought they were parochial, difficult, doctrinaire, and impossible to lead (I tended to agree with Lanigan). They welcomed his withdrawal.

After months of seeking a strong community-based candidate, the reformers—the Village Independent Democrats (and, my God, were they independent!)—finally selected an aggressive young lawyer, Edward Koch, to run against De Sapio. Koch had taken a stunning defeat the year before in a primary for assembly against a former De Sapio protégé, when Senator Lehman and Mayor Wagner were persuaded to support Koch's opponent at the eleventh hour.

To Koch's eternal credit, he recognized that *this time* he needed Wagner's and Lehman's support, and he publicly apologized to both of them for some remarks he had made when they came out for his adversary the year before. Although his club correctly held me partly accountable for the Lehman and Wagner endorsements of their adversary the year before, Koch, again to his credit, was prepared to forget the past, accept all help tendered in good faith, including mine.

In late June and early July, I had a poll taken. The campaign was then well under way, although primary election day was two months away. That poll cost fifteen hundred dollars. The county had no funds to pay for it—nor could it, probably, legally do so. Ultimately I personally borrowed the money necessary to get delivery of the poll results. The anti-De Sapio heroes (all but one—who lent me the money) looked the other way when asked to help. (I never paid the loan back. After the victory, the lender forgave the debt. If Koch had lost, I don't know what the result would have been.)

The poll was a great one. It showed that everything that Koch and his supporters were doing was losing votes, and that if the election were held at that point, De Sapio would win by at least fifteen hundred votes. I suspect Carmine De Sapio had taken his own polls before he started his campaign and that they showed the same thing. Indeed, De Sapio's campaign was obviously geared to the same information our poll revealed.

What precisely did it reveal? The projected De Sapio majority was the least important fact. The important facts related to the attitudes of the voters. In an earlier day, district captains could accurately report voter sentiment. This was Tammany's great strength. But in today's Democratic Party, possibly because of population mobility, the impersonality of city life, and the breakdown of the machine, the party dare not rely wholly on itself in this kind of intelligence gathering. Hence, the pollster.

Here is the kind of information the poll developed and the impact it had on the campaign.

In the first place, the poll indicated that 68 percent of the Democrats likely to vote in the primary identified themselves as "regular Democrats." Only 32 percent identified themselves as reformers. Accordingly, it was clear that if Koch ran as a reformer pure and simple and got all the reform votes, De Sapio would win. In fact, Koch's whole campaign, like the French Maginot Line, was geared to an old war—to the issues of the 1961 campaign, when "reform" was a magic word. He was running as the instrument of "reform" and the Village Independent Democrats, not as Ed Koch, boy lawyer, civic leader, and friend of the Village.

Secondly, the poll showed that the VID drew the support of less than a majority of the likely Democratic voters as against De Sapio's Tamawa Club. The exclusive identification of Koch as the VID candidate was therefore also a losing and not a winning tactic.

Third, the poll revealed great voter resentment of both Koch and De Sapio because of outside political influences—in Koch's case, outsiders who called themselves reformers, telling the voters what to do; in De Sapio's case, his outside interests, i.e., his desire to use the leadership as a new steppingstone for a new political career outside the Village.

The poll revealed many other details of voter reaction. Koch's anonymity was a serious handicap—he should be on the streets instead of in the clubhouse—Villagers were more interested in certain specific local problems than in ideological differences—and so on. Essentially, however, the poll indicated voters were tiring of the reform-regular dispute and were more interested in the capacity of the candidates to be effective in dealing with local problems.

The results of the poll were revealed first to a handful of Koch's supporters. A "Mobilization for Reform" planned by Koch's campaign managers, which would have brought every reformer in town into the district and undoubtedly would have lost the election, was quickly scuttled. Instead, a "Democratic Mobilization," 80 percent of which consisted of First Assembly District South Democrats, was quickly put together. (De Sapio, apparently armed with secret information as to the composition of the projected "Mobilization for Reform" promptly charged that three-quarters of the people involved in the Democratic Mobilization came from outside the district. This was true as to the projected "Mobilization for Reform" but not true of the campaign group which was substituted for it. Chalk up one for Koch.)

When Koch was told of the poll's result, he showed his true colors. He could have said, "It's wrong." He could have said, "It's right, and I'm licked." Or he could have said, as he did, "I think it's right. What should I do to win?" Needless to say, I acquired great respect for his intelligence and his courage. He was smart enough to turn his strategy inside out halfway through the campaign, strong enough to turn a losing campaign into one that could be won.

I do not want to suggest the poll was magic. On the contrary, it was Koch's imaginative use of the material revealed by the survey, his very hard work in convincing his supporters to change their approach, and his own redoubled efforts that brought victory.

Only eight or ten people ever knew of the existence of the poll, let alone its content. Only two people ever had copies of parts of it; and only one, the author, had a copy of the complete text of the poll. Its existence was unknown to the press and to the voters. It affected the final result only by making available detailed information on voter attitudes to the candidate. Koch won because he used the poll wisely.

To this date, I suspect that Carmine De Sapio stopped polling at the time we started, sure of victory, and is perhaps still perplexed about what happened to the fifteen-hundred-vote margin he held in early July.

There are many other examples of the proper use of polls. The material published in the newspapers—the "laundry list" of voters' candidate preferences—is almost useless in planning a campaign. Indeed, in a political poll designed for use by politicians, the "laundry list" is the least important information. It constitutes perhaps 5 percent of the data. Voter attitudes, important issues, views on public officials, local discontents, ideological positions—these are the materials the political leaders use. They are a valid, useful and wholly proper tool when properly used.

The first piece of advice for any prospective candidate is to take a poll in order to find out who he is—if anyone—in the minds of the voters, and what these voters who might be his are thinking about. Then, and only then, is he in a position to decide whether to run at all.

The cost is relatively cheap, between $1,500 and $2,500 for local candidacies, and up to $7,500 for a state-wide canvass in a state as big as New York. That move—to survey the terrain at the start—can save a fortune in wasted campaign expenditures. It is an investment, moreover, that can produce, as it has in a number of cases with which I am familiar, a successful candidacy and the sweet launching of a political career.

19. The Use of the Press as a Political Tool

✻✻

There may have been a day when the contents of the daily newspapers were the product of hard-working reporters who diligently dug out the facts of politics and faithfully reported them without regard to the political result. It would have been difficult for Benjamin Franklin to credit such a circumstance. It is at least as difficult for me. The Golden Age, in any event, is long since past. Political leaders simply do not keep their mouths shut before reporters, mutter "no comment" to every question, and defy the press to uncover the truth. "Political news" no longer consists, if it ever did, wholly of the raked muck of exposed political misconduct, or reports of speeches delivered to thousands of voters by candidates orating under red-white-and-blue bunting. Newspapermen today no longer find it necessary to beat down the closed doors of politicians or dig out their material all by themselves.

Today the press is one of the principal tools of a political leader. He uses it as he uses his captains and district leaders, or money, or campaign literature. For the market has shifted: where once reporters and politicians were essentially antagonists, the former snooping into the private conduct of the latter—who wanted NO publicity—now reporters and politicians sometimes seem to be co-practitioners of the same trade.

The reporter is deluged with releases, statements, hot tips, and other material eagerly furnished by publicity-seeking politicians. The main problem for a reporter is not to find news, but to distinguish between the volunteered information that is news and the volunteered information that is not. To make that distinction, newsmen must know as much as their news source about what's really going on—if not more. And so newsmen turn more to political leaders than to officeholders for guidance, for "background," for "off-the-record" data. Whether or not there is a current story popping, the newsman checks in weekly or perhaps more frequently with his political sources to keep his information current, his fingers on the political pulse, his judgment sharpened. If there is a story produced by such calls, it's an unexpected dividend.

If a politician is in a position where he is the recipient of such inquiries, he can destroy himself quickly—by lying, by misleading, by refusing to say anything at any time, or by trying to push a wholly self-serving or merely mischievous story. But if he establishes a rapport, if his information is valid (and the press will check it), if he is discreet and not a blabbermouth, if he does not try exclusively to push himself, he creates a great ally and finds a great tool.

If his credit with the press is good, then when he needs it, when he has a valid story (or sometimes one he wishes were valid), or when he wants to float a balloon—i.e., push a candidacy without personally supporting it—the press is a tool that can advance a political cause far better than any other instrumentality. There are many concrete examples of this phenomenon. In each case news was created, and the press was prepared to push it; it was on the front page—not the last.

For example, the abortive candidacy of Judge Bernard Botein for governor in 1962 was 90 percent the product of careful news management.

Judge Botein was not privy to these maneuvers. Indeed, I am told on reliable authority that he visibly blanched at some of our antics. But he was the subject of a candidacy handled almost exclusively through the press and about ten individuals. And this campaign, but for Judge Botein's insistence on observing the canons of judicial ethics, would probably have succeeded. This was the timetable:

STEP 1: As county leader, I was to urge the state chairman, in a carefully drafted letter, to consider the desirability of a Botein candidacy. Before I wrote this letter I spoke to no one except those who were planning the Botein candidacy—all of them significant state party figures—and the state chairman. This letter was carefully prepared in my office, drafts reviewed and revised, and delivery was to be on "Saturday-for-Sunday" (i.e., on Saturday it would be released for Sunday's papers).

STEP 2: The letter was released on a dull, summer Saturday. (I don't think I ever actually sent the letter itself to the addressee, but maybe I did.) All major papers had a political writer on duty who had been alerted to look for the release when it came in to the City Desk. Result: Front page, not back.

STEP 3: On Sunday, I was on a television interview program. Naturally, the major subject was the Botein candidacy. Result: All day Sunday the Botein balloon occupied the news programs on radio and TV, and as item Number 1 or 2, not buried at the end as a filler.

STEP 4: On Monday, front-page follow-up stories on Sunday's TV show.

STEP 5: No news released Monday-for-Tuesday.

STEP 6: On Tuesday, an upstate leader was prepared to and did announce his agreement to my suggestion. This was a "Tuesday-for-Wednesday" release. Result: Front page, as alerted reporters picked up the story.

STEP 7: No Wednesday news.

STEP 8: On Thursday, another upstate leader or two announced. This was a "Thursday-for-Friday" story.

STEP 9: No Friday news. (Saturday is a deadly news day, especially in summer.)

And so it went. When Herbert H. Lehman returned from Europe, all other endorsements were held back to give his statement for Judge Botein center stage. The flow of news thickened. It continued for almost two weeks as the endorsements and the stories carefully poured forth.

There were a few setbacks. Mrs. Roosevelt said she didn't know who Judge Botein was; a county leader with his own candidate leveled his sights at the balloon and blasted away. But the balloon stayed aloft.

The clincher was due a few days after the mayor returned from vacation and indicated his approval of the suggestion. One of the largest counties in the state was to join the bandwagon ("Sunday-for-Monday"). The county leader wanted only to be able to say *truthfully* to his district leaders, "I know Judge Botein"—and he didn't. So could he drop up to say hello to Judge Botein?

The judge, faithful to judicial ethics, which forbid political activity by a judge, declined. He was not a candidate. If nominated, he would resign from the bench and run (so I was told; I never discussed any of this with him until long after the whole thing collapsed). But meeting district leaders and county leaders beforehand was a form of political campaigning, and as a sitting judge he would not do it.

His rectitude—which was further evidence to me of his value as a public servant—would not permit cute evasions. And so there was no endorsement from the key county whose leader couldn't honestly say he knew Judge Botein.

The Botein balloon collapsed, and its proponents found a new candidate and started a new series of "Sunday-for-Monday" and "Tuesday-for-Wednesday" releases.

The Robert F. Kennedy prenomination campaign for U.S. Senate in 1964 was similarly planned and executed. A newspaperman's by-lined account of the maneuvers (he was obviously himself a participant in the operation to be able to write such an intimate account) appeared in the New York *Times* shortly before the nomination.

While incomplete, the account magnificently demonstrates the use of the press as a political tool. For it is plain that the natural result of confiding such data to a newsman was to enable him to command the front page of the New York *Times* day after day—and the Kennedy candidacy benefited accordingly.

The same account, incidentally, also reveals the extent to which the source of the confidences can indirectly affect the content of the stories. One of the Kennedy endorsements that made national news was one I released while on a brief vacation in New Hampshire. That it had more than local New York State interest was clear, because the statement, which I repeated *ad nauseam* over the telephone for radio stations, was heard repeatedly in New Hampshire and Vermont, in Portland, Boston, Springfield, and almost as quickly on national radio network news roundups. It was picked up in the New Hampshire papers, from which it spread as it got stale to the inside pages of other New England papers.

But the carefully written summary of the press campaign which was printed a week later included no reference to this unplanned "Sunday-for-Monday" release, largely because the reporter's contact in Kennedy's headquarters was not aware of my endorsement until it was public knowledge, and also because the same contact was a recent opponent of mine (I had endorsed his adversary in a primary in which he lost). The point, of course, is that the content of press coverage, as well as its timing, can to some extent be controlled.

Part of the technique of enlisting the press as a political tool is not to be too eager, never to tell outright lies to the press, to give an occasional exclusive, and, if you don't want to be identified, to say so.

The result? Well, for example, in the spring of 1964, the New York *Times* carried an exclusive front-page story: "Democrats Consider Stevenson Candidacy" or something like that. The story reported that important New York County Democrats were considering Stevenson as a candidate for the United States Senate. Actually, the notion had come from one of my close friends, and I thought the best way to explore it was by leaking it. The reporter checked elsewhere, found support for the idea, and he had a story. It stimulated editorials, news stories, ultimately a Stevenson withdrawal, a renewal of Stevenson interest, another withdrawal, and finally futile efforts by anti-Bob Kennedy Democrats to get Stevenson to agree to run at the last minute.

The press carries such stories daily. "Informed circles"—"informed sources"—"it is reported"—"political authorities agree"—and so on. As often as not, the "informed circles" who report what Politician A is thinking consist of Politician A himself.

A wonderful example of this kind of use of the press took place in the summer of 1965, when the New York *Times* reported on its front page that Republican U.S. Senator Javits had received a letter from Republican State Senator John Hughes condemning Governor Rockefeller and urging Javits to lead a fight to remove Rockefeller as a candidate for re-election. The letter had been written months earlier, and was leaked after an inside story appeared reporting how Rockefeller had allegedly prevailed upon John Lindsay to run for mayor while Senator Javits had sat on the sidelines calculating his own ambitions.

No source was ever revealed for any of the stories, which caused a series of minor explosions. As Barry Gottehrer of the New York *Herald Tribune* (July 13, 1965) reported:

"The Hughes letter was around for weeks but not for publication," said one [wholly unidentified] New York Republican yesterday. "When the *Newsweek* story appeared, [unidentified] friends of the Senator made it available for publication."

Asked about the stories, Javits just grinned last week—and changed the subject. "Nelson and I are close friends," he said.

There is of course great danger in this technique and practice. It permits anonymous sponsorship of candidates and programs for which someone should be willing to take the responsibility. It also permits anonymous distortion of the facts. For example, when I finally resigned from politics, every effort was made to prevent any knowledge of my intentions from leaking, lest "informed sources" who once before had succeeded in anonymously leaking a proposed resignation, assigning unattractive reasons for it in the process, might do it again and make the exit appear to be a forced one. It was fun to time things—using "modern communications techniques"—so that no one knew I was resigning until it was too late for anyone to sneak in with an "exclusive" demeaning version of the reasons for terminating a political career.

It is a matter for grave concern, however, that the press sometimes co-operates in anonymous character assassination by reason of its apparent acceptance of its function as a political tool. The use of such a technique, moreover, is not limited to politics but extends to purely government activity. For example, the forced retirement of New York's superintendent of schools in 1965 was "leaked" and became the lead story in the New York *Times*. Anonymous sources revealed the reasons for the forced resignation. The fact that the "anonymous source" was a key official of the Board of Education was never revealed by the press, although his identity was acknowledged privately. Certainly the identity of the high official of the Board of Education who was the source of the anonymous charges was news, but it was never printed. It seems to me that the press is permitting itself to become too much of a tool in politics and government when it thus suppresses information that should be public knowledge.

In any event, the significant fact, insofar as understanding of the political process is concerned, is that in the planted story, the anonymous source is frequently—but not always—highly reliable, and that the story is almost always a move in some political or government program whose sponsors wish to remain anonymous for reasons that seem good and sufficient to them.

There is one other area in which the press is a valuable political asset—the editorial page. That page reflects whatever belief the newspaper is prepared to proclaim it holds. And the belief is reflected both editorially and in the selection of "Letters to the Editor." Both are a natural and proper target for politicians.

"Letters to the Editor" is easier to use than the editorial column, although both are susceptible to political effort. The fact is that most newspapers are *not* inundated with literate communications from readers. Since newspaper publishers and editors *are* literate, literate letters receive a warmer reception than others. And while it is questionable how many people read the "letters" column, probably those who do are somewhat more influential than those who do not. Doubtless they (and their spouses) are well-heeled members of the business, communications, and professional communities. And so well-planted letters can be helpful.

On occasion, letter-writing efforts are organized. Someone with a "big name" is persuaded to sign a letter to "answer" an editorial, and it is published. A sense of fair play leads editorial editors to tend to publish mildly critical letters from "big names." Strongly critical letters are almost never published, and if they are, they are frequently edited—on occasion without the author's consent. But, resort to the "letters" column is an effective technique and is frequently used. In one campaign I remember, the "letters" column got to be a bit of a game. Dealing with a couple of New York papers that were frequently critical of the party's major candidates, and weren't moved by "big names," an effective operation was set up to produce two dozen letters a day from "small names" to counterbalance the daily editorial page blasts. Towards the end, some of the signatories were, I am afraid, fictitious, but every two or three days one or two favorable letters were published. Among the few who were aware of the extent to which the letter-writing had been pushed, there was a daily betting pool to identify the fictitious letters from the genuine ones.

The editorial columns are harder to crack. Editorial writers are far less well informed about what is going on than their own political reporters, with whom they apparently never communicate. Indeed, political reporters early become accustomed to apologizing to their political informants for the contents of their editorial pages. But editorial writers are human beings too. They walk, they talk, they laugh (occasionally), they eat and drink. And they are not impervious to facts or to personality.

Editorialists regularly lunch with significant public figures. The lunches, to the victim at least, seem to be high state occasions. A visit to the President of the United States is far less awesome than an editorial lunch with the top staff of the New York *Times*. This is probably unfortunate. Perhaps less austerity would produce more effective communication. However, the skillful politician who is aware of the nature of the formal encounter and of the possibility of less formal and more informative ones, and is willing to "take his hair down," can make friends, and if he is really good at it, he becomes an "editorial saint"—which is at least one level above Gertrude Stein's "publicity saint."

The best example I know of an "editorial saint" was Robert Moses. Until recently, he could do no wrong. How much off-the-record "background" confidential disclosures produced this status for Moses is hard to judge.

A final factor in editorial attitude—although the subject is an unspoken and ambiguous one—is the extent to which a particular newspaper enjoys the political patronage of legal advertising. The publication of "legals" (notices of election, lists of polling places, lists of candidates) is a profitable form of advertising, and there is always a discreet scramble for it—not infrequently communicated via political reporters. The lesson is never lost on the person who has the power to name the designees, particularly the marginal ones.

Some of these legal advertisements are placed after consultation with party leaders. Others—judicial notices and so on, are printed in the paper designated by the judge with jurisdiction over the matter, and some judges rely upon the political leaders to name the papers to be thus blessed.

Some local neighborhood newspapers are particularly dependent upon legals, and don't hesitate to say so. The editor of one West Side neighborhood weekly was from time to time during his tenure in contact with me about the possibility of my persuading a judge or two to designate his sheet as the place for legal advertising or notices. Usually the calls followed a particularly vitriolic editorial or unfair news article. He got no advertising. And not too much later the editorials and editorial policy ended when he was, to my considerable satisfaction, fired.

Most of the press, to be sure, is *not* for sale. Here and there a political reporter may be reputed to be on the take. One had a "sick brother-in-law" who was trotted out from time to time to justify a "loan." Here and there a local paper is available to the highest bidder. But by and large, the use of the press as a political tool requires ingenuity, intelligence, tact, and a good and truthful—or at least not wholly untruthful—story.

20. Financing Politics and Campaigns

The Achilles heel of every honest political organization is the necessity to finance itself. The major problem of every candidate is how to finance his campaign.

There was a time when the problem—for candidates at least—was probably less acute. In an era when an assemblyman ran for re-election every year, and when the costs of campaigns did not involve enormous expenditures for mail, advertising, printing, sound trucks, and the like, financing was easier. Supported by a well-heeled organization, a candidate could by a politic modesty permit himself to mix his name and photograph with the head(s) of the ticket and so he was carried into office.

As for the well-heeled organization, its funds came from wherever they came from. The son of a leader of Tammany Hall of bygone days once told me of the pre-election day "spread" on the family dining-room table—over $500,000 divided into piles, $400 per election district, one for each leader to pick up and deliver to his captains. This was the captain's pay—for his own time, his staff of runners, his election-day expenses, and perhaps for his political operation for the ensuing year. For in an era when the local bar was the election district's social center, a good captain had to spend a fair amount of time there making friends, and, incidentally, picking up tabs. In addition, there were local charities, indigent families, policemen assigned to the polls, and a host of other expenses, many of which tended to cluster about the pre-election period. Then, but not now, the political organization filled a community function. Neither the captain nor the leader said "no" to legitimate requests for financial aid. I am guessing, but I suspect that the principal financial burden of a campaign fell upon the organization and

229

the leader—not the candidate—although the candidate did his part when he could.

Where the money came from, I do not know, except that I have read many, many exposés, investigations, and muck-raking reports that indicate that the fund-raising methods did not overlook any illicit source of cash. Have times changed? Ah, yes. The notion of the organization raising and distributing $400 or $300 or $200 or $100 per election district is laughable. The highest I ever hit was $30 or $35 per district. The campaign budget for the county organization never exceeded $60,000—and that was its very highest point, in the 1964 Presidential election. (Of course, on top of that another $75,000 had to be raised for regular operating expenses, including the paying-off of debts.) In addition, the local candidates running for election in New York County usually account for the expenditure of at least another $100,000 to $200,000. Where does it come from? How is it spent?

The Source of Funds

There are four separate, but overlapping, fund-raising operations involved:

1. COUNTY GENERAL FUNDS: to pay rent, telephone, staff, and other operating expenses—budgeted at about $60,000 a year.

2. CLUB GENERAL FUNDS: for the same purposes, except that most have no paid staff—estimated at $300,000.

3. COUNTY CAMPAIGN FUNDS: spent for printing, sound trucks, advertisements, telephones, headquarters, and also in part (over 50%) disbursed to local clubs for election-day expenses—$60,000 to $70,000. (Some campaign bills inevitably are paid out of county general funds: increased telephones, meetings, miscellaneous expenses, and so on.)

4. LOCAL CAMPAIGN FUNDS: spent by four congressional, six state senate, and sixteen assembly candidates: estimated at at least $200,000.*

* In 1960, the Democratic candidate in one congressional district spent almost $100,000 in that district alone—and lost. Probably my estimate for the whole county is low.

The total is over $600,000 per year, and probably far higher. Since there are over 375,000 enrolled Democrats in New York County, the political cost is a little under $2 per enrolled Democrat.

Anyone examining these figures with a properly skeptical attitude, especially if he has had the benefit of a conventional education about politics in a good academic institution, will tend to assume that portions of the organization—the county, and one or two clubs—are easily purchased. When such a skeptic wants to run for Congress or assembly or something, he sets about buying support. He is known to professional politicians, who have some pride in themselves and their craft, as a "pigeon" and if he is eager and obnoxious enough he will be plucked, only to discover at the crucial moment that the "other leaders" turned him down. Or, if he is a shrewd pigeon and wants to hold back his funds until after he's *got* the nomination, he is a "tight s.o.b." and for that reason the "other leaders" will turn him down. A gentleman with money who knows the art of politics, and has respect for those leaders who are entitled to respect and toleration for those who deserve no more, can use his money as a legitimate asset in building a political career. And he is a useful asset to the financially shaky political party. But "pigeons" and "tight s.o.b.'s" are merely amusing diversions.

There are obvious theoretical limits on the amounts of his own money a candidate himself is allowed to spend on a campaign. But none of the statutes were seriously drafted to achieve their stated purposes. They are never violated, but they never limit the amount of money spent on campaigns. If the statutes had been seriously intended, they would not have been deliberately drafted to invite evasion. Perhaps someday we will have seriously drafted statutes with reasonable limits on amounts to be spent and upon amounts that can be contributed, but there isn't one on the books today. Like so many of our good-government devices, they are window dressing, and the only concern anyone gives them is to insure that contributions are made in a form that does not violate the statutes.

That really isn't very hard.

While I have dismissed the rich candidate as a dominant factor in politics, the threat posed by a candidate of great wealth should not be disregarded. Besides money, the very rich have other tools denied to their poorer competitors—private airplanes, often paid for by their corporations as tax-deductible business expenses, to get around; public relations men on corporate payrolls, whose salaries are likewise deductible as business expenses, although the bulk or all of their activities are devoted to promoting the political image and political career of the company president. And of course, a wealthy young man with great resources has a greater opportunity to finance "charitable" or "good-government" committees with valid tax-deductible objectives—which, incidentally, enhance the political image of the benefactor.

The "rich man in politics" is a threat to democratic government. If "patronage" is evil, and if only those with enough money to live without working are eligible for politics, we will have very strange politics in the years ahead. Fortunately, we have been lucky in the wealthy men who have succeeded in politics—Senator Robert Kennedy and Governor Nelson Rockefeller, for example. Add to the list Congressmen Scheuer and Ottinger from New York, both of whom were elected from New York in 1964 after expenditures in the pursuit of a two-year congressional term of over $100,000 apiece, derived from their own or their family's funds.

Somehow men like William Randolph Hearst never quite made it. Nor did Rockefeller's wealth win him nomination for the Presidency.

Probably the best protection against the unprincipled or unreliable wealthy young man has been the political party officeholder who is prepared to say, "I don't care how much he's got. He's a jerk." I have heard that said, and said it myself, on more than one occasion, about potential candidates whose only serious qualification for public office was a bankroll. Indeed, in 1965, more than one potential candidate for city-wide office bit the dust with that epitaph.

County General Funds and County Campaign Funds

General county funds are raised through one major fund-raising event a year, a $60- to $100-a-plate dinner ($60 for club members; $100 for others). It can net anywhere from about $35,000 to about $100,000, depending upon the time, place, guest of honor, status of the leader, relative power of the party at the time, its significance in the governmental scheme, and its relations with the President and governor and mayor.

In a county like New York, there are people who regard it as their obligation to buy a table every year, whatever the state of the party; for this is their token of loyalty to an ancient political institution. There are others who will participate out of a desire to honor the particular county leader or what he stands for. By the end of my tenure as county leader, I had built up a substantial group of this kind—people who for personal reasons were happy to see me at the helm of the party. There are others who do business with the city (or whatever governmental unit is involved) who feel it is either an obligation or good business or both to support the party in power. (More and more, elected public officials keep these prospects for themselves, awaiting the day when they themselves will want to call upon their special supporters for financial contributions to their campaigns for re-election.) Finally, there are those who participate so that they will be in a position, if they need help with a government official, to use the good offices of the organization to meet and talk to him under favorable auspices.

During my two and three-quarters years as county leader, I estimate that I raised well over $300,000. I sometimes received requests from contributors: Help in preventing the razing of a commercial building for a new civic project; introduction to various city officials, in the housing field particularly; a favorable word for a candidate for appointment to a good position who was a close friend of a major contributor; appointment to some honorary, nonpaying commission; opposition to proposed legislation that affected a contributor's business. But these were not *quid pro quos.* They were by-products of membership in the same organization.

There were occasions when a contribution was promised provided certain results were obtained. These offers were ignored.

There were occasions upon which all of a sudden someone became very friendly and helpful—and a few months later he was back asking for some impossible favor like appointment to a highly honorific commission by a chief executive who had contempt for the contributor. When this was turned down, he disappeared and was never seen at headquarters again.

There were also candidates for the judiciary whose names were spawned by some nonpolitical group and who were well educated and so realized that the "politicos" had to be dealt with. They came around, eager to line up the politicos, asking, "Just tell me what I have to do." (I was supposed to translate this into "How much will it cost me?") Decent people, misled, and unwittingly insulting.

The worst problem on the county level is the competition. There was a time when every good and wealthy Democrat who felt deeply about the party would pay his annual visit to his county leader or to his state chairman and make a contribution, after which the county and state committees, after caring for their own needs, would make a contribution to the Democratic National Committee.

But all that is changed. The glamour of local political leaders is dimmed, and the route to the national committee—indeed, to the President—is direct. Instead of proceeding through the county and state organizations, the contributor goes direct to the White House via the President's Club, which accepts contributions of a thousand dollars or more. To this kind of contributor, the local party is frequently nothing but a cause for disdain because of its inadequate campaigns and second-rate, under-financed candidates.

A second source of competition is the public officeholder who has his own campaign coming up next year or the year after. In 1964, a number of old party contributors privately told me that they were holding back because someone had told them the mayor had let it be known that they should go easy in order to save their money for next year, when he would be running for re-election. All I had to do was to get the mayor to tell them to help and they would. The mayor never told them, although he did help in other ways.

Then how do you get the money? I don't know. I could never reproduce in a compact narrative the frenzy of the last two weeks of the 1964 campaign when I spent fourteen hours a day on the phone and in person, cajoling, begging, demanding, writing letters, sending panicky telegrams, doing everything that I had ever learned how to do, in order to raise some thirty thousand dollars to meet my campaign budget.

As far as the general county funds are concerned, they are raised in the spring. The last ten days before the annual dinner is spent on the phone—one call after another—until one is dizzy, and the names mean nothing, contacting all the people who our records indicated at one time or another had supported the party. That, too, becomes a blur—a blur which comes to focus when the seating arrangement for the banquet is finally prepared and it is clear that a capacity crowd will attend.

An unspoken element in both operations is the notion of power—that the leader has some mysterious power, and that in deference to it everyone should say "yes"—at least a small "yes."

Club General Funds

How do the clubs raise their funds? By pretty much the same techniques as the county does, but on a smaller scale. Some clubs publish a "journal"—a printed volume of advertisements in which public officeholders, local businesses, friends of the leader and club officers, captains, and so on, buy "advertisements" —a full page or less—saying something like "Compliments of Your Assemblyman, Joe Flub."

Other clubs simply run dinners or theatre benefits or dances, or publish and mail out local business directories. They solicit their members for dues and additional contributions at campaign time. Others use the $20 or $25, $30 or $35 per election district, which the county headquarters distributes on the day before election day, to close their budget gaps. (In the case of some clubs, like the Lexington Democratic Club, for example, the reform club in the Ninth A.D., the 1964 election-day check from the county was $2,520. The Riverside Democrats, a reform club on the West Side, liked to write letters to its members telling them to double their contribution because the county organization wasn't helping the club. In actual fact, they regularly received their checks. In 1964 they received $1,620.) The total New York party election-day distribution in 1964 was over $35,000, a far cry from the $500,000 of years ago. But for the guy who raised it (plus an equal amount spent county-wide), it was no small potatoes. This money—$30 to $35 a district—is not used to buy votes. How could it be? What it does buy is coffee and sandwiches, taxis to get someplace fast; it tips a co-operative doorman or telephone operator; it hires kids to distribute literature—and so on. If anything is left, it buys a few drinks for the captain and his staff.

The Candidates

And that leaves the candidates to scrounge for what's left. How do they finance their campaigns?

Remember that, as a rule of thumb, an assembly campaign in a close district costs $5,000 to $10,000, a state senate campaign $10,000 to $20,000, and a congressional campaign $25,000 (minimum) to $125,000. In districts where the Democratic nomination is the equivalent of election, the amounts are probably less, and are often limited to election-day "expenses" for the captains —anywhere from $10 to $40 per election district. For a normal assembly district of 65 election districts, this amounts to $650 to $2,600. For a safe district, the expense probably mostly comes out of the candidate's pocket and out of the salary he will earn. In a close district, however, the candidate must set up his own fund-raising operation—friends, classmates, political associates, family, clients, what have you.

The most fruitful source of contributions is the candidate's own bank account, or that of a member or members of his family. A rich father-in-law is useful. A wide and admiring acquaintanceship is helpful, and deficit financing is an appropriate fiscal technique. Many losing candidates spend a year or more paying off debts. Those who are lawyers may receive help from sympathetic judges, who appoint them as referees, special masters, and special guardians. But the help comes from where you can find it.

Doesn't this mean that the candidate—and the party—are for sale? Don't the bribers move in? Don't underworld figures offer to pick up the tab?

They once did. There was a time—not too long ago—when reputed underworld figures actively participated in political financing. But public exposure, and replacement of the generation of political leaders who accepted such help, has put an end, at least temporarily, to such practice. As for buying candidates, that too is passé—for the time being anyway. Part of the reason may be that a man who can be bought has the bad habit of not staying bought—he becomes a statesman—and underworld figures prefer safer investments.

May this mean that a political leader is tempted to sell the nominations he controls? Yes, it may. Some undoubtedly give in to the temptation, or at least allow their judgments to be colored by the easing of financial problems offered covertly, if not openly, by a wealthy candidate. Indeed, the money problem is the soft underbelly of political morality. It creates more problems than anything else for the political leader. By nature and necessity it allows the possibility of a return to some of the bad practices of earlier years. (Although things will never get back to the practices of the Tweed ring. To the extent that anyone wishes to corrupt government, it has been adequately demonstrated that the corrupters can deal directly with government— e.g., gamblers dealing with police—without the intervention of political leaders.) But if there is a relapse—and I doubt that there will be—it will come only because the party members, the *enrolled* Democrats and Republicans—are quite content to accept the benefits of party membership (nominating party candidates and electing their political organization leaders in primary elections) but are unwilling to pay their share of the cost of operating a party.

I never failed to be amused by some of the complaints we received from some of our enrolled Democrats—who never contributed a dollar to any campaign. "Why don't you people send out more mail during the campaign?" (This in a campaign where one mailing costs over $1,200, and we've managed to raise enough for only one and a half.) "Nobody called me on the phone" (at six cents per call). "The Republicans sent me three letters, and you sent only one"—and so on.

Efforts to organize door-to-door "dollars-for-Democrats" drives have not worked in New York City, largely because of the resistance by party workers, who instinctively hesitate to ask voters for money (after all, *our* tradition is one of giving money to those who need it and asking only for votes on election day). Their feeling comes partly because they assume that there will be voter resistance (which I doubt), and partly because of inability to make an ancient institution reverse its attitude so startlingly. Perhaps in a few years the effort will be successfully made. Other counties—particularly suburban Nassau, under the leadership of a very able and imaginative young leader, John English—have had great success with door-to-door fund-raising efforts. Perhaps an alternative is to say to those who wish to enroll in the party and control its affairs, "Fine—the dues are one dollar a year." That alone would solve all the financial problems—though it would probably create political problems.

The best solution may involve government financing of campaigns. At the very least it should involve indirect government subsidization—making political contributions tax-deductible, for instance, not up to $10 but up to $100 or $500. But, I admit, no immediate solution is at hand.

While there is no point in overlooking the problem, it should not be exaggerated. There is still cash in the political financial stream, though in relatively small amounts. It is frequently there for decent and understandable reasons (a resident of another county does not wish his county leader to learn that he made a contribution to New York County larger than the amount contributed at home). There are leaders who might be bought—and there are candidates who might be had. Since the era of the muckrakers, however, the sudden and unexplained wealth of a political leader is a source of suspicion and heavy public discussion. When it occurs, it is usually the cause of early—and involuntary—retirement from politics.

Yet the risk of corruption is there. It cannot be ignored.

It is not too much to say that a permanent defense against the flexible ethics of Tweed politics will never be secured until the problem of financing is solved in such a way that the integrity of the organization does not depend *virtually exclusively* upon the individual integrity of the man or men who raise its funds. From my own experience, I can only say that despite a badly divided organization, despite the competition of the President's Club, despite the absence of genuine co-operation from many public officeholders, and despite an organized boycott by most of the reform wing of the party and many of its supporters, I was able to liquidate the deficit I inherited, to reactivate a host of old party supporters, and to keep the organization functioning with increasing adequacy, if not luxury. I did this by selling the notion that the Democratic Party of New York County was an honest party organization, and that it was up to those who wanted such a party to do their share.

Given party unity and freedom from boycotts and personal feuds, I believe an urban party can finance itself and its candidates on a platform of integrity without resort to dirty dollars.

21. On Campaign Literature

Every campaign of any size generates thousands of pieces of paper. Each contains hundreds or thousands of words. All are intended to get votes for the candidate who issues them.

In recent years radio, television, and newspaper advertisements have played increasingly important roles. The attractiveness of these media is that the message gets delivered to the home of the voter without having to rely upon what relatively few political foot-soldiers there are to hand-deliver a brochure. Whether the message is heard, read, or understood is, of course, another question, but at least it gets to the home of the voter. For the same reason, there has been an increasing use of the mails to deliver literature to the voter's home.

Delivery, however, is a separate difficulty. The basic problem is what to say, how to say it so that it will be read (or heard), and how to be persuasive.

There are some guidelines, which are regularly flouted. First, the message should be short. Almost every piece of political literature is too long. A fifteen-minute radio or television speech is too long unless the speaker is a major figure—a Stevenson or a Goldwater or a Kennedy. Most voters, although they *should* read or listen to serious statements on public affairs, simply won't pay attention for fifteen minutes. Thus one reaches perhaps 5 to 10 percent of the audience with a lengthy statement.

Second, the basic literature (and here I include radio and TV) should all be directed to the same campaign theme—and that means the candidate must *have* a theme—a one-sentence reason why the voter should vote for him.

Kennedy's "Let's get the country moving again," Stevenson's "Talk sense to the American people," Rockefeller's "Fiscal Integrity," Wagner's "Beat the Bosses," Roosevelt's "New Deal" (a political theme before it came to describe a collection of government programs), Johnson's "The Great Society" are all examples of a central theme into which everything else could be integrated.

Third, the message of the piece must be distilled into one opening sentence that provocatively summarizes the purpose of the literature in a way related to the theme of the campaign.

These generalizations are all well and good, but far more can be said by giving specific examples of good and bad literature and television promotion.

The best piece of political literature I ever saw was issued by John Lamula, a Republican who was running for the Republican nomination for the office of councilman-at-large in Manhattan against Richard Aldrich, a cousin of Governor Nelson Rockefeller's. Lamula, a former assemblyman, a Republican district leader, and for many years an active party worker, was a logical candidate and would have been a popular one. The word slowly leaked out, however, that Governor Rockefeller wanted his cousin to be designated by the Republican leaders. Charges and countercharges—a free choice had been promised and now the promise was broken, pressure and arm-twisting were being used—filled the air and the press. Finally, a majority of the Republican district leaders, under the unhappy guidance of the Republican county chairman, designated Aldrich.

Lamula promptly declared his own candidacy and entered the primary. He was first ruled off the ballot on some technical ground in a lawsuit brought by the Republican county organization, but was restored to the ballot by the state's highest court. (While all this was going on, Aldrich was in Chile on a ski trip.)

On the day before the primary, Lamula's piece reached the enrolled Republicans in the county. This piece was almost Lamula's entire campaign, since except in the lower East Side he had no workers and no campaign. Moreover, he was fighting the whole Republican organization, which under Nelson Rocke-feller's gentle prodding had decided to support Rocky's cousin, Richard Aldrich.

The full text of Lamula's brochure (except for the back, which consisted of endorsements culled from old letters from such Republican luminaries as La Guardia, Eisenhower, and Rocke-feller) is reproduced in the insert between pages 244 and 245.

Lamula lost the primary by less than ½ of 1 percent of the votes cast. He got over 49 percent of the vote largely on that one piece of literature. Twenty more captains working for him (in 20 of the 1,074 election districts in Manhattan) undoubtedly would have won the election for him.

Another of the very best pieces of literature I have ever seen was used by Democrat Fred Berman when he successfully ran for state senate from the silk-stocking Twentieth Senate District in Manhattan in 1964. The district substantially parallels the congressional district then represented by John Lindsay and had been represented by a Republican ever since its creation in 1942. It had a basic Republican majority but a liberal Republican orientation. Berman's campaign did not take off until his op-ponent, veteran State Senator MacNeil Mitchell, made it clear that he was supporting Goldwater. This was Berman's opening, and he grabbed it. The front of the piece of literature he pre-pared is reproduced between pages 244 and 245.

The rest of the piece was not as good as Lamula's. It was too wordy, covered too much, and used too many adjectives. But it was okay, especially in light of the effectiveness of the cover.

The words on the front cover (the literature is put into the envelope so that the cover is what the voter first sees) are the *most* important words in the entire piece. That is what most people read to decide whether to read the rest of the piece or not.

Berman used the same theme on posters which were stuck up all over the district. They said, simply:

"Most Republicans are shocked
that my opponent, MacNeil Mitchell,*
is supporting Goldwater."
—Frederic S. Berman,
Democratic Candidate for State Senator.

Other Democrats in similar districts (Eighth Assembly, Sixth Assembly) had similar opportunities. Their Republican-incumbent opponents likewise supported Goldwater. But these Democrats didn't exploit the fact as Berman did. They mentioned it in literature and posters, but it was lost among a dozen other facts.

And so, though Johnson swept these districts by well over 60 percent of the vote, and Berman carried his, some obscure Goldwater supporters won their own races on the Republican line.

One of the difficulties in a tightly fought local campaign, where literature has been extensively used, is that many voters, spotting the political source or nature of literature, throw it away. The problem has often been to disguise it so that the voter will open and read it.

One of the most effective pieces of this nature was conceived by Len and Mort Weber, two old friends of mine, who run an advertising–public relations company specializing in public events and public affairs.

In 1959, Jean McCabe (now Jean McCabe Angell) and I were running for re-election as district leaders. We were endorsed by the Citizens Union, a nonpartisan group that is highly respected by the voters, which increasingly in recent years has made its views known on the caliber of candidates for party office. The endorsement came shortly before primary day. Since the endorsement was highly regarded by our voters, I wanted it distributed to every voter in a form they would read even after having been deluged with literature.

Len and Mort Weber came up with the answer. They prepared a telegram to announce the endorsement, which we sent

---

* The popular notion that it is a mistake to mention your opponent's name doesn't apply when you are going for the jugular, especially when running against an opponent who is far better known.

to the Webers. They photostated it, deleting their names as addressees, leaving the rest of it plain. On the back, the essential information as to how to vote was set forth with admirable conciseness (see illustration between pages 244 and 245).

It was effective. Western Union later complained, but we pacified them and agreed not to do it again unless we got their consent.

Another *good* piece (but with too many words) was our basic piece in that campaign. The center fold contained a picture of each of us and a biography of each. (In later years we cut down on the biographical data.) In this one we emphasized our status as *Democrats*. And "Tammany" was still an affirmative word with many of our constituents, so we weren't afraid to use it. Two years later the word was a negative.

The back cover contained endorsements and a summary of our "achievements."

Endorsements can be significant. In 1957 we used only two, as follows:

"If my efforts have resulted in one Club such as this, I deem them to have been worthwhile."

ADLAI E. STEVENSON

"It is incumbent on a party leader to assert himself whenever he thinks it is in the best interests of the party. I support Ed Costikyan and Mary Reed."

CARMINE G. DE SAPIO

The voters may not know you, but they may know your endorsers.

There are, of course, many other examples of good "basic" literature. And there are other kinds of literature.

For example, some voters do read and think and worry about issues. In the 1956 Presidential campaign, Adlai Stevenson made a great speech on the dangers of unlimited atomic-bomb testing. Politically this was a mistake because the subject was too complicated to raise for the first time in the middle of a campaign. It came as no surprise, therefore, that the voter reaction was negative. They simply didn't understand what the Presidential candidate was after.

Dear Fellow Republican:

Will you be my Cousin on Primary Day?

John Lamula
Candidate for
Councilman-at-Large
in Manhattan

■ Front of mailing piece used in Republican primary campaign,
September 1963

"IT is not fit [that] the public trusts should be lodged in the hands of any, till they are first proved and found fit for the business they are to be entrusted with." —MATTHEW HENRY

NOW—LET'S LOOK AT THE RECORD

ALDRICH		LAMULA
Living in Rhode Island	1943	Elected to New York State Assembly (1st Republican to win any office in Al Smith's old district)
Living in Rhode Island	1944	Original sponsor of New York State Rent Control Law Sponsored bill to create Gov. Alfred E. Smith Houses
Living in Rhode Island	1945	Legislative Representative—Joint Rent Action Committee Small Business Trade Association to Control Commercial Rents
Living in Rhode Island	1946	Executive Director—All American Committee for Re-election of Governor Thomas E. Dewey
Living in Rhode Island	1947	Campaign Manager to Keep Proportional Representation (P.R.) (Chosen by League of Women Voters, Citizens Union, City Club of N.Y.)
Living in Rhode Island	1948	National Director—Committee for a Just Peace for Italy
Living in Rhode Island	1949	Elected Republican Leader in Lower Manhattan (Still serves in this office)
Living in Rhode Island	1950	Chairman—New York State Minimum Wage Board—Cleaning & Dyeing Industry. Appointed by Governor Dewey
Living in South America	1951	Chairman—Business Support for Motorist Protection by Compulsory Auto Insurance Program
Living in South America	1952	Director of Foreign Language Division Citizens for Eisenhower & Nixon
Living in South America	1953	City Wide Campaign Coordinator—Riegelman for Mayor
Living in South America	1954	State-wide Campaign for Javits for State Attorney General & Ives for Governor
Living in South America	1955	Led & Won Fight for Renewal of Business & Commercial Rent Control to Keep Business & Employment in New York
Living in South America	1956	Delegate to Republican National Convention
Living in South America	1957	Chairman—All American Committee Republican Mayoralty Campaign
Living in South America	1958	Appointed by Speaker of the Assembly Oswald D. Heck as Deputy Clerk of the State Assembly & Assistant to the Speaker
Living in South America	1959	Deputy Clerk of the State Assembly & Assistant to the Speaker
Living in New York — Did not vote	1960	Deputy Clerk of the State Assembly & Assistant to the Speaker
Living in New York — Did not vote	1961	Deputy Clerk of the State Assembly & Assistant to the Speaker
Candidate for Congress—First vote in New York	1962	Deputy Clerk of the State Assembly & Assistant to the Speaker
Candidate for Councilman-at-Large in Manhattan	1963	Candidate for Councilman-at-Large in Manhattan

WHO DESERVES YOUR VOTE ON PRIMARY DAY, THURSDAY, SEPTEMBER 5, 1963?

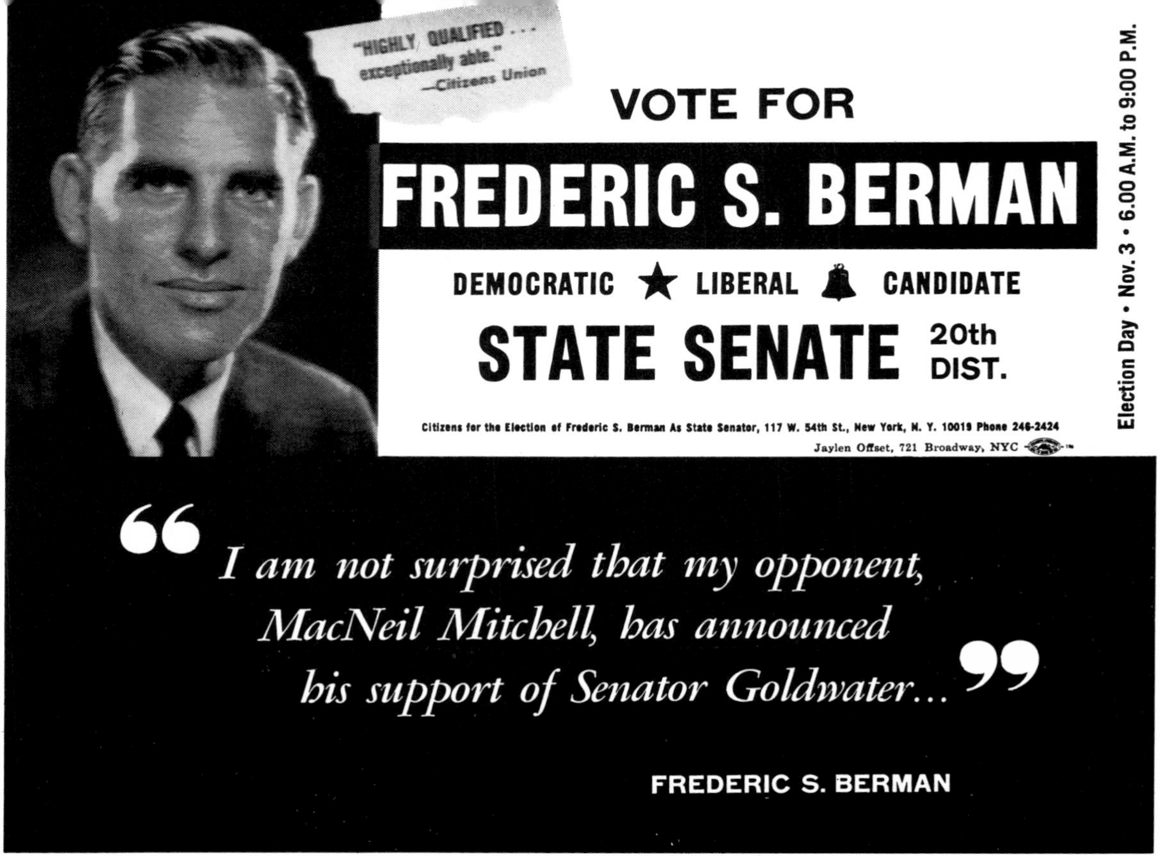
"HIGHLY QUALIFIED . . . exceptionally able."
—Citizens Union
VOTE FOR
FREDERIC S. BERMAN
DEMOCRATIC ★ LIBERAL CANDIDATE
STATE SENATE 20th DIST.
Citizens for the Election of Frederic S. Berman As State Senator, 117 W. 54th St., New York, N. Y. 10019 Phone 246-2424
Jaylen Offset, 721 Broadway, NYC
Election Day • Nov. 3 • 6.00 A.M. to 9:00 P.M.
"I am not surprised that my opponent, MacNeil Mitchell, has announced his support of Senator Goldwater..."
FREDERIC S. BERMAN

■ Mailing piece used in election campaign, November 1964

TO ALL REGISTERED DEMOCRATS,
EIGHTH ASSEMBLY DISTRICT SOUTH.

FLASH -- NON-PARTISAN CITIZENS UNION RELEASES CHOICE FOR
1959 PRIMARY, AS FOLLOWS: "FOR THE LAST FOUR YEARS, MR.
COSTIKYAN HAS BEEN ONE OF THE MOST ENLIGHTENED OF THE
CITY'S DEMOCRATIC LEADERS, HAVING DEFEATED THE DISCREDITED
CONNOLLY MACHINE, OF CRIME COMMISSION FAME, IN 1955.

"MR. COSTIKYAN IS A FORMER SECRETARY TO FEDERAL JUDGE
MEDINA, AND PRESENTLY A STAFF MEMBER OF THE LAW FIRM
OF ADLAI STEVENSON ... MISS McCABE IS A PROBATION SUPER-
VISOR IN THE MAGISTRATES' COURT. SHE HAS BEEN ACTIVE IN
CIVIC AFFAIRS.

"MR. COSTIKYAN AND MISS McCABE HEAD A PRACTICAL AND
FORWARD-LOOKING POLITICAL ORGANIZATION."

CITIZENS UNION FINDS THAT ELECTION OF OUR OPPONENTS "WOULD
UPSET A NEW POLITICAL REGIME OF EXCEPTIONAL PROMISE WITH
NO LIKELIHOOD OF PUTTING ANYTHING COMPARABLE IN ITS PLACE."

WARNING -- TWO YEARS AGO, OUR OPPONENTS FLOODED THE
DISTRICT, AT THE LAST MINUTE, WITH HANDOUTS MAKING FALSE
CLAIMS AND STATEMENTS. ALTHOUGH IT WAS TOO LATE TO REPLY
WITH THE TRUTH, ONLY A VERY FEW VOTERS WERE DECEIVED.
THIS YEAR, BE SURE YOU ARE NOT TAKEN IN BY THESE TACTICS!

REMEMBER, THE POLLS ARE OPEN FROM 3 PM TO 10 PM ON TUESDAY.
BE SURE TO VOTE LINE ONE - THE TOP ROW - ALL THE WAY ACROSS.
FOR THE REGULAR DEMOCRATIC CANDIDATES --

EDWARD N. COSTIKYAN AND JEAN McCABE

■ Inside spread of mailing piece used in Democratic primary campaign,
September 1959

AS DEMOCRATIC DISTRICT LEADERS, 8th A.D., South
RE-ELECT COSTIKYAN AND McCABE

and vote the rest of Line 1
— THE TOP ROW —
all the way across!

	1 Male Assembly Dist. Leader—Part A Vote for one	2 Female Assembly Dist. Leader—Part A Vote for one	3	4 7th Election District County Committee Vote for 3	5
			Frances H. Costikyan	Elinor MacNaughton	Lawrence H. Traubner
LINE 1	1 Edward N. Costikyan	2 Jean McCabe	3	4	5
LINE 2	1 Opponent	2 Opponent	3 Opponent	4 Opponent	5 Opponent

BE SURE TO VOTE ON PRIMARY DAY

at P.S. 73, 209 East 46th Street (bet. 2nd and 3rd Aves.)

TUESDAY, SEPTEMBER 15th — POLLS OPEN 3 PM TO 10 PM

Take this sample of the voting machine into the polls with you and
pull down all the levers on Line One—the top row all the way across.

129

■ Back page of the same mailing piece

■ Poster used in Democratic primary campaign, September 1961

PRIMARY DAY

The New York Times

SEPTEMBER 7th

FIVE CENTS

VOL. CX... No. 37,509.

NEW YORK, WEDNESDAY, NOVEMBER 22, 1961.

DE SAPIO'S OUSTER AS TAMMANY HEAD ASKED IN PETITION

Two Reform Democrats Put Plea in Circulation Among the District Leaders

A petition to oust Carmine G. De Sapio as leader of Tammany Hall has been placed in circulation among Manhattan district leaders by two members of the Democratic reform faction.

A memorandum distributed to district leaders in advance of the petition contended that Mr. De Sapio had become a liability to the Democratic party.

"Good candidates with good records will be defeated, both in primaries and in general elections, merely by their opponents' tying them to the present county leadership," the memorandum predicted.

"We were indeed fortunate this year that 'anti-De Sapioism' was used only sparingly by the Republicans. It is perfectly obvious that it will not be used sparingly next year, come either the primaries or the general election."

Both the memorandum and the petition were drafted by Edward N. Costikyan and Mrs. Jean McCabe, leader and co-leader, respectively, of the Eighth Assembly District South, which takes in the East Side of Manhattan from Queensboro Bridge to Yorkville.

...since joined by WAGNER, BEAME and SCREVANE

RE-ELECT
ED COSTIKYAN
JEAN McCABE

REGULAR-REFORM DEMOCRATIC CANDIDATES for

District Leaders – Eighth Assembly District, South

VOTE LINE 2 ALL THE WAY – POLLS OPEN 3 to 10 pm

Candidates of THE NEW DEMOCRATIC CLUB - Regular Democratic Organization

This is a sample literacy test. It's very easy.

Read this paragraph:

THE RED CROSS

In 1863, 25 people in Switzerland founded the International Committee of the Red Cross. These people chose a white flag with a red cross as the sign of their organization. They did this to honor Switzerland, whose flag has a white cross on a red field. On the flag of the Red Cross, the cross always stands alone. The Red Cross workers help the victims of war, flood and famine.

Answer these questions:

1. How many people formed the International Committee of the Red Cross?_____

2. In what country did the International Committee of the Red Cross start?_____

3. What are the two colors of the flag of Switzerland?_____
4. What always stands alone on the flag of the Red Cross?_____
5. Name one kind of victim that Red Cross workers help._____

Easy.

The literacy test at the polls is just as easy.

Take it. Register. Vote.

REGISTER OCTOBER 7th • 8th • 9th • 10th

VOTE FOR JOHNSON • HUMPHREY • KENNEDY

New York County Democratic Committee   Edward N. Costikyan, County Leader

■ Newspaper ad used in Democratic Party registration drive, October 1964

To no avail, I begged county and state headquarters for an information piece on it. They had no one to write it—because they had no one who understood it. Nothing came from national headquarters or from the Citizens for Stevenson-Kefauver. And so, in desperation, we searched for someone who could explain it. My wife has given the history of the piece in Chapter 5. It never looked pretty, but it was effective. It was the only piece I know of on the subject ever used in the campaign.

There are also posters—snipes, we call them—the bills put up at night on empty stores and walls marked POST NO BILLS. Their purpose is to spread the candidate's name around. Sometimes they also have pictures, but the general rule is to avoid pictures and text and concentrate solely on the name of the candidate, the office for which he is running, and the date of the election.

In 1961, we violated all these rules, and produced a kind of poster so different that people stopped to read. (I used to love to watch them do it.)

That was the year of the "Beat the Bosses" campaign. Since Jean McCabe and I had been the first leaders to actually seek De Sapio's removal as county leader, months before Wagner joined the fray, we decided to capitalize on it.

Using the front-page New York *Times* story of our efforts to remove De Sapio as the base, Len and Mort Weber designed a poster which is reproduced between pages 244 and 245.

People used to walk close to read the fine print. And our faces were thereafter well known and well recognized in the district (which they really hadn't been before).

What of bad literature?

Let me start with the worst I ever saw. In 1959 our opponents for district leader put out the following:

Front cover as it came out of the envelope read

ELECT

The rest of the front read

THOMAS J.
MURRAY

FLORENCE
LENISTON

The center fold read

TOM MURRAY

Air pollution caused by factories and utilities in the neighborhood. A vital service for health protection.

✸

Police Protection—This service is sorely needed in the neighborhood.

✸

Playgrounds are of utmost importance in combatting juvenile delinquency.

Housing—Endorse middle income housing for those desiring to remain in the neighborhood.

✸

Fire Protection—The absence of an Engine Company in our District is a distinct hazard and needs correction.*

FLORENCE LENISTON

Devotes much time to the promotion of Boy and Girl Scout activities.

✸

Taxes—Will endeavor to improve the tax situation for my constituents.

✸

Family picture—Is the devoted mother of seven children.

Charities—Has arranged and participated in numerous drives and movements for various charitable works.

✸

Traffic—Will endeavor to improve traffic situations and obtain protection for children attending school in our District.

---

* Actually, plans were then almost completed to put a firehouse in the district, and within a month this was done. The trouble was, it was on a one-way street and no fire engine could apparently get anyplace within miles of the firehouse without going up and down a series of one-way streets. After this had happened about twelve times in the middle of the night, waking every resident, my opponent soft-pedaled this issue.

Above each platform plank was a picture of some kind, including a Cape Cod cottage (in the middle of New York!) being destroyed by a fire.

The pictures used did neither of the candidates justice. The content was confused, the promises were unconvincing (for example: "Taxes—Will endeavor to improve the tax situation for my constituents.").

The back page was the climax. Divided into four boxes of small, close-set type, it read as follows:

Framework of American Democracy

RIGHTS OF EVERY CITIZEN

Every citizen has the right to:

1. Freedom of thought, speech, and the press, provided he does not injure others.
2. Freedom to worship as he desires.
3. Assemble peaceably with other citizens for peaceable purposes.
4. Join and work with any organization whose purposes are lawful.
5. Petition the Government to correct injustices.
6. Be protected from loss of life, liberty, or property without due process of law.
7. Be safeguarded when accused of crime by being: informed about charges against him; faced by his accusers; tried by jury; free from excessive bail and unusual punishment; and protected from having his life placed twice in jeopardy for the same crime.
8. Be protected from slavery or involuntary servitude except in prison.
9. Be protected by the Federal Government if a state tries to limit his constitutional rights.
10. Help choose the officials who direct governmental affairs.

DUTIES OF EVERY CITIZEN

Every citizen has the duty to:

1. Live peaceably, and support law and order.
2. Respect public and private property.
3. Serve his country as his abilities are needed.

4. Respect the opinions and rights of others.
5. Respect the rights of minorities, and help safeguard the rights of all religious, racial, and nationality groups.
6. Honestly study and form intelligent opinions on issues before the country.
7. Support views which he believes are right.
8. Vote in all elections, and support the best qualified leaders and representatives.
9. Support leaders properly elected, and abide by majority decisions.
10. Respect the Flag.
11. Assist public officers in preventing crime and detecting criminals.
12. Assist the courts by giving evidence.
13. Accept service on juries.
14. Pay taxes and other obligations to the Government.
15. Carry out contracts and agreements to which he is a party.

Political Democracy in the United States

PRINCIPLES

1. Supremacy of the Constitution as the law of the land and the obligation of the Government to enforce it.
2. Obligation of the Government to hold its authority within the limits set by the Constitution and the laws.
3. Right of the states to be dominant in their own field, subject only to the Constitution.
4. Right of the Government to protect itself against those who endanger it or attempt to change the system by revolution.
5. Changes in Government personnel and organization only through regular constitutional methods.
6. Supreme authority of the citizens expressed through regularly scheduled elections.
7. Right of every legally qualified citizen to vote.
8. Right of every voter freely to express his choice.
9. Right of minority groups to oppose the majority which is in power.
10. Right of every citizen to seek any office for which he is legally qualified.
11. Right of citizens, individually or in groups, to petition the Government for correcting injustices.
12. Separation of church and state.

ACHIEVEMENTS

- A democracy which has worked effectively for 170 years.
- Changing of Government by peaceful and legal means to fit new needs.
- Acceptance of and respect for the decisions of the Supreme Court.
- Popular control over state and local government through initiative, referendum, and recall.
- Peaceful acceptance of changes in Government's powers, organization, and personnel by all political groups.
- No ruling class—officials drawn from all walks of life.
- No governmental interference with activities of minority groups except for the security of the Nation.
- Widening of the suffrage until it includes most men and women.
- Constant improvements to protect voting rights.
- Constant improvement in election procedure.
- Full and free discussion of issues and candidates.
- Constant improvement of methods for training citizens.
- Increased efficiency of public employees through the Civil Service.
- Our form of government voluntarily copied by other peoples.

The faults in the literature were almost complete: no identification of who the candidates were, unflattering pictures of them, no theme, too many words. The whole of it was crammed on a four-fold sheet measuring 8½ by 11 inches and looked as appetizing as a lease.

There are many other examples of bad literature. Sometimes the message and the format don't match. For example, in 1956, Mary Reed, who was the woman district leader with me in the Eighth Assembly District South, ran for the assembly. She produced what I then thought and still think was the most attractive piece of political literature I ever saw.

It was a ten- or twelve-page pamphlet, beautifully written, beautifully laid out, beautifully printed and illustrated. I had expected her to run well ahead of the ticket, but she came in only slightly ahead. She was overwhelmed, along with the other Democratic candidates, in the Eisenhower landslide. Apparently the literature had had no impact. (It is doubtful of course that any piece of literature for a Democratic candidate could have done much good that year. Still you learn what you can.)

Later I speculated that the trouble was that the *format* of the literature—a twelve-page pamphlet—appealed to the middle- and upper-income voters who were mostly Republicans in that district, while the message—a good statement of a dozen bread-and-butter Democratic programs—appealed to the lower- and lower-middle-income voters, who were preponderantly Democratic. The format attracted those to whom the message was not appealing, and failed to attract those to whom the message would have been appealing.

Sometimes literature just misses the boat and must be killed. This happened in the 1964 Presidential election, when the national committee produced a television commercial in which a little girl was shown pulling petals off a daisy—"10, 9, 8, 7, 6, 5, 4, 3, 2, 1"—whereupon an enormous atomic mushroom arose. This was followed by an appeal to vote for Johnson to keep the bomb in safe hands. Party officials who saw it were appalled, complained vehemently, and the commercial was quickly killed. It was just too raw. (The same fate was suffered by a Goldwater film on decadence in American life, which featured strip-teasers and beer-can-strewn highways, for the same reason.)

Another type of bad literature is the kind that is jam-packed with copy and pictures. Like a Sears Roebuck catalog, it tells too much and therefore gets across nothing. The mail order catalog works perfectly for its purpose; those who go to it are positively primed, they know what it is they want to check out. The recipients of campaign literature are, if anything, negatively primed. It's all you can do sometimes to succeed in getting the piece of literature into their mailboxes or under their doors, much less in their hands.

Most political literature, however, is neither good nor bad; it doesn't hurt, but it does little good. The most common fault is that it deals with subjects the candidate thinks the voters *ought* to be interested in, rather than those they *are* interested in. For example, child day-care centers, where working mothers can leave children during the day, are socially desirable. But a candidate running in an upper-income, low-child-population district achieves nothing by making child day-care centers a central issue in his campaign.

In short, if it is to be successful, campaign literature, like campaigns in general, must direct itself to subjects that are of interest to the voters. If the candidate feels strongly on a subject his constituents care little or nothing about, he is fortunate if the issue never comes up in his campaign, and if he and his campaign manager are wise, it never will. If, on the other hand, the issue is one his constituents care about deeply, he had better bring it out into the open fast. If he can convince his constituents that there is more to the question than they thought—and that he is right—he may have saved his seat or gained his opponent's.

A campaign, it should be remembered, while it has some educational value, is not basically an educational but a persuasive process. Thus, in 1964, one candidate whose district was in quite an uproar in opposition to the school-busing program was asked his views. His answer: "I'm opposed to it." So far, fine. But he continued: "But I think we should all look deep in our hearts to discover whether it's the trip or what's on the other end [Negro children] that really bothers us." I applauded the candidate's character and candor. But I knew he was licked. I asked him: "What in hell did you say *that* for?" His answer: "It's true." My answer: "I know it's true. But you are not a preacher trying to improve the souls of your constituents at this point in the campaign. If this was your issue, you should have started on it last year. Now you must persuade them, not challenge them."

Campaign literature too often challenges the voter instead of trying to persuade him. That kind of literature doesn't work. Except in rare instances like the Lamula and Berman pieces, moreover, it has relatively small impact.

After the 1959 election, I had the Murray piece discussed above framed and hung in my office as a constant reminder that literature really doesn't make much difference. For, in spite of that piece, Murray still got 40 percent of the vote.

22 * The Mythology of Patronage

✳✳✳

The greatest obstacle to effective political activity created by conventional education and social attitudes is the attitude it engenders towards "patronage." "Patronage" is, by traditional standards, evil. The word conjures up pictures of the hordes of Jacksonian politicians descending upon Washington, D.C., to devour the spoils; of a President assassinated by a disappointed office-seeker; of fat and bloated Boss Tweed in the Nast cartoons; of incompetents lounging about government offices; of "political hacks" outrageously rewarded for devious political activity at public expense.

If "patronage" is a dirty term, "judicial patronage" is worse. It calls to mind the image of venal political lawyers living off the meager estates of widows and orphans, receiving exorbitant fees for doing nothing. On the other side of the coin, the "Tammany boss" (me) should have had the power to see that thousands of the party faithful were hired, and the unfaithful fired.

Alas, that myth is indeed a myth.

The reform approach to the whole subject reflects these stereotypes—so much so that when, in 1959, the author drafted a series of proposals to modernize the Democratic Party, for submission to the then county leader, he was forced by his reform associates to rename a "Patronage Committee" as a "Government Appointments Committee." This euphemism, fortunately, deceived no one, and the proposed committee continued to be described, except on formal occasion, by its proper name.

Any serious analysis of patronage as a political tool suffers not only from the images the word evokes, but also from an almost total lack of understanding of what is involved—how many jobs are involved, what kind of jobs they are, what sort of people get them, what do such people do once they are hired, how much they are paid, and how long do the jobs last?

A proper starting point is: Does patronage serve any useful and proper governmental, or any valid political, purpose? The answer, it now seems clear to me, is clearly in the affirmative.

The education that led me to this conclusion commenced with a remark made by a distinguished New Dealer, public servant, and good-government exponent, Isadore Lubin, at a forum in 1960. He said, in substance, that patronage was an essential tool for a public officeholder in maintaining some control over the political party that elected him. He noted that, lacking some device of this kind, the legislators, having been elected on the executive's coat-tails and platform, were quite free to fashion their own programs after election, and thereby to deprive the chief executive of the power to keep his promises.

He noted that since 1938, when postmasters were placed under Civil Service, no President had been able to induce Congress to observe the party's commitments, or, indeed, to get much through Congress at all except the barest minimum of programs for which bi-partisan support had been generated.

In the Eighty-eighth and Eighty-ninth Congresses, however, greater executive influence over the Congress has been apparent. The explanation that Lyndon Johnson has some mysterious power over legislators has been generally accepted. I suspect, however, that initially the death of President Kennedy and the desire, somehow, to atone for earlier shortcomings, and later public enthusiasm for the anti-poverty program and the multitude of new jobs it and related programs created had as much to do with the increased Presidential power over Congress as any Svengali-like persuasiveness.

The next step in my education was an appraisal of the kind of jobs, the pay, and the duration of the jobs that make up the overwhelming bulk of the available positions. As we shall see, they are, by and large, lowly and underpaid positions with poor tenure, and do not attract the successful, effective, well-educated citizen. Yet these jobs are essential to the operation of government, and the marginal government servant who fills them is a necessary participant in the governmental process.

True there are some higher paid, policy-level jobs, which on occasion are filled by people recommended to the government officials by a political officeholder. But the availability of non-politically-sponsored appointees has resulted in an extremely high level of competence being required before a politically-sponsored candidate can secure acceptance. On this level, political sponsorship tends to be more of a liability to the candidate than an asset.

Governmentally, patronage remains a highly useful tool. A chief executive can achieve some degree of party control and at the same time staff the government by filling interstitial civil-service vacancies (where there are no civil-service eligibles) and even policy-level jobs through political channels.

What of the political uses of patronage? Is it a proper tool in the exercise of political leadership? When I became county leader of New York County, I entertained some simple notions about the proper use of patronage. All would be dealt with equally. Patronage would not be used to buy or maintain support for the leadership. The guides would be the size of the district, the number of present jobholders, and the availability of qualified candidates.

Although these notions were modified in some ways as time passed, they do not today seem to be inappropriate guides on an over-all basis—subject, however, to some very strong exceptions. I put aside the fact that in most cases the qualifications (for chauffeurs, laborers, clerks, typists, filing clerks, messengers, traffic-device maintainers, etc.) are such that judgments as to relative competence between candidates are impossible. I also put aside the fact, which I early learned, that the size of a district has little to do with its patronage needs (a wealthy district like the silk-stocking district doesn't need jobs for clerks, laborers, chauffeurs, etc., to perform its political functions, while a leader in a low-income district is expected by his constituents to be helpful in these areas and he needs such jobs to maintain his club's status as an honest-to-God Democratic club).

But the basic lesson I quickly learned was that a political leader cannot afford to insult his supporters by rewarding his opponents. Right or wrong, his supporters expect that obstructionists will not be treated in the same manner as those who try to be helpful and co-operative.

The problem becomes especially acute when supporters have as much cause for unhappiness with the state of political affairs as the obstructionists, but nevertheless hope for the best and do their best to find common ground with the leadership and to submerge their frustrations. If, after all that effort to co-operate, the supporter finds that an obstructionist is treated like everyone else, and if a position for which a supporter has made a recommendation goes to the obstructionist, there is hell to pay. So some of the obstructionists necessarily were rebuffed when they sought patronage rewards—as they all, with one exception, did.

I learned that it was still possible in many cases to adhere to my original principles about disregarding opposition to my leadership, and to recognize patronage requests from opponents. I made it a point to see that specific opponents fared reasonably well in patronage terms—as the figures below demonstrate—where other political factors justified it. So long as I had a good reason, my supporters were not offended. (Once the "good reason" I gave was that I had "goofed"—which was true—and my supporters quietly accepted it.)

Another difficulty in the use of patronage as a political tool is the inability to know, currently, how you are using it. Recommendations are made and weeks and months pass before one knows what happened. Perhaps the person was hired, but somehow word doesn't get back. The flow of recommendations builds up for a particular leader, but anything short of an annual or bi-annual review reveals nothing, other than good intentions because the flow of responses to recommendations is so slow.

This problem becomes even more confused when a leader for one reason or another insists upon recommending total incompetents for a particular job, because he equates "patronage job" with "incompetence." One such leader (a reformer) insisted on recommending a series of fifth-raters for a court position. When I remonstrated with him, his bland response was, "After all, it's a patronage job." To this day I am sure he blames his failure to get a job for one of his people on our mutual antagonism. In fact, however, I was embarrassed by the low quality he insisted on supporting, and ultimately the job went to another reform club, whose leader had a better understanding of the patronage process and gave me a qualified man. For those who are recommended simply will not be hired unless they are able and willing to do the job.

A similar attitude was exhibited by another leader. She had taken the "Ryan pledge"—that neither she nor any member of her family would accept a patronage position. Despite the pledge, she recommended her husband for appointment to a nonpaying Regional Manpower Commission appointment. When I questioned her about the pledge (after all this was a patronage recommendation in my book—though paying only expenses, it carried prestige with it) her response was simple:

"But, Eddie, he's qualified."

Sic transit pledges mundi!

And so, recommendations are made, then the slow wheels of government turn, and some survive but most do not.

To complicate matters, when known vacancies exist, a quick recommendation of a qualified person must be made. In those circumstances, the recommendation is made in terms of the current attitude of the leader. When my secretary, Mrs. Halloran, would advise me of some "spot," I might say:

"I haven't done anything for so-and-so lately—call him."

Or: "Let me see the book—I think so-and-so needs a little help." [The book was the record we tried to keep on all recommendations and appointments—two large ledgers.]

Or: "So-and-so lost out on that other job. See if he has a man for this."

Or: "So-and-so has begged me to find a spot for X. Have him find out if X is interested."

Or: "So-and-so was promised that Y would be appointed as a deputy in Z Department, but it's been held up. Maybe Y would fit here."

Or: "We've got to increase the uptown group's position [the

Negro, Puerto Rican, Italian, and Irish leaders north of 110th Street]. Ask A if he has a man."

Or: "We haven't given anything to the reformers lately. Try B."

Months later the result of these necessarily quick decisions are reviewable, but basically only trends (of recommendation) are apparent as you go.

Of course, the major problem is learning just how much patronage is really available. There are no statistics to consult. Many of the jobs are "provisionals"—civil-service positions for which the pay is so low that no current civil-service lists of qualified persons exist. These jobs last for six months to two years. Then a new list comes out and the provisional employee is dropped. In order to be hired in the first place, the provisional employee must meet civil service requirements for the job—i.e., education and training prerequisites—though he need not take the appropriate tests. When a list of those who have passed the test finally comes out, the problem is to try to keep these provisionals on the payroll by finding some other provisional spot. About 50 percent can usually be saved. The balance are "out" and hopefully will find other employment or sweat it out until the civil-service list is again exhausted. Some become career provisionals—able people who for one reason or another—age, lack of ambition, fear of exams—never take the civil-service tests. I had one who went to work in 1955 and is still a provisional auto machinist—now close to retirement. Others take the tests, pass them, and become permanent employees.

Finally, there are many positions that are hard to define in patronage terms. Is a nomination for a judgeship or for Congress or for the state legislature in a sure Democratic district "patronage"? In a way, it surely is. But it is hard to analyze such a position in patronage terms, and the subject can be better dealt with elsewhere.

What about a nonpaying honorific position, like membership on some federal or city or state commission? (Board of Regents, Library Board, Board of Correction, and so on.) Again, these partake of the nature of patronage, but they are more like frosting on the cake, and my experience with them is so slight that I can do no more than mention them. Suffice it to say that, with the breakdown of party government, control of these honorific appointments is more and more retained by the public official for his private purposes and benefit. The party has little to do with them.

All government appointments, however, fall within the same problem area: how does one secure good government with good people, and strengthen a political party through the use of the power to appoint people to government office? This is the basic problem in dealing with "patronage," and it is one which our mythology prevents us from dealing with effectively.

The statistics amassed in my thirty-two months of county leadership, which are discussed in the next chapter, cast a good deal of light upon the dynamics of the patronage process, upon the nature of the patronage demands a modern political party should meet, and upon the relatively small dimensions of patronage as an aspect of political leadership.

These statistics do not deal with judicial patronage at all. That is a subject that perhaps illustrates best the black-and-white thinking of the good-government tradition, and demonstrates the difficulty of a rational attempt to deal with the whole subject when the mythology of politics, to which all decent and educated Americans have been subjected, obscures what is being dealt with.

Before turning to the statistics, therefore, it would be wise to have a word about the greatest alleged evil of them all—judicial patronage.

In this country from the beginning, judges have been charged with the duty of conducting adversary proceedings. The roots of this duty and power are found in Anglo-Saxon jurisprudential doctrines, which accord to the judge the status of an arbiter, and to each counsel the duty to put his client's views forward with vigor and devotion. Out of this adversary clash, truth is supposed to emerge.

By and large, the system has worked well, but it has so permeated our jurisprudential theories that judges are expected to make it possible for the adversary system to develop truth by creating adversaries where there are only smiling, agreeable, and consenting counsel before them. This is especially true in the case of accountings of trusts and estates, where remotely interested children may be benignly represented by their parents, and where the parents—as often as not—have interests different from the children's and seek judicial approval of their acts.

Who in such situations will protect the children? Why, the surrogate will appoint a special guardian for them—a lawyer, who will zealously defend their rights against all comers. Of course the special guardian should be paid. The state appropriates no money for this purpose. And so why shouldn't the estate or the trust in which the children have an interest pay them—just as the estate or trust pays their parents' lawyer?

In theory, the practice is beyond criticism. If the accounting is correct, and the children have been dealt with fairly, their special guardian so reports and the judge or surrogate can accept the accounting, confident that the adversary system of litigation has revealed no misconduct in the administration of the estate. In practice, however, there has been much criticism. The special guardians, it is said, are political hangers-on who are grossly overpaid for doing nothing.

As in the case of the excesses of the 1870's and 1880's, the good-government mythology has confused a symptom—the presence of politicians in the process—with a basic disease—a misapplication of approved judicial standards for setting fees.

Such standards are generally directed to the fixing of fees in light of the difficulty of the task, the importance of the matter ("how much money is involved"), the standing of counsel at the bar, the results obtained, and the time necessarily spent. In fixing fees for special guardians, the courts have tended to place great and probably undue emphasis upon the "importance of the matter" (how much money) and insufficient emphasis upon the time necessarily spent and the results obtained. So the fees awarded to special guardians have often justifiably been criticized as being far too high.

But the obvious cure—a restatement by the courts of the applicable standards so as to emphasize time spent and results obtained—has been totally disregarded by everyone. Instead, there has been a continuing effort to eliminate recommendations by political leaders. These efforts have been successful largely because the judges have been perfectly content to survive without recommendations from political leaders, and instead to appoint their friends, acquaintances, old associates, and even relatives.

But I don't think the fees are any lower, or the children any better served.

I had hoped at the inception of my term as county leader to achieve, through the use of an existing political power, a basic improvement in the system of recommendation for such appointments. Each lawyer to be recommended was required to submit a résumé—just as if he were a candidate for appointment to public office. Many were personally interviewed (most I knew already from legal and political contacts).

Many hours were spent preparing recommendations setting forth the basic elements in the qualifications of each lawyer: years at the bar, nature of prior experience, exposure to the field of trusts and estates, capacity for responsibility, and so on. And it was made clear to all concerned that requests for excessive fees would not be tolerated, that the result would be no more recommendations.

In the case of recommendations for appointment as counsel in homicide cases (for which the state pays $2,000 per defendant) the author undertook to eliminate the former practice of appointing four lawyers to share the fee (equally—so that no one assumed the basic responsibility of managing the case), and to substitute the more lawyerlike arrangement of appointing a senior and a junior, the former to bear the principal responsibility and to be paid accordingly.

These efforts came to nothing.

A minority of the reform group (over the opposition of the *majority* of reformers) declared a well-publicized war upon the symptom—political recommendations—and so embarrassed the courts and the party that whole effort was abandoned.

This was not progress.

This was not reform.

Nevertheless, the program had some impact. Some judges

continued to entertain recommendations. And, in the criminal courts, most of the judges shifted to the senior-junior system on homicide assignments. But the sources of their recommendations were no longer political ones. Whether the ones appointed were better than the ones we could have recommended is a question I cannot answer.

But for better or for worse, the fact is that the only effective restraint upon the exercise of discretion by judges—some control by political leaders—was eliminated. Not even publicity as to the identity of such appointees remained as a possible control, since an earlier requirement that their names be published in the official court newspaper, *The New York Law Journal,* had been eliminated some years earlier by reason of the co-operation between the Association of the Bar of the City of New York and the Republican-dominated legislature—both of which apparently hoped for a greater share of judicial appointments under the veil of secrecy. I doubt that they got it.

This ill-fated attempt to improve government perhaps best illustrates the extent to which rational thought processes are destroyed by inherited myths about politicians. Why not have a system which permits duly elected political leaders to recommend lawyers whom they know and trust to serve, at fair fees, for minors? I know of no objection to this other than the assumption that politicians are crooks. Many lawyers spend extensive compensable time on a form of public service—political activity— while many of their brothers at the bar are spending all their time cultivating clients and working for them ten to fourteen hours a day. Why shouldn't the courts recognize this public service by appointing these lawyers to do work they are qualified to do—thus replacing for them the clients they could have obtained in the time they have given to public service?

I have seen no improvement in the basic problem involved in "judicial patronage"—unduly high fees—by the elimination of politicians from the process. If anything there has been more direct pressure upon judges, more possibility of illicit arrangements, and more possibility of nepotism and favoritism.

The volume of possible judicial patronage is unknown to me.

I suspect it could be a highly useful and effective tool in attracting to political activity the kind of people who should be participants in the process.

But, short of a revolution in public understanding of the role of the political leaders (and failing a close personal relationship between judges and the political leaders—which could produce its own problems), I see little hope for the effective use of this political tool in the public interest.

23 * The Reality of Patronage

Immediately after my election as county leader, a former law-school professor warned me that I would get lost in a morass if I attempted to deal with a multitude of requests for small jobs which he anticipated I would receive. He thought them useless politically, in terms of the results obtained and in light of the time spent on securing them. He was both wrong and right. Right that there was a multitude of requests, right that I could get into a morass, but wrong that this area is not useful politically, and wrong that I'd get lost in it.

I early learned that the way to deal with the volume of requests was to delegate authority. If the request was backed with facts—a résumé for a job, a justification for a promotion or a transfer—my secretary, Mrs. Halloran, "put it through." The smelly ones, the troublesome ones, the questionable ones, the cases where two requests came for one vacancy, she passed on to me. She checked with City Hall on vacancies, ascertained pay and experience requirements, and advised me of what was open. I told her which leaders to call to see if they could fill the vacancy—and who to call next if the first leader was not interested. She followed up on recommendations when there was no response. And she maintained a record of all recommendations processed and of the ascertainable results—"approved," "appointed," "rejected job," "not qualified," "no response when asked to come in," and so on.

She and her assistants, Vicki McGarry and Elsie Cortes, created a system that worked, that kept leaders reasonably satisfied, that dealt with the problem efficiently, and compiled a body of statistics which, I think, is unique in the annals of city government. It also, I suggest, places the whole patronage ques-

tion in a proper context and demonstrates the relatively interstitial (although significant) role played by patronage in a
modern political party.

The statistics are not entirely precise. We often didn't hear
the result of a recommendation for months, and then perhaps
learned that 5½, or 15, months earlier the applicant had been
hired or promoted. In some cases we never learned at all. Some
recommendations were made by me directly and orally to the
mayor, and approved, but I sometimes forgot to tell Mrs.
Halloran, and neither the recommendation nor the result were
recorded, or perhaps only one or the other was recorded.

Frequently the same man or woman was repeatedly recommended without success, so that the total number of recommendations far exceeds the number of people involved.

It would take a perfectly programmed computer to make a
wholly accurate analysis of what took place, and I am not such
an instrument. Instead, I have made a count of the number of
ledger sheets and number of lines used on each and reached a
figure for "total recommendations": I counted the number of
"new jobs" (with an expected term of six months or more) and
"temporary new jobs" (less than six months) recorded. A job
with a probable term of at least six months was counted as a new
job. Jobs reported to us as "temporary"—such as tabulators at the
Board of Election for twenty days after election, or literacy
clerks for a summer registration program, or Christmas post-
office jobs—are not included *anywhere*—in part because our records never caught up with the results of these recommendations.
We believe most of them resulted in employment. Jobs that we
later learned had short tenure—ambulance drivers, summer jobs,
and the like—are classified as temporary jobs.

The total number of recommendations includes recommendations for promotion, transfer, inquiries on public housing applications, and so forth. Probably less than 75 percent of the
recommendations were for new employment.

Finally, we attempted to obtain an inventory of existing jobs,
by clubs. Some leaders reported judges and assemblymen who
had been nominated with club support. Others (Adam Clayton
Powell, for one), reported nothing. Other sources revealed to us

the names of public officials living in the particular district and we added their names to the book.

In my analysis I have made *ad hoc* judgments as to which of the existing officeholders should be included in an inventory of patronage or quasi-patronage positions. Many of these office-holders did not secure their jobs through political activity. Some of the jobs are civil service. Finally, many of the "new jobs"—perhaps as many as 35 to 40 percent—were replacements for existing jobholders—and so not "new" jobs at all.

And so, while the calculation is a rough one and based to some extent upon subjective analysis, it nevertheless is revealing of the paucity of patronage available in a heartland of Democratic power, New York County, under a Democratic city and federal administration.

In tabular form, the figures are (for the period of March 1962 to November 1964):

Existing Jobs *	*New Jobs*	*New "Temporary" Jobs*	*Total Recommendations*
522	378	102	3,699
[Approximately one for every 2 election districts]	[Approximately one for every 3 election districts]	[Approximately one for every 10 election districts]	

We averaged:
about 12 "New Jobs" for each of my
32 months in office;
about 11 jobs per club over the 32-month period;
about 1 "New Job" for each 10 recommendations
(including recommendations for promotion,
transfer, and housing).

* This figure is high. It includes some elective officials who should not be included and many civil servants or mayoral appointees who happened also to be members of a club. I have used the figure because I think it represents the maximum patronage effectiveness of the party. A change to a Republican administration would probably affect no more than 200 of these 522 at the most.

The level of jobs is even more revealing.

Most paid under $5,000 a year. In one well-patronized regular club with 23 "existing jobs" (including 2 judges), all but 3 were at salaries of under $6,000 a year and only 2 above $7,000 a year. In another, also with 23 existing jobs, all but 3 were under $5,000 a year.

Most of the jobs lasted two years at most; some were only worth six months of employment. Probably no more than about 20 to 25 percent of the "New Jobs" had any tenure. Only a handful of the "holdovers" were in federal jobs, which is an insignificant source of patronage.

The most interesting aspect of the patronage process was the ratio of jobs obtained to recommendations—approximately 1 to 10 over-all. The overwhelming bulk of recommendations came from low-income regular districts. Reformers accounted for 649 recommendations resulting in 75 jobs, and the nonreformers accounted for 3,050 recommendations and 303 jobs.

Four reform districts, the Tenth South, Tenth Middle, Tenth North, and Sixth South accounted for 47 of the 75 reform jobs, but these were all lower-income areas, with high numbers of recommendations.

The income levels of the jobs obtained also reflected the economic level of the reform and regular clubs. For the Eighth North (reform), the average new job was above $10,000 a year; for the Third Middle, a regular district, slightly above $5,000. The same ratios applied elsewhere.

A conscious effort to increase the number of Puerto Rican and Negro jobholders is reflected in the job-recommendation ratio. Over-all, the ratio was about 1 to 10; for Puerto Rican and Negro districts it was better than 2 out of 10.

Most clubs, however, strangely enough, were at the 1 to 10 ratio. The exceptions included the Puerto Rican and Negro clubs, noted above, who did better than average, one reform club whose leader managed to be so difficult that I felt I could not honor its recommendations and at the same time avoid insulting the other ladies and gentlemen on the committee (including my supporters and my opponents). In addition, I just couldn't get myself to move his recommendations after a little while had passed and I had learned that he regarded patronage as something for people of a low level of competence. That club did worse than average.

There were other deviations from the 1 to 10 ratio including:

one leader's refusal to make recommendations;

an inadequate number of recommendations from one club to justify any conclusions;

a desire on my part to help particular clubs—one reform club (the Sixth North) and one regular (the Third Middle) were well ahead of ratio for this reason; there were others where special quick assistance by pushing job requests was important to the leader in solidifying a newly-won leadership;

an unduly high number of promotion and transfer requests, which distorted the ratio;

one club whose leader had great skill in locating jobs, and would then place the request with us for the sake of formality so that his ratio of jobs obtained to recommendations was close to 5 to 10.

And so on.

My own club fared badly. Always sensitive to my delicate power position, and aware of past abuses by past leaders in favoring their own clubs, I consciously avoided allocating jobs to my own club; so much so that on occasion Mrs. Halloran used to remind me quietly.

"What about *your* club, Mr. Costikyan?" When *she* said it, I knew it was time to allocate a job to the New Democratic Club.

So much for the statistics.

Obviously an organization with 66 district leaders, 1,074 captains, 1,074 co-captains or co-workers, 33 club presidents, over 300 other club officers, and countless other functionaries, does not exist on this volume of jobs. Nor can it be expected to.

Nor can discipline be maintained by firing the few jobholders susceptible to such treatment. The press and public wouldn't tolerate it.

But patronage is still a useful and proper tool. It brings prestige to the local leader, and shows his acceptability to his superior party and public officeholders. To some small extent, it encourages support of the leadership, but not very much, and it exposes the leader to very human problems—a small promotion, a job when in extremis, a helping hand with the rigidity of civil-service bureaucrats.

I remember one low-paid employee who was to be discharged for gambling on duty. This ingenious explanation—"the boys" were merely drawing cards to see who would pick up the coffee money in the middle of the table and go out to get the coffee ("how could the guy have figured we were playing blackjack?") —was so imaginative that I was able to save his job. After all, it was Christmastime and he swore, swore, swore never to do it again.

I remember Patsy Carito, one of the best captains of one of my district leaders. He was then seventy-five and facing an already delayed enforced retirement from a city job, but full of beans, full of vigor, and angry at the notion of retirement. We kept him on for almost another year.

The over-all place of patronage in the political structure is not—as its vehement opponents say—evil. It is not—as its old-fashioned proponents claim—essential. It is not—as my law-school professor feared—a morass.

It is a useful government tool.

It is a useful political tool.

But it just doesn't involve what traditional students of government have always assumed it did—a raiding of the public treasury to support incompetents who devote their time to operating a political machine.

If the party had to depend on the jobholders, it would disappear.

24. How to Run a Campaign

Most candidates, most politicians, and most voters believe a political campaign is an occult process that makes the mysterious difference between victory and defeat. The amateur candidate, selected out of a nonpolitical background and in the full clutch of his belief in the mystery of it all, invests, reinvests, and re-reinvests in a campaign headquarters. By the end of the campaign, 80 percent of the campaign funds have been invested in renting headquarters that are too large by far, and hiring campaign aides, who waste more money on telephone calls, purchasing supplies that are never used and other useless campaign boondoggles.

One congressional candidate in a losing campaign spent over $90,000 (and his opponent over $120,000). By election day he could contemplate a buzzing headquarters jammed with people (many of them full-time paid assistants), dozens of items in gossip columns (each time a candidate reads his name he smiles, as if it meant votes), hundreds of cocktail parties, generally attended by loyal Democrats who would have voted for him come what may (unless he said or did something which *lost* votes at the parties, which usually happens)—and not enough votes to get elected.

This phenomenon is repeated year after year on every level. With all due deference to Senator Robert F. Kennedy, who on his own behalf is far more a statesman than a politician, the greatest campaign boondoggle I ever saw was his campaign for the Senate in New York County. Three headquarters, hundreds of people, co-ordinators by the dozen, confusion rampant, all because the campaign planners were operating in a vacuum; they did not know enough about the New York State political structure to know what was needed in order to activate it, they had no contact with the voters, direct or indirect, they did not seem to know New York politics, and, finally, they were not politicians—i.e., not one of them had been an election-district captain or a district leader in New York, and they had no idea of how to utilize the existing political army.

Item: There was no usable literature on Kennedy in sufficient quantities to make a distribution until two weeks before election day.

Item: The literature that was produced was unusable (a political tabloid, which weighed too much to get out of the clubhouses via captain manpower, and a slick biographical piece which told too much about him).

Item: Until mid-October Kennedy ran "alone"—i.e., he was the sole candidate named in his literature, although every pro knew that in 1964 the key to success was to be part of the Johnson-Humphrey anti-Goldwater team.

Item: Kennedy was afraid to attack his opponent lest he appear to be "ruthless." As a result, his opponent ran free and clear for six weeks as a great "liberal," although his opponent's record was spotty and inconsistent, as conservative as it was liberal.

Yet Kennedy won—not only on Johnson's coat-tails, but also because three weeks before the election, he found his self-confidence, went after his opponent on his opponent's record, and so held enough Johnson votes to produce a substantial majority. But he did it the hard way, because he did not use the political structure that was available but duplicated it (poorly) where it was essential, leaving it immobilized where he couldn't duplicate it.

For example, a captain simply will not ring a doorbell for a candidate unless he has a piece of literature to leave. Why? Partly because the captain wants to make up his own spiel from something in print—not just his own theories. The official line in print is an assurance that he is safe in saying what he says, and he has something to fall back on when he meets a truculent voter. Indeed, the piece of literature is a final protective line against the truculent constituent: there is no better exit when faced with a voter who is angry than to thrust a single piece of literature in his hand and say, "Look, I know you feel strongly, but please read this before you make up your mind." It covers a graceful retreat, and makes it possible for the shaken captain to leave with his dignity intact and ring the next doorbell with confidence.

The first task, therefore, to mobilize the captains and workers is to create a usable piece of distributable literature in sufficient quantities. In New York County that means 300,000 copies distributed in varying quantities to thirty-six clubs. For all five of the counties that make up New York City, over a million and a quarter copies are necessary.

The next step is to get it to the captains in time for them to use it. One must allow a minimum of a week from printing to distribution. Ten days is safer.

None of these practical logistical problems are within the ken of most candidates, who tend to view the campaign from a wholly egocentric viewpoint—as if they had to do it all themselves. And, in many cases, they do it all—via television, direct mail, street tours, *ad infinitum*. But the cost in headquarters staff is staggering—and unnecessary.

In 1964, the New York County Democratic organization ran an effective campaign that even personally antagonistic leaders acknowledged was first-rate. Cost of headquarters and headquarters staff? Under a thousand dollars—one secretary, rent for one extra room, four extra telephone lines, and one assistant to heave literature around. The results showed that New York County produced a vote for Johnson and Humphrey of over 80 percent, and for the first time in years it was again the banner county in New York State—indeed the nation. Why and how?

First, early in 1964 we recognized the importance of stimulating the registration of potential Democrats who simply hadn't bothered to register or vote before. Most of these voters were in lower-income areas. So throughout the summer we flooded these key areas, through our clubs, with literature and placards urging registration and telling the potential voter where and how to register.

Every leader was made aware that we were following the

registration figures in his area. Sound-trucks were hired, and nonpolitical groups working on registration received co-operation and in some cases indirect financial help.

We discovered that the biggest obstacle to registration was the fear of literacy tests, so we printed up thousands of samples of the literacy test for distribution. Ultimately, we took a full-page ad reproducing the test in the paper with the largest circulation in New York to show how simple it was (see illustration between pages 244 and 245).

The results were startling. For the first time since World War II, and perhaps earlier, New York County's registration was higher than four years earlier; a forty-year trend was reversed. Kings (Brooklyn), traditionally the leader, had a decline, and not even a growing county like Queens surpassed our showing. These new registrants showed up on election day—and made the difference between the 74 percent Johnson vote of Brooklyn and the Bronx, and the 80 percent showing of Manhattan.

So much for the registration campaign. It cost about $15,000 at the most. It was the best-spent money any party ever spent.

The second task in running a campaign properly is more obviously political. New York County for years has seen its campaigns ruined by rivalry between "citizens committees" and the regular organization. Every Presidential campaign saw the creation of a host of local headquarters, manned by local residents under the banner of "Citizens for Kennedy" or "Volunteers for Stevenson." A year later, in two cases out of three, the local chairman of these groups would suddenly emerge as a reform or insurgent candidate for district leader, using the remnants of his volunteer group of a year earlier to mount a campaign.

Thus, during every Presidential campaign until 1964, both the organization and its putative opponents spent as much time and energy fighting with each other as they did fighting Republicans.

During the years from 1955 through 1960, I kept up good terms and working relations with both groups, and I found that a good part of the time in all meetings was spent listening to the complaints of local representatives as to how either the organization or the Citizens Committee was functioning. The high point of all this took place in 1956, when one leader complained bitterly and at length at a meeting of the county Executive Committee about the "beatniks" who, he asserted, were lousing up the party in his district, operating out of the local Volunteers for Stevenson headquarters. His opposite number, the Volunteers chairman, some months later, confided to me that he had indeed been disturbed by this problem, and that in the Volunteers headquarters there had been a group informally referred to as "Beatniks for Stevenson."

With this pattern implicit in New York County political history, I was determined that in 1964 we were not going to waste precious campaign time and energy (and money) in such squabbling, and that only where the local Democratic club was ineffective would there be a local "volunteer" headquarters. To foreclose the possibility that someone else would set up a "Citizens Committee for Johnson," I caused it to be set up and financed myself.

It was effective and efficient. Manpower was utilized centrally. The committee forwarded names of volunteers to local Democratic clubs. It held coffee klatches, locally and centrally; addressed mailings for local clubs as well as for the Citizens Committee itself. And no more than thirty minutes was spent—and that by only a half-dozen lady leaders and myself—on conflicts between the organization and the citizens groups throughout the entire campaign. Net cost? About $4,500. Net benefit? No squabbles, a lot of people put to work, mailings addressed, a county-wide motorcade, and some able new people *in the clubs* instead of getting ready to fight them.

By early September, the outlines of the campaign were clear. The registration drive was rolling—with no one in charge except the county leader and the district leaders and six legislators who were given the initial responsibility for co-ordination in their areas. The Citizens Committee was in existence and out of the organization's hair.

It was then clear that President Johnson was headed for a victory, and Goldwater to a bad defeat. The more votes we could get out, the more there would be for Johnson, and for all his running mates. So our strategy was simple and straight-forward—and, strangely, it was in the most venerable tradition of New York's Democratic Party: maximize the vote; get every-one out; don't worry about selectivity—three out of four voters are with us (we were wrong, it was four out of five).

That meant we should spend our money and energy on registration and getting out the vote. We forgot about fancy literature. After registration was closed, we spent our money and energy on the last weekend through Tuesday, election day, whooping it up and distributing every cent we could find to the clubs to see that they and their captains were functioning on each of the last five days at peak effectiveness. Almost two-thirds of our total expenditures was spent in the last four or five days—half on the last day alone.

To execute this campaign, I selected one of our district leaders, Assemblyman Frank Rossetti, as campaign chairman. Once a lieutenant of De Sapio's and still his friend, Frank was a veteran political leader. No one had to tell him how long it took to mobilize a district and its captains for a rally, or to distribute literature, or to do anything. He had been a captain, he was a leader, and he had been a successful candidate for the assembly in every election for almost twenty years.

Some reform eyebrows were raised when I appointed him, but they came down fast. Within six weeks, if the leaders had been permitted to vote their own choice for county leader, they would have picked Rossetti.

The reason was simple: he is a pro. Every leader to him was as important as every other. If one needed literature for his captains, Rossetti got it—if it existed. If a candidate was touring a district, Rossetti made sure the leader knew it. Crazy ideas from a candidate's headquarters were quashed. Reasonable complaints from any source were dealt with. Literature was ordered and distributed in sufficient quantities for each club.

Cute maneuvers were quelled. For example, Adam Powell's people had a habit of requesting four times the amount of literature they could use. We sometimes used literature requests as a thermometer to measure "who was playing with Powell."

The campaign culminated with a Saturday-night-before-election-day Madison Square Garden rally, co-sponsored by New York County and the state committee, the first time in twenty years that the county had done this.

New York County provided over two-thirds of the attendance at the Garden. The captains and leaders had preferred seats. They felt important. None were angered by their treatment. (Rossetti handled tickets too.)

And on election day our people were "up." They did their job. The vote turned out in record numbers. The margin—80.4 percent for LBJ, was the greatest in our history.

I think that if we had done nothing the margin would have been between 65 and 70 percent. That 10 to 15 percent (probably closer to 10) is about the maximum that any political organization can contribute to a campaign.

Usually 5 percent is a fairer figure. (In 1964 New York County had an unusually heavy new registration, part of which should have been registered years before.) And in a race where the disparity between candidates is not so great as it was in 1964, the effective organization probably swings 3 percent of the vote at best. But that 3 percent is enough to change the outcome of one out of three elections.

In 1964, the New York County campaign required the services of a dozen people. As county leader, I was in charge, and the staff at county headquarters (my secretary, Mrs. Halloran; our receptionist, Elsie Cortes; and Mrs. Halloran's assistant) spent part of their time on campaign problems. Over-all supervision and finances were my responsibility; operations were Rossetti's. (He had a secretary who was hired for six weeks, and a former sanitation man assisted on literature breakdowns. Whenever a load of literature—anywhere from 100,000 to 600,000 pieces—came in, it was divided into predetermined allocations, one for each of our thirty-six clubs, and promptly shipped out.) Judge Hilda Schwartz, on leave of absence as treasurer of the City of New York, and Robert Lounsbury, general counsel of Kennecott Copper, headed the Citizens Committee with the help of one paid assistant.

A young lawyer, Tom Purcell, headed a Young Citizens Division.

A former assemblyman, Bentley Kassel, handled speakers and sound trucks.

The Madison Square Garden Rally was handled by a group which included Jerry Finkelstein, our finance chairman, a businessman who was addicted to politics; George Daly, our recently acquired public relations adviser; and Len and Mort Weber, our consultants on public events. Our law committee quietly and efficiently handled its function of preparing election-day instruction forms. And that was it.

It was an ideal campaign: 99 percent of the people were "on the outside," and 90 percent of the money was spent "on the outside." There was little concern about "newsbreaks." An infinitesimal amount of time and energy was wasted on internal squabbles. There was a campaign director who knew what he was directing and knew how to use the organization—who knew what it could do and what it couldn't.

The best advice I can give any candidate for any office is to find a Rossetti: find a captain, find someone who understands what can be done and what can't, what is needed and what isn't (four extra telephone lines sufficed for the county organization—another headquarters with far less to do put in an eighteen-line switchboard), how much time is needed to get one piece of literature to a voter from the printer (at least ten days), what the voter will do with it (especially when it's an eight-page tabloid), what voters care about, and the limited area in which a candidate has to operate (a swing of 10 percent of the voters will guarantee victory in almost any election; 70 to 80 percent of the voters usually have their minds made up before anyone is nominated).

For campaigns are not mysteries or magic: money spent means nothing unless it is spent to achieve an objective. A hotel-floor full of "workers" may mean nothing more than a big rent bill, a large room-service bill, and too many people wasting their time. It does, however, cheer up the candidate with the illusion of activity. More candidates have spent more money to sustain this illusion than for any other result.

Stripped of illusions, however, a campaign is simple. It is

designed to get votes. People who vote are not stupid; they are not automatons; they do not react to magic.

Every step in a campaign should be directed at a voter. Yet I have heard a thousand proposals in campaigns that have absolutely no relation to this objective.

"We ought to rent ten more rooms." Why? How many votes will it mean?

"We need a veterans' division (and so-and-so in charge, and a secretary and a desk and a telephone and another room, and a letter to veterans)."—How many votes?

"Why doesn't the candidate give a cocktail party for the staff?" —How many votes?

One campaign manager I knew said to his workers: "These headquarters are empty on Saturdays. We got thirty rooms for you people. I want to see you in those rooms working on Saturday and Sunday afternoons." (Too many rooms, too many people.)

One campaign I remember had a "policy meeting" once a week with twenty-five to fifty people in attendance. It flattered the attendants but made no policy, and it cost money to rent a room in the hotel large enough to take care of the group. And so it goes. The tendency to bureaucracy, which affects every unit of government, is carried over to the political arena. If it takes 200,000 people to run the city government, you *must* need 500 to run this campaign.

And it's all nonsense.

Part of the reason it's nonsense is that most candidates do not know the political process: they expect to win by magic, and the best magic (they think) is lots of people in a headquarters—then if some work comes in to be done, someone will be there to do it.

In addition, many political leaders are themselves unsure of what ought to be done. Until recent years, many had not had to run in a contested primary, or in a close election race, since they were first elected.

My experience was different. In every year from 1951 until 1963, with only one exception (1956), I was involved in a hotly contested primary. In two I was a district captain. In four I was the candidate for party office. In the rest I played a key role. When I retired as county leader, few other active district leaders had been so exposed to primaries or closely contested elections.

But I learned, year after year, that the process was simpler and simpler, less and less costly. Instead of the frenetic activity I hurled into the first two campaigns when I was the candidate for district leader, I was ready by 1961, on the fourth, to take a position about expenditures and activities that defied all tradition: spend little, keep the headquarters empty, and keep workers out in the districts. But we won by three to one—the greatest margin we'd ever had—spending less money and using fewer people at headquarters than we ever had before.

Campaigns are not magic. Campaign managers whose associations look good in the press (the president of such-and-such corporation) but who are not experienced from the election district up, are expensive façades. Beware of large headquarters. Don't spend money just because you have it, or because someone says "we need it," * or because it's traditional.

Above all, keep your mind on one question: "How many votes do you think *that* expenditure, *that* program, *that* office, *that* mailing, will produce?" Half of the costly ventures proposed in every campaign are disposed of by an honest answer to that question.

* One day in 1964, a wind-up planning meeting was held to complete plans for the Madison Square Garden rally. I was told that sound trucks were needed to publicize the rally. Would the New York County organization supply them? While I was pondering whether they really were needed, one of the young assistant campaign managers brusquely announced "We need ten sound trucks." "Ten?" I asked. "Why ten?" (Our "saturation" figure for Manhattan—i.e., "all you can effectively use in each district"—was eight.) "Make it six," said the assistant. "Why not sixty?" I asked. For it was clear that the figures ten and six had not been determined on the basis of need but on the basis of what sounded good. We ultimately used four trucks, and the Garden and the surrounding area were jammed.

Part Seven

The Relation
of Politics to
Government

Introduction to Part Seven

Political activity is part of the governmental process. Half in and half out of government, the politician sees both government and constituency with a sympathetic eye. Subjected to the pressure of constituents to secure government action, he sees the failures and shortcomings of any administration better than any critic of that administration. Aware of the frustrating problems of government, he sees the demagoguery and unreasonableness of its critics far better than any newspaper editorialist.

But from his constituents and his counterparts in government he acquires a sense of the functioning of government, its shortcomings, its achievements, its limitations which no amount of theoretical study can produce.

What follows is a distillation of some years of observation of the governmental process at work in New York City.

25 * How New York City Is Run

Any politically sophisticated New Yorker will tell you, with great certainty, that New York City is, of course, ungovernable. Indeed, so it seems—one administration after another. But if it *is* ungovernable, which I doubt, it is largely as a result of the attitudes about government, politics, and mayors, about "permanent problems" and the city, about reform and reformers—in the face of all of which generations of sophisticated and unsophisticated New Yorkers have muttered a familiar mixture of apathy and contempt.

For a presumably rational breed, most of us behave surprisingly irrationally. The first area of irrationality is in the city officials; the second in the populace.

The City Officials

Any sensible executive of a substantial enterprise with adequate but not unlimited resources learns that the first requirement for effective direction of his affairs is the determination of priorities between competing demands. The second is the selection of personnel to execute policy and program. He learns that it is necessary to concentrate his resources on the achievement of the selected priorities and to eliminate unnecessary expenditure, to maintain contact with and receive information from the lower echelons and to make sure that the bureaucracy functions well enough to carry out his programs. Finally, he learns early that it is necessary to preserve his position of power.

New Yorkers accept governmental leadership that concentrates almost exclusively on the last element—the preservation of power and position—and pays little attention to any other element.

Decision-Making

In a large city like New York, one would expect some rational system of determining priorities. One would expect to find some official exercising judgment to determine the relative importance of the competing demands for governmental action.

The police need a new stable; the Harlem community needs ten new schools. To maintain a decent level of employment, the construction trades need a huge new project such as the Lower Manhattan Expressway; the city must create a surplus of housing to bring rents down, in order to permit the removal of an obsolete rent-control system which after almost twenty-five years is still necessary to protect tenants who cannot afford to pay uncontrolled rents.

Residents of crowded areas need local recreational areas where the children can play rather than in the streets. The city in twenty years will need a new public beach on the ocean for residents who can afford a subway ride but no more for a day in the sun.

The variations are endless. But the decisions between priorities basically are never made at all. No one says: "fifty schools this year, twenty next, then five a year for replacement"; or: "starting in three years, 200,000 new housing units per year for three years, and then 50,000 a year for replacement"; or: "starting in six years, arterial highway development for three years, and then recreation facilities in high density areas for five years; then development of outlying recreational facilities."

For no one exercises any qualitative judgment on priorities. Indeed the priorities are hardly evident—if they exist at all—in the pattern of city expenditure, except to the extent that they reflect the quantity of support that can be generated behind a particular proposal.

For example, in 1963, the city administration was blitzkrieged into a decision to acquire land in an outlying area of Queens on the Atlantic Ocean for eventual construction as a public park. The area—Breezy Point—is undoubtedly admirably suited for public recreation. The cost is substantial and, given the city's not unlimited resources, the allocation of funds to Breezy Point necessarily reduced those available for other public necessities— schools, housing, and police protection.

Ninety percent at least of the Breezy Point protagonists were people who never in their lives would think of using such a facility. Most, at least almost all of the principal movers, resided in the Silk-Stocking District—a heavily Republican and very wealthy area in midtown including Fifth and Park Avenues. They quite properly felt that the Breezy Point acquisition was an opportunity to create a public facility which ought to be very nice for the residents of the city who couldn't go to East Hampton for the weekend.

So they organized. They hired public relations counsel. They got editorials. Many of them had been heavy financial supporters of liberal candidates like the mayor; they talked to the mayor. They blew up a storm. And the city administration went along.

Why?

Because the Breezy Point adherents understood the city's system of determining priorities: How much pressure has been built up? Once a sufficient head of steam is created, once the Board of Estimate is inundated with speakers whose credentials are distinguished, once hundreds and hundreds of people mill about in the hearing room, once picket lines form and are backed up by a demonstration or two of dubious spontaneity, once enough substantial supporters whose financial help will be needed at the next election have added their names to the project—then the proposal becomes worthy of consideration and approval.

This is the system that has become the principal method of establishing priorities in a city teeming with urgent and unsolved problems. It is heartbreaking for several reasons, not the least of which is that it turns its back on a great tradition of political creativity, which better than anything else summons the loyalty of the Democratic and independent voter to the Democratic Party. Without a proper system of priorities, genuine political leadership is impossible. Mayors and their administrations are meant to be more than pressure gauges. The present system is a confession of helplessness, a helplessness responsive to the worst myth of all—the myth that effective urban government is impossible in New York City.

There are hundreds of examples of how the current system works. The Lower Manhattan Expressway, once dead as a doornail, was resuscitated when key unions, fearing a decline in work for their members, pressed and pressed and pressed for reinstatement of that project, which would provide plenty of work for a number of years.

Under the focus of pressure from a variety of private interests, streets are widened—or not widened. Overpasses are built—or not built. Baseball stadiums and baseball teams are created—or not created. The police force is increased—or not increased. Housing projects are authorized—or not authorized. All on the basis of the amount of pressure brought to push one problem, regardless of its relative importance, to the top, where in the glare of publicity it must be dealt with.

This is the way New York City establishes priorities. No other rational form of organization so abdicates the function of judgment in favor of a system of spurious priorities in which noise and movement give a problem the illusion of importance.

If this process is not arrested, it will mean that our officials will merely reflect the views brought to them most effectively, most vociferously, and under the most auspicious sponsorship. While public relations counselors are exercising a legitimate function when working for a client, the public reaction they create is no substitute for the kind of objective judgment that the city government should exhibit if—at long last—it is to be capable of providing proper government for our ever-enlarging urban center.

The Selection of Personnel

Like most cities, New York cannot select the personnel to govern it except for a small handful at the top. According to Sayre and Kaufman in their authoritative book, *Governing New York City,* the number of positions the mayor of New York can fill in the entire city work force of some 250,000 is a few hundred. Moreover, the people when they vote can elect exactly six city officials, including their local city councilman.

The rest—except for a relative handful appointed by the mayor—are civil servants, whose tenure in office is virtually unbreakable. Only thievery, for all practical purposes, justifies their removal. Incompetence, laziness, insolence—none of these result in removal.

This state of affairs is a tribute to the great fear among the populace of the chicanery of political leaders. The civil service is the great bulwark erected against bad government in the wake of the excesses of the Tweed ring and similar periods of corruption. It has been a fairly effective protection against the loading of the payroll with incompetents sponsored by politicians, but it has produced its own brand of bad and inefficient government— the bad government of insensitivity to the need for action, for economy of operations, and for procedural efficiency.

No modern business could survive on a civil-service system modeled on the one in use in New York City government. No management expert would recommend it as the best way to get a job done. Yet it survives as the essential personnel mechanism of our urban government. Has any one ever heard of a civil-service job being abolished? And yet it must be that some of the problems of twenty or thirty or fifty years ago no longer require the bureaucracy which was created to deal with them.

The elimination of civil service is neither a sensible nor a feasible proposal. However, if we expect our elected officials to be rational and efficient executives, they must be given far more flexibility in dealing with the civil-service establishment— which, incidentally, is a far more effective political organization today than any political party. The power to fire or transfer on grounds of competence, devotion to duty, common courtesy, and need for the job must be substantially increased. Flexibility in assignment and reassignment must be expanded.

Pay scales should be—and could be—increased on the basis of productivity as well as in recognition of the fact that civil service is not necessarily a lifetime job leading to a pension. Low pay, moreover, cannot be justified by a guarantee of a lifetime job.

When a department head is appointed today, it is not uncommon to create one or two positions outside the competitive civil service on top of the existing bureaucracy, in order to give the department head one or two people whom he may appoint, so that he will have a close associate or two with whom he can work and on whom he can rely.

Small wonder that the budgets go higher and higher, year after year.

Another aspect of the personnel problem is the creation of new departments (the Department of Relocation, for example) and new positions to make a place for a significant supporter. The result is the creation of a new group of protected public servants; for the newly created jobs, filled on a political basis, are as soon as possible frozen into the civil-service structure.

This kind of personnel management makes no sense. Designed to keep the political leaders out, it doesn't even do that.

If city government seriously hopes to deal with the growing problems of increasing urbanization, a reappraisal of the whole theory of personnel recruitment and personnel protection must be conducted.

But more than mere reappraisal is required. There is probably a fair analogy between the unnecessary and redundant work of many city departments and the overstaffing of poorly run political campaigns. There is as much need for the reduction of staff sizes and the retraining of personnel in some parts of urban government as there is in some industries where automation promises both greater productivity per man and greater economy of operations. To embrace these two opportunities need not mean that employees with long records of service be fired in mid-career. The needs of city government for personnel can be phased out over the foreseeable future. Retraining and transfer of able civil servants from jobs subsiding into obsolescence to new and vital jobs should be given as much if not more attention as the creation of new bureaus or departments created to get the job—whatever it is—done.

Concentration of Resources and Elimination of Unnecessary Expenditure

The combination of the present *de facto* system of establishing priorities according to the degree of real or manufactured public pressure with civil-service employee policies makes it almost impossible to concentrate available financial resources on first priority projects. Built-in personnel allocations to particular departments carry with them inevitable expenditures. No one's departmental budget ever gets seriously cut.

Moreover, in an economy of scarcity of funds in which every city government must function, given the competition for the tax dollar afforded by superior government units, the result must be waste of funds, or at least the failure to concentrate them where they can do the most good.

New York City, for example, has a Department of Water Supply, Gas, and Electricity, a department of increasing importance in an era of increasing demands for water and power. It also has a Board of Water Supply, a creation of the years when the city faced an increasing demand for water and needed an agency to plan how to get it. The Board of Water Supply survives, but it does little if anything. The available water supply is now largely determined by the uncontrolled and unmetered use of water by city residents, who squander it, and the uncontrollable rainfall in the watersheds. Indeed, we were told by this board some years ago that New York City had enough water to meet its needs through the year 2000, only to run into the worst water shortage in years. But no one blamed the Board of Water Supply, and it survives with its lifetime jobs at good salaries, which are attractive plums to take care of devoted friends of retiring mayors.

Some of the figures are startling. For example, the Board of Education has a staff of 465 working on school design. And yet the Board completes only a few schools per year.

The Housing and Redevelopment Board, which in 1964 saw the completion of about 500 apartments, or housing for 500 families, had a staff of 574.

There is really no legitimate reason why the cost of government should be as high as it is. A staff of twenty architects doubtless would be sufficient to supervise the construction handled by the Board of Education's 465. A 500-family project can be supervised by far fewer than 574 people.

Part of the problem of excess staff is the effort to eliminate fraud. Not one, not two, not three, but ten or twenty or thirty different people review each project, each step, each proposal, on the theory that with that many people on the job, by God there'll be no thievery (occasionally, of course, there still is).

This duplication is precisely what paralyzes action. Meetings, conferences, checks and double checks, one group saying yea, the other nay and both with jurisdiction, requires a third group to resolve the issue. And so government grinds grandly along, its personnel safe in their jobs, vulnerable only to provable thievery charges, each person guarding his flanks with care, moving with an inevitable slowness to a safe and unchallengeable conclusion.

I once represented a department store, famed for its low prices, whose management had discovered that shoplifting cost something like 1.5 percent of the gross per year when there was a large staff of private eyes roaming the premises, and 1.75 percent (or something like it) when there was only one per floor. As the chief executive said to me: "It's cheaper to let 'em steal a little more. We saved money by getting rid of the private detectives."

Perhaps, in terms of the present needs of city government it would be cheaper to eliminate all the duplication of work. The duplication is supposed to, but does not and cannot, completely eliminate fraud. With duplication eliminated, it might be possible to speed up the process of government. This would decrease the pressure on some corrupters to corrupt and the time during which the public servant is exposed to corruption. This would mean taking the risk that some corruption will sneak through, in the expectation that the city would get a lot more action in solving its problems. I think it's worth the chance.

Maintaining Contact with the Electorate

Any rational democratic government must have some technique for maintaining contact with the voters—to know what problems concern them, what needs must be met, what programs should be instituted.

Taxi drivers alone do not furnish this information, nor do newspapers. Nor do occasional expeditions "into the street." Some mechanism for measuring the significance of individual attitudes as part of the mass is necessary. Once the political parties, with their hierarchies for dispensing patronage and money down the hierarchy and information and support back up, served this function. Charles Murphy never needed a public opinion poll to tell him what was bothering a majority of voters. Sifting and weighing the reports of his leaders (derived from their captains, who were authentic local foci of opinion and help) gave him the equivalent of today's public opinion polls.

Political parties are no longer used for this purpose. Indeed, only when a problem becomes so critical that the leaders scream to an otherwise deaf chief executive is the politician recognized as having a significant contribution to make in the formulation of public policy.

On rare occasions I have seen the old contributory process work. Once, in response to uniformly outspoken reactions and requests from regular and reformers alike, I registered a party position in opposition to the Lower Manhattan Expressway. That time the city officials took the same position. In contrast, however, twice the party's Executive Committee adopted deeply felt views in favor of a civilian police review board, but when these views were passed on to the appropriate authorities they were not only disregarded but, I felt, resented.

One other party issue I fostered was the restoration of free tuition in units of the state university. I got the distinct impression that the city educational authorities regarded the party's intrusion in this area as unwelcome, and that our efforts to make free tuition mandatory throughout the state were contrary to the city education line, which would have been satisfied with mandatory free tuition in the city alone.

Similarly, frequent attempts to create a single housing-inspection agency were rebuffed (until an election year), as were almost all the other proposals which grew out of the direct exposure of our leaders to problems at the grass-roots.

The best example of the contributory process is perhaps the education problem, which was bothering most of the leaders in 1962, 1963, and 1964. Because of this concern, during those years the Executive Committee made a halting attempt to deal with the problem of adequate education in Harlem. Careful soundings convinced me that the majority of Negro as well as white parents opposed the "busing" programs which were supposed to integrate our schools. Every effort, however, to communicate the notion that the proposal for busing white children into Harlem was no more than a convenient way to demand some guarantee of quality education ("If the white kids are here in school, the white community won't permit these conditions for *their* children") was rebuffed. Instead, the Board of Education bureaucracy talked of "busing" as a solution to the educational crisis. Busing was a panacea. In fact, it created more problems than it solved.

Why the rebuff? The answer was clear. Education was off limits to political leaders. Eighty years ago the Tweed era politicos placed unqualified supporters and relatives in the schools as teachers, and since then a line had been drawn. We should not cross it.

Many years ago, I am told, some members of the Board of Trustees of Columbia University had placed themselves on the faculty, and that led to a rule banning faculty members from serving as trustees and vice versa at the same time. But at Columbia the excesses of eighty years ago have not resulted in the trustees today refusing to listen to faculty members or vice versa.

But in the city education system the wall is high and the counsel of community-oriented political leaders is disregarded. Thus the Board of Education has been racked by crises it could have avoided in large part if it had among its members people trained in politics, or if it could and did listen to the advice of

political leaders. To reason together on problems of mutual concern, after all, is hardly to capitulate to the goblins of Tammany.

There is no reason why political leaders should have to
operate in the educational area with anonymity if they are
permitted to function at all. Nor is there any reason why the
education system should adhere to eighty-year-old attitudes,
close itself off from access to an effective device to measure
significant local attitudes, and attempt to solve its own in-
dubitably political problems without utilizing the services of
men and women equipped by training, experience and instinct
to handle political problems. Indeed, the major problem of the
city's educational system is its persistent inability to solve its political problems because it is staffed by political amateurs, who
simply fail to understand the political problems it faces or to
use the political techniques and talents necessary to solve them.

In order to keep Honest John Kelly from placing an incompetent relative on the payroll, the nonpolitical Board of Education, dominated by the bureaucracy of the system, muddles
through in its nonpolitical way, attempting to direct and control
that same bureaucracy, which directs a school system less and
less able to deal with the city's education problems. To spite
dead Honest John Kelly, we have created an elaborate educational institution from which more and more of our citizens are
turning away—in large part because that system is out of touch
with the people and unwilling to use the available mechanisms
to determine what the needs and desires of the mass of people
are, and to translate educational policy into satisfactory political
terms.

In this attitude the Board of Education is similar to every other
department of City Government (except that it is so far more
independent since it is a state not a city agency. The city merely
appoints and finances it).

If political advice on problems and their solutions is forbidden,
what *are* the methods used by government to gather information
on citizen and community attitudes? First, the louder and more
concentrated the noise, the more weight is attached to it. Enter
the extremists—from Vito Battista and his Taxpayers Party
through Milton Galamison and his school boycotters—who seize

the initiative, are listened to, and help to formulate government decisions.

Second, the elected officials, facing re-election every four years, turn to public opinion polls. As a result, every fourth election year, as the polls confirm what the political leaders already know and have vainly tried to report, urban government launches a host of new programs. More police, a central housing-inspection system, more funds for education. The costs are higher because the problems, so long disregarded, are worse.

In 1965, both major mayoral candidates recognized this problem. But, rather than turn to the existing hierarchies of political clubs and their leaders, both proposed the creation—at governmental expense—of "Little City Halls" throughout the city. This proposal may help solve one problem—access to information—but will bring with it many more. For these offices will not be staffed by locally elected party officials but by appointees from City Hall. And they will inevitably become local *political* offices, acting *politically* for the mayor—all at public rather than private expense.

A new "nonpolitical" device has been created to protect the city from the evil politician. It will, inevitably, bring with it a new political organization, maintained at government expense, to sustain the party in power.

Finally, there is political instinct, which "tells" an official what issues and problems concern the mass of people. This is a tool, necessarily singular and variable in its efficiency, that nevertheless serves some political leaders and public officeholders well enough from time to time.

The net result of separating the political leaders from the government they serve is that the information-gathering aspect of city government functions sporadically for three years, and then vigorously through the medium of public opinion polls in the fourth, or election, year. In that last year in office, of course, no administration is in a good position to launch programs that can seriously deal with complex urban problems. What is forthcoming is usually little more than a rhetorical palliative.

This sad cyclical circus is not really a very sensible way to run a city. It is certainly no way to govern one.

Making the Bureaucracy Function

I really doubt that much need be said on this subject, because the resistance of bureaucracy to action is so well known that it needs no documentation.

One example should suffice. When Mayor Wagner decided to support the Breezy Point Park development, he issued a statement to that effect. The statement specified some of the steps to be taken by key departments, and he had copies of the statement sent to the department heads involved. Many weeks later one of them was asked what steps he had taken to effectuate the project, and he replied, "None."

"Don't you know," he was asked, "that the mayor has announced that this project has been approved?"

"Yes—I heard about that," was the reply.

"Well, why haven't you done anything to carry it out?"

"Listen," was the reply, "he may be for it, and he may have told you he's for it, and he may have told the press he's for it, but he hasn't told *me* he's for it."

Maintenance of Political Power

This is the only area in which modern urban government is effective. With political leadership roles and government leadership roles united in one man, a chief executive is in a strong position, especially when he seeks re-election. Again, not very much need be said, for the whole analysis of the political structure in this book demonstrates the many ways in which the combined public officeholder–political leader maintains his position.

If the governmental and political power thus created and preserved could be directed at governing a city instead of being directed almost exclusively to preserving the political power of the possessor of the power, the city would undoubtedly be governable. The priorities could be established and the information on needs and demands could be obtained, and the decisions could be executed. But given our traditions, our attitudes about politics, politicians, and city government, most public office-holders would far prefer to use their power for self-survival than to attempt to use it seriously for the purpose that justifies the existence of that power in the first place—proper government.

Popular Irrationality

Most people regard politics as a dirty business and politicians as dirty people. The public generally expects a poor quality of government—largely, I believe, because the public, including the businessmen, the lawyers, the doctors, the preachers, as well as the laborers, the street-cleaners, and the taxi-drivers, enjoys a sense of satisfaction in being able to look down upon those who exercise power over it.

In socially minded churches, we hear ministers remarking with condescension, "But the politicians tell us . . ." In socially minded newspapers, our editorialists assure us that some piece of asininity is the product of "politicians"—as if that explained everything. Our high schools and colleges continue to bequeath to their students an unearned cynicism about politics and politicians—a sure deterrent to any desire in the normal and moral young to participate in political affairs.

I once enjoyed the experience of being told by a "good-government" citizen of New York, whose interest in politics and government was voracious and whose attitude about my activity in politics was not unfriendly, that notwithstanding all this he did not want a man active in politics as his lawyer—and I was out a good client.

Similar examples are legion.

Given these attitudes, what citizen has the right to complain if the quality of urban government does not meet high standards? To me, it is surprising that so many good people disregard the conventional public attitudes and persist in their political activities.

Politics can be a noble profession. It has produced many of the great men of our heritage. Jefferson, Madison, Jackson,

Lincoln, Cleveland, Theodore Roosevelt, Wilson, Franklin Roosevelt, John Kennedy—to name but nine. It is well to underscore the fact that these men were products of politics, not accidents of the political process.

A profession that produces such men—and Al Smith and Fiorello La Guardia, and George Norris and Herbert Lehman—is not inherently bad. That the list is hardly begun by these two strings of names is no small tribute to American politics.

If our urban citizens are to dare even hope for better government, they need to re-evaluate their attitudes and prejudices. Having re-evaluated them, they need then to see that the best of the politicians available—and the best in each politician—is stimulated to creative action, instead of fostering the notion that politics is a house of ill repute whose occupants are to be pitied or scorned depending upon one's attitude against or appetite for sin.

I think Professor Theodore Lowi of the University of Chicago stated the whole problem best. He said that our attitudes about politicians are such that politicians have been all but eliminated from the governmental process, and that as a result, "New York is well run, but ungoverned."

26 ⁎   The Locus of Corruption

Just as our ideas about good city government are largely the product of confusing a symptom of bad government with its cause, so our defenses against the symptom of bad government—corruption—are the product of the same confusion. In narrow obedience to our tradition, the principal defense against corruption continues to be an attempt to keep political leaders out of the government process. Nothing more is thought necessary to mind the store.

This defense presupposes that political leaders as a group are less honest and more likely to engage in nefarious conduct than other groups such as lawyers, businessmen, and civil servants. The evidence to support this assumption is flimsy at best. I do not have the statistics, but I suspect that the percentage of political leaders convicted of crime is far less than the percentage of political leaders in the population. It is not, for example, unusual to read in the press of businessmen or lawyers or doctors convicted of income-tax evasion or some other crime of corruption. The back pages usually suffice to carry this not unusual news. But let a charge of corruption be even leveled at a political leader and it is front-page news. Even the prominence accorded to such news is not sufficient in itself to justify the assumption that underlies our defenses against government corruption: that the political leaders are the likeliest causes of the disease.

I reject this assumption.

In my experience it is not true.

That is not to say that all political leaders are honest and incorruptible. They are not, and I know they are not, but I reject the popular assumption about the frail honesty of political leaders, even though I acknowledge that they, like all human beings, are corruptible and from time to time are corrupted.

Indeed, the last thing a serious practitioner of the political process can afford is to be naïve about the possibility of corruption. There is nothing worse than having your own people stealing behind your back. If they do steal, the defect, while hardly yours at law, does not make them less your people in the public's eye. And the public—though it may forget and forgive— will not be wrong. They were your people. You put them there. That you called the police, and they were fined and their offices cleaned out as soon as possible, does not quite take the smell out of the air. For his own effectiveness, then, as well as for his own self-respect, the politician may never forget that men and women who can be corrupted are always in sufficient supply.

A serious politician allows his power to be exercised by subordinates only so long as he trusts them. The flow of power to a subordinate responds with the utmost delicacy to the eddies of disquiet which corruption—or the suspicion of it—inevitably sets in motion.

It is not a particular group of people that is the magnet which attracts corrupters. Power, and power alone, attracts. The natural locus of corruption is *always* where the discretionary power resides. It follows that in an era when political leaders exercised basic power over the government officials whom they controlled, the locus of corruption was in the offices of the political bosses— Tweed, Croker, Kelly, and the rest. But as power has shifted from the political leader to the civil servant and the public officeholder, so the locus of corruptibility and of corruption has shifted. The evidence demonstrates this clearly, and yet little attention is paid to the evidence, because the old myths and preconceptions are too strong.

Let us first put aside the few cases that invite public attention because the items involved are so easily understood. For example, an Oriental rug given to a political official is something the ordinary voter comprehends. Many millions of dollars in a Dixon-Yates contract (involving no political leaders) is not. A bathtub given to a political leader is understood. A television-antenna franchise awarded to businessmen is not. A deep-freeze given to a political leader is understood. Stocking a substantial part of a retired general's farm with cattle from wealthy friends is not. But the deep-freezes and the vicuna coats and the bathtubs and the Oriental rugs are not the great danger to honest government. It is the relationship reflected by these gifts that causes the problem.

The question of whether Sherman Adams used his public power to help his friend Bernard Goldfine is more disturbing than the hospitality enjoyed and gifts received by Adams. Indeed, these gifts are neither the stuff with which corruption is accomplished, nor the subject matter of political deals. The real corrupters rarely leave tangible evidence of where they have been and what they have sought.

Those who seek the benefit of licit and illicit government favors are nothing if not perfectly attuned to shifts in power, and they instinctively go where the power is. What needs to be made clear is that the power is no longer in the hands of political leaders. It has been transferred to the hands of public officials and civil servants long since.

So why deal through a political leader when you can go direct to the source of power? Why contribute to the party when you get more consideration by making your contribution to the candidate himself? Why deal with secondary sources when the primary source is an independent, uncontrolled civil servant?

When a parking-meter company's public relations expert sought to create a "bribe plot," in order, as it later developed, to pocket the bribe himself, the person whose name he invoked as the recipient of the bribe was a former career civil servant, then high in the city government, not a political leader. In 1961, one newspaper, intent upon attempting to discredit the Wagner administration, ran a box-score of "scandals" day after day; I remember that it got as high as twenty-one or twenty-two "scandals." With *one* exception, every one of the "scandals" involved civil servants, not political leaders or appointees. By the same token, Republican strategists, in early 1965, before Congressman John Lindsay decided to run for mayor, were reported to be disheartened at the prospects of "fusion" because fusion had never succeeded in the absence of widespread *political* scandals.

Does the absence of political scandal mean there is no corruption? Of course not. It means that corruption has taken new forms and found a new locus.

By "corruption" I mean not only the use of a consideration such as money to persuade government to do something it shouldn't, although that is one form of corruption. There are other forms: The exercise of discretion to award a government privilege to an old friend as against an equally or better qualified applicant is a form of corruption. The tender treatment of a regulated industry by a regulatory commission whose members look to an ultimate future in private industry is a form of it. In short, corruption is the exercise of governmental power to achieve nongovernmental objectives.

From the point of view of the public and competing aspirants, what difference does it make whether the consideration for such an exercise of power is cash, or friendship, or future campaign contributions, or a future job, or nothing?

For example, since World War II a massive government-sponsored housing program has been carried on almost continuously in one form or another. The essence of the slum-clearance program has been to encourage private enterprise by almost guaranteeing builders a substantial profit and perhaps a windfall. The essence of the program—"Title I" or "urban renewal"—is for government to acquire slum properties at market value and resell them (or make them available) to private builders or sponsors at a lower cost. The subsidy is supposed to permit the construction of housing that will rent—or in the case of co-operatives, sell—at lower prices than would otherwise obtain.

The rule is that the sponsor is selected through the exercise of discretion among a host of applicants who are for all measurable purposes equally qualified. Why is A selected, instead of B or C, to sponsor or build such a development? There is no public bidding; no objective measure of who ought to be selected is applied.

Under current practices a "project" for a given area is developed by government officials and approved. A "sponsor" of the development, who is in charge of carrying it out and controls it, is then selected by government officials. The sponsor selects a builder, an architect, a lawyer, an accountant, insurance broker, and all of the rest of the retinue needed to build a complex of buildings, hires them through a corporation organized to build the project, secures financing, and sees that the development is created.

The power to designate these participants is a valuable one. The architect, the lawyer, the insurance broker, may be prepared to share their profits with the source of business. The possibilities for profit to the sponsor are substantial. Certainly the builder, the lawyers, the architect, and the insurance broker are all well compensated.

"Title I," urban renewal's predecessor, was administered by Robert Moses, that conspicuous agent of good government. He and his varied Public Authorities, accountable to no one ("since there are no politicians involved, it must be honest, so why should it have to account?") are a monument to the anti-political good-government tradition of "keep the politicians out and it will be okay."

Moses' administration of Title I was so unsatisfactory that the program was killed. If a political leader had made one-tenth of the mistakes Moses made in that program alone, he would have been destroyed, defeated, out of business. Arbitrariness; designation of favored associates for choice patronage, high salaries, limousines, and chauffeurs; and invulnerability to any requirement of public accountability or auditing of accounts are the earmarks of an entrenched machine. Moses' Public Authorities have them all.

Moses' reward for so directing his many enterprises has been continuing editorial adulation, new jobs, constant praise, and finally the opportunity to run the greatest boondoggle of them all, the 1964–65 New York World's Fair—again, because he is politically pure and deemed to be "efficient."

The potential for abuse in such a set-up could not have escaped the attention of those who seek the pleasures of governmental favor. Who would not prefer the favors of an anonymous Public Authority, which is not subject to public accountability, to the friendship of a political boss. (Moses' critics have repeatedly suggested that his authorities should be subjected to methodical public examination. All to no avail.)

Probably the reason is Moses' accepted and undisputed personal honesty in money matters. But this begs the question. Personal honesty is the *first* requirement for public service, not the only one. And, as noted above, corruption as I have used the term does not require cash as a consideration. There are subtler and more utilitarian forms—future support, campaign contributions, honorific appointments, even ill-defined debts and obligations available for later redemption, or merely old friendships—or whim!

The irregularities in the Moses operation of Title I are well documented elsewhere. Their significance, however, as a demonstration of the new locus of corruption has been generally disregarded—except, I suspect, by the corrupters.

What of Title I's successor—urban renewal? Here again a sponsorship is a valuable asset. Anyone schooled in traditional notions about good government would expect to find the politician's heavy hand allocating sponsorships and designating builders, architects, and the like.

There were political leaders involved in the process, but as supplicants for favors, not dispensers of them. My successor as county leader, J. Raymond Jones, a Harlem political leader, was the most notable of these. Jones's dealings in urban renewal projects—he became a sponsor of at least one major project—came to light when he and Congressman Adam Clayton Powell had a falling out about one project, and a lawsuit was started in which Powell claimed that a sponsorship which was to have been awarded to a company in which they were both interested was at the last moment awarded to a company in which Jones was interested but Powell was not.

Decisions on sponsorships of these projects were made on the very highest level of city government—not by any political leaders. The political leaders, except occasionally as supplicants, played no role in the process. But I cannot believe that their absence rendered the projects $99 \frac{44}{100}$ percent pure. For the discretionary power to designate sponsors carries with it all the conditions that inevitably lead to "influence" and influence-peddling. If indeed these sponsorships have value, why shouldn't they be *sold* by government to the highest bidder, instead of given away? If an FCC license to operate a television station is of great value, why not have the government *sell* it, instead of giving it to one of half a dozen equally qualified applicants?

The gift of public privileges by government officials on a discretionary basis in the absence of public bidding is the greatest source of corruption, quasi-corruption, influence-peddling, and demeaning of the governmental process in America today. That distribution of public largess is more and more nonpolitical does not make it any better. Indeed, as in so many other cases, the division of power between political leaders and public officeholders might tend to diminish the opportunities for overt corruption in the dispensation of such government favors. But the greatest preventive would be to charge for the value of the government privileges being dispensed.

A classic example of the whole problem is the tale of the television-antenna franchise in New York City, which briefly attracted public attention in the spring of 1965. Six applicants sought the privilege of running master television antennas beneath New York City's streets, and charging residents at stipulated rates for connecting into the master antenna and thus securing first-rate reception. In some areas of the city where high buildings block reception (especially public housing projects), such a service was badly needed.

The proposed charges and rates varied from a $60 connection charge to $19.95, and from $20 a month service fee to $4.50. Some of the applicants had had extensive prior experience in operating such systems and some had not. Lo and behold, the two approved franchisers had the least experience and the highest charges of all the applicants. According to the New York *World-Telegram and Sun*, one of the two successful applicants had some unexplained connection with a former legislative representative and close confidant of the mayor. This mayoral friend had been involved in the process of securing the franchise. The other successful applicant was a firm headed by another old mayoral friend. Both had cut their proposed fees (although they were still well above those of the other applicants). What is more, according to the New York *World-Telegram and Sun*, the cuts had been made by the head of the Bureau of Franchises at the *mayor's* suggestion. No political leaders were involved in any way with the successful applicants (what a departure from the days of Boss Tweed!), so it was okay. One unsuccessful applicant was represented by the law firm to which New York County's former law chairman belonged. And one of my partners—by then I had retired as a political leader—represented another unsuccessful applicant.

If the myths were true, should not the ex-Tammany law chairman's client and the ex-county-leader's partner's client have triumphed—especially since their rates were lowest and their experience greatest?

The point, it seems to me, is clear. The pathway to government preference no longer passes through Tammany Hall or the internal political leader's office. It goes direct to the source. This phenomenon of modern urban government has hardly been noted by the theorists or the specialists in good government. They seem to be so convinced that civil service and growth of the public officeholder's independence have created such impregnable fortresses of rectitude that they have devoted all their attention when discussing corruption to looking for political leaders in the governmental process. Noting their absence, the good-government forces viewing a veritable parade of nude emperors have been satisfied that corruption has disappeared.

Indeed, not long ago this preconception so dominated the thinking of those investigating the city government that they laid a colossal egg. In 1959 the state legislature created a "Little Hoover Commission" to investigate New York City. The commission's activities were supposed to expose enough political corruption to lay the basis for a 1961 fusion movement to defeat Mayor Wagner. The Commission and its staff honestly believed, I think, that New York City was beset by the same conditions of political corruption that had laid the basis for the 1933 election of La Guardia. The staff apparently immersed itself in the literature of corruption, particularly that revealed by the Seabury Commission, which uncovered and documented the shenanigans of the political leaders of the 1930's. They had fixed judges and commissioners, sold contracts, and generally operated the city through the public officeholder nominees they controlled. (When one of their designees, Mayor O'Brien, was asked in 1933 who his police commissioner would be, he replied: "I don't know. They haven't told me yet." And he was telling the truth!) But thirty years later, the pattern wasn't there. The corruption was among civil servants—usually lowly ones—and it was minor nickels-and-dimes stuff, not the classic corruption of the Tweed era.

Yet, obsessed by their preconceptions about what *ought* to be wrong (i.e., crooked politicians, not dishonest civil servants), the investigators never realized that what had been established was a shift in the nature and locus of corruption from the socially despicable politician middleman to the socially acceptable reform product—the civil servant, the career government servant, the elected public official who was free of domination by the machine. What had happened was that the corrupters, like water, had found their own level—underpaid and frustrated civil servants who yearned for a more affluent life, or ambitious public officeholders hoping to make affluent friends upon whom they could call when campaign funds were needed.

The frustrated civil servants do not represent any real threat to government. Their number is low and the graft is comparatively small, and no serious student of government would attribute to this kind of activity the manifold faults of modern urban misgovernment.

Of course, petty corruption remains a heavy burden to the person who must endure it. The construction of buildings in New York, for example, is still reported to involve substantial amounts in ten- and twenty-dollar payments to inspectors. How much of this gets to the inspector and how much is an excuse for the builder to get a little tax-free income ("petty cash" in his books) is anyone's guess.

But several things are clear. First, the supposition that such bribery exists, whether the supposition is true or not, saps popular confidence in government. Second, none of the principal defenses built up to protect government from corruption—the

isolation and elimination of the politician from government—
have had any success in eliminating the occasional bribery of
civil servants.

My own belief is that the amount of such corruption is
exaggerated, that the overwhelming bulk of civil servants are
honest and that, like politicians, they have about the same
percentage of corruptible people as the population at large—or
less.

The real threat posed by corruption to good government is the
fact that, as the form and locus of corruption has shifted from the
middleman politician to the civil servant or elected official, so has
the technique of receiving discretionary governmental largess.

The corrupter seeking to lease the Brooklyn Bridge for a dollar
a year in exchange for $100,000 in cash, or engaged in an effort to
accomplish such misbehavior, is a political and governmental joke.
Nobody pays any attention to him. Moreover, the political graft
of the Tweed and post-Tweed eras—liquor, prostitution, police
protection and the like—is simply nonexistent (unless it is a direct
deal between criminal and civil-servant policemen).

"Graft" today, if it can be called that, is the kind described by
George Washington Plunkitt as "honest graft"—only now it is
more "honest" by far. In short, the political plums today are
nonpolitical: urban-renewal projects, contracts to build schools
and public buildings and roads and sewers, franchises to install
community television antenna systems, and what have you—all
involving government funds or privileges, with contracts given
for value received with built-in profit of varying amounts, and all
disbursed on a *discretionary* basis.

When the time comes to raise funds for the public officeholder who dispensed that favor, or this sponsorship, he has a
ready-made list of potential contributors, just as Charles Murphy
and Boss Tweed and their predecessors did—the recipients of
discretionary public largess.

Should a portrait be painted and presented to the city? Run
down the list! And before you know it a patron has hired a
portraitist. The patron, moreover, has a tax-deduction. He is, of
course, a public benefactor, not a political wheeler-dealer.

Sometimes the cloak of purity achieved through association

with public officeholders instead of dirty political leaders reaches ridiculous proportions. For example, one prominent citizen, who, unlike the late Vice-President Alben Barkley, would far rather "sit at the feet of the mighty" than be a "servant of the Lord" is famed for his ability to move fireplugs on Park Avenue. The basis of his celebrity arises from the desire of Park Avenue building managements to have a "no parking" area near their front doors, so that tenants don't have to crawl between parked cars as they come and go. The best way to achieve this is to have a fire hydrant right next to the awning—that guarantees twelve feet of "no parking" on each side of it.

And so this scion of civic virtue specializes in securing fireplug movements in exchange for long-term retainers. He accomplishes these results (and Park Avenue's fireplugs have seen a fair amount of movement lately) not because of any relation with political leaders, but because of his nonpolitical, good-government status and his close friendships with significant public officeholders.

The locus of corruption is always where unrestrained power exists. The political leader's present function in the scheme of corruption is to be a scapegoat, who shields the self-styled public vindicator of political morality from public scrutiny. After all, so long as the "bosses" exist, their opponents, being saints, should be protected. So long as the political leaders are excluded from the process, why is it necessary to inquire why fire hydrants are moved or how urban-renewal-project sponsorships are allocated?

Of course, I am sufficiently skeptical to be unable to believe that corruption will be eliminated from the conduct of human affairs, either by eliminating the power of political leaders or by restoring their power to what it once was. But I do believe there are ways to minimize the improper exercise of governmental power—ways that would make it more difficult for the corrupter to corrupt and easier to uncover him and his activities.

The first step is to realize that the locus of corruption is where the power is. The second is to destroy the stereotypes that brand the political leader as thief and the public official as saint. The third is to eliminate the discretionary distribution of governmental privileges—Title I housing projects, urban-renewal sponsorships (and construction contracts), public architecture contracts, and so on—without competition for either quality (where the arts are involved) or quantity (where money is involved).

Is there any good reason why every architect who wants to should not submit a design for a school or a courthouse and have the winning design selected on the basis of the merit, utility, and decent cost ratios of the design, and not because of the name attached to it? Why should not an urban-renewal sponsorship, worth a million dollars to the sponsor, be awarded on the basis of price paid to the city, instead of unexplained "discretion"?

The reason why such discretion is granted to public officials—especially the "nonpolitical" ones—is the public supposition that since they are outside the traditional political structure, they, rather than the politician, should have power—and by some magic, rectitude will be achieved.

What has happened is that a new politics has been created, certainly no better and in some ways worse than the politics this "nonpolitical" politics has replaced. It is indeed time to re-examine the post-Tweed-era assumptions which have led to this new form of urban mismanagement.

The ideas I am suggesting seem at first blush to be radical, perhaps half-baked, certainly unusual. But it seems clear to me that in a city where the power is in the bureaucracy, the locus of corruption must also be there. And the discretionary exercise of power by bureaucrats is to be feared and needs to be dealt with at least as much as—probably far more than—the venality of Boss Tweed's successors.

Part Eight

The

Human Side of

Politics

Introduction to Part Eight

Politics is not all grim, mechanical, and serious. On the contrary, it is a source of humor, of pride, of excitement.

It has its own styles, its own stories, its own kinds of heroic action.

It involves people, and therefore it is irredeemably human.

No one who has been in politics can escape its humanity or stop telling its stories. There have been, I suppose, close-mouthed politicians and for good cause. But more often than not eyes twinkled above such shut mouths and ears were open to the stories politicians love to tell. There are as many styles to politics as there are to any serious pursuit. Such styles reflect, of course, the character of a man's commitment and so embody more than the way he laughs or cries. Taken together they exhibit the human side of politics.

27 * On Political Styles

Throughout this book, there runs the question, what makes the political leaders do what they do? The answers are as varied as there are kinds of people.

Of course, except very temporarily and by accident, there are no people in political office whose outlook on life, shall we say, is governed by their opposition to vivisection or fluoridation, or who believe that they are being secretly attacked by Russian radio waves. We must, at the outset, exclude from the political spectrum, or at least from any serious analysis of it, those who have a paranoid reaction to particular problems and who go off like rockets whenever given nerves are touched.

We are not dealing with the nuts but with the less emotionally disturbed portion of the population. And the variations are great.

Fifty years ago, this astonishing variety of types did not pose a problem for analysis of the political process. The practitioners were essentially soldiers—or company and battalion grade officers—in a para-military organization, an organization where the leader's word, whoever he was and however he discovered it, was law.

In the old Tammany, the leader's word was the decisive factor. In Edward J. Flynn's book *You're the Boss*, he bluntly notes that he, as the leader, even decided who his district leaders would be and, if they did not see eye to eye with him and made their disagreement plain, he had the power, he quietly notes, to cause the underlings of the leader to select a new one.

But times have changed. The old monolithic power, first eroded, has now largely disappeared. For that power was based upon an organizational concept that put the organization, as directed by its leader, above personal desires where those desires could not, temporarily at least, be satisfied. The district leader who lost out in the allocation of candidacies would in due course find his loyalty to the organization recognized and rewarded by a subsequent nomination or appointment for one of his supporters.

Among many of the district leaders, this faith and loyalty to the organization survives. For example, in 1963, Italian leaders and Lower East Side leaders were faced with a county ticket consisting of a Negro, two Jews, and one reform Irishman—no Italian and no Lower East Sider. Yet, despite muttered (and shouted) discontent, they worked for this ticket as if they had liked it. Their reward and recognition came the next year with the nomination of a Lower East Side Italian for county-wide office.

But the majority of leaders, having seen the destruction of the organization, are more likely to function with an independent, nonorganization orientation. The result can create a rather complex situation in the internal politics of the party. One day in 1963, for example, when the Executive Committee selected four different candidates to run in the primary, it was necessary to put together four different majorities, each composed of different combinations of leaders; and in each case the separate stimuli that led a particular leader to each of the majorities—or to two or three of them—varied candidate by candidate.

That operation took six weeks of work before the meeting and a good deal more as it went on. The meeting itself started at 12:30 P.M. and ended at 5:00 P.M. It was marked by frequent recesses while I went to work to round up the next majority by pressure, pushing and cajoling, arguing, begging, and occasionally shouting. If I had to reproduce what happened on that day, I couldn't. There were too many cross-currents, too many discussions, too many recesses. All I really remember was that at the end of the day I remarked to a friend: "That was quite an exercise. But I'd just as soon never have to put a ticket together *that* way again."

What were the individual variables? Here are some:

Leader A: Loyal to me and the mayor, but unwilling to support candidate 1 because the leader suspected candidate 1 would nevertheless support the leader's opponent in his own campaign for re-election.

Leader B: Opposed to the nomination of judges "in principle" but unwilling to vote against candidate 2, a Negro, who was nominated for judicial office.

Leader C: Anxious to do what he thought was right, but hamstrung by his reform affiliations from voting for candidate 3.

Leader D: Willing to vote for all four candidates in the hope that a recommendation of his would be approved.

Leader E: Basically an organization man, who saw the four candidates as a reasonable compromise of conflicting forces.

Leader F: Recognizing that candidate 4 was a public relations liability to the county leader, he was willing to see him nominated in order to embarrass the county leader, but not willing to vote for him, and therefore abstained.

Leader G: Had hoped for a nomination for his club, knew he couldn't get it, so went along on a what-the-hell-maybe-next-time basis.

Leader H: Genuinely concerned about the qualifications of candidate 1 but lacking sufficient provable facts to make an issue of it.

Leaders I and J: Mad at the mayor—therefore no votes for any of *his* choices.

Leaders K and L: Reformers who needed regular votes to nominate a reform candidate for one of the four vacancies, thus willing to trade their votes to a regular for nomination of a reformer in exchange.

And so it went. In each case there was another side of the coin. Some stimuli—a past favor, some known asset in the candidate, a hope for tomorrow, a feeling of loyalty, a feeling of futility, distaste for the tactics of the opposition, general policy orientation, ethnic considerations, or a desire for peace within the party—resulted in an affirmative vote on one or two or three or even four of the candidates.

The techniques of leadership vary with the leader employing them. Some use brazen arrogance, specific threats, and naked power to coerce support. They rarely last long in these days, for their maneuvers stimulate opposition. Others make promises of future benefits. Others encourage a cult of personal loyalty.

But the expert politician knows each individual, his likes, dislikes, prejudices, emotions, loyalties, obligations, ambitions, attitudes, and character, and like an organist he knows which stop to pull to make each leader say yea at the opportune time—if it exists. Sometimes he may think he knows the stop, pull it, push the key, and discover that it doesn't work any more because of a change in circumstances, whereupon the search for a new stop must begin.

In this sense he is manipulative, and in this sense politics involves manipulating people. Yet the result in the end can be harmony and effective government, and *should* involve summoning from each person the best that is in him.

True, this is an ideal. It may rarely be accomplished. There are baser considerations which can produce a majority. The self-centered man who sits at the console may find the lowest common denominator far easier to achieve than the highest. But this ideal—seeking the highest rather than the lowest common denominator—is what distinguishes the political statesman from the political hack.

James A. Farley—and to a lesser extent Edward J. Flynn—probably best epitomize the political statesmen of the last generation in New York. To their company should be added the late James Finnegan of Philadelphia, David Lawrence of Pittsburgh, and Jacob Arvey of Illinois.

Farley's reputation was founded on two simple but almost unique traits: he told the truth and he kept his word. He was concerned with the quality of the products of his political machine, but his basic orientation was to the organization. It, not he, was most important. This being the case he always "voted the ticket," at the same time neither forgiving nor forgetting those who broke his rule and lied to him.

Part of Farley's greatness is that he created an image of the politician that was essentially affirmative—an honest man who kept his word. He was one of the first political leaders in this country who emerged from the process with his record for integrity unimpaired. There were no whispers, there was no gossip, no suggestion of ill-gotten gains. He left the profession and the reputation of politics and politicians better than he found it.

Other political leaders of equal if temporary eminence never matched Farley. De Sapio was obsessed by an ego that led him to place himself farther and farther out front, until he became an obvious and irresistibly vulnerable target. Unlike Farley, De Sapio loved to delay decisions and to spring things at the last minute. Farley, I am told, preferred to move fast in order to minimize competitive dissension within the organization when a vacancy was to be filled. Indeed, if De Sapio in 1958 had announced his support of Hogan for the United States Senate nomination a month before the convention, the Buffalo debacle and De Sapio's ensuing downfall would never have occurred. At least half and perhaps three-quarters of the Finletter supporters—the source of the reform movement—would have swung to Hogan without any problems. But De Sapio liked to keep it quiet and close, and then leap. In Buffalo he leaped into oblivion.

Nor did De Sapio place the organization first. A self-centered man, most of his decisions included a substantial personal ingredient.

Soft-spoken, an easy promiser, De Sapio rarely made threats. He governed via a mixture of gentle blandishments, quiet persuasion, and delay until the last moment, when his decision was the only option on the table and time was too short to put a vote together to defeat it.

His greatest shortcoming, however, was his unwillingness to defend himself against his attackers. After the 1958 Buffalo convention, he seemed to be paralyzed—in part by the intransigence of his own supporters, and in part by the intransigence of his opponents—as he watched the opposition grow. At the annual county-organization dinner in 1960 or 1961—or perhaps at both—he contented himself with a rousing attack upon his tormenters. But he never really fought back.

He never, for example, told his side of the Buffalo convention story, although he had a reasonable story to tell. He never really hit back until the spring of 1961, when in a half-hour television show he did a devastating job on his opponents. But it was too late. He was by then "the Boss," the symbol of bossism, and he led his supporters to the final glorious battle in the 1961 primary to unseat Mayor Robert F. Wagner—by then his enemy. In the final months his egotism demanded that he reply to each of the mayor's repeated attacks on De Sapio and bossism, so that the issue became Wagner vs. De Sapio (just what Wagner wanted), and De Sapio's candidate, Arthur Levitt, was all but lost in the shuffle.

De Sapio's conqueror, Robert F. Wagner, was a unique and different political personality. Wagner was and is essentially a public officeholder, not a political leader. Like De Sapio, he loved to delay and delay and delay political decisions until what seemed like long past the last possible moment. His sense of timing in retrospect, however, always seemed just about perfect.

As a public officeholder his orientation was personal, not organizational. This is a common characteristic of public officeholder types. Their names are on the ballot, they seek public recognition for themselves, not their associates and not their party, and ultimately the question for each public officeholder— who needs the votes for himself when he runs—is "what's good for me?" The political leader can afford to be far less selfish because he doesn't have to run for office in quite the same way.

By 1961, Wagner's orientation was almost entirely personal. Facing the battle of his life for his political life, he had little time and less inclination to ruminate on what might be good or bad for the organization. By 1961 Wagner had served almost eight years. During that period he had done precious little—if anything—to build a party oriented towards him or his governmental programs. Where other similarly placed chief executives might have fostered the careers of his supporters within the party and in the public office arena, Wagner had done nothing.

Indeed, the degree of his almost complete self-devotion is revealed in a comparison between his years as mayor of New York and the period during which Hubert H. Humphrey emerged in the politics of Minnesota, first as mayor of Minneapolis and later as United States senator. In the period just before and during his three and a half years as mayor, Humphrey was deeply involved in the movement that rid the Farmer-Labor Party of Communist infiltrators and welded it and the Democratic party of the state into *one* united and winning party, the Democratic–Farmer Labor Party (DFL). In contrast, in New York an essentially similar division among natural allies between the Liberal and Democratic parties has been perpetuated with Wagner until 1965 presiding over both but each kept separate and divided one from the other. One legacy of his personal brand of public-officeholder politics was the needlessly divisive 1965 mayoral campaign in which natural allies of the Democratic Party and thousands upon thousands of normally Democratic voters were arrayed against it.

In his years as mayor of Minneapolis, Humphrey was instrumental in producing an organization that included men and women like Secretary of Agriculture Orville Freeman, Arthur Naftalin, Ambassador Eugenie Anderson, and United States Senator Eugene McCarthy. Indeed, out of the Humphrey group have come one vice-president of the United States, one cabinet officer, a governor, and two senators—from what used to be a Republican state. I suspect the reason is that Humphrey, a man of excellence in mind, spirit, character, and courage, was not afraid to surround himself with men of excellence. He did not regard them as threats to himself but as allies. Together they have gone far. The Minnesota Democratic–Farmer Labor Party is one of the healthiest in the nation. It has a remarkably large number of men equal to high public office, all of whom—U.S. senators Eugene McCarthy and Walter F. Mondale, Congressman Donald Fraser, and Mayor Naftalin of Minneapolis are typical recent examples—have been developed in a party that knows it must constantly restore itself if it is to survive.

In contrast, in twelve years as mayor of the largest city in the country, with worlds of talent available, Wagner has yet to foster and develop or produce from his administration one assemblyman, one state senator, one congressman or one U.S. senator, let alone a cabinet officer or a vice-president of the United States.

It is this phenomenon of careerist self-absorption more than anything else that reflects the Wagner political style: create no potential opponents, eliminate those who appear, take care of yourself, and never make a decision until it can't be avoided.

As a result of this pursuit of the politics of self-protection, Wagner in 1961 had only a small group of associates to call upon—almost none within the regular party. In Manhattan, only four out of sixty-six district leaders were genuinely for him, in Queens only one (with whom he later had a falling out), and in the other three counties none.

There is, however, another side of the Wagner political style. He is a difficult man to count out. For alone, apparently licked, isolated and surrounded, he has a stubborn, indomitable, imperturbable confidence that pushes him on and through a campaign. "It isn't," as someone once said, "that he knows what the man in the street thinks—he *is* the man in the street."

And the man in the street in 1961, faced with a choice between dogged, amiable, honest, familiar, "fighting" Bob Wagner and Boss De Sapio, chose Wagner. For Wagner this result had been predicted by his favorite pollster eight months earlier. But many such predictions are made, and half of them are always wrong. It was Wagner who made the poll come true.

What of his style since 1961, when he became the acknowledged leader of the party? Like his counterpart—Richard Daley, mayor of Chicago—since 1961 the mayor of New York has occupied the position of chief of party as well as chief public officer. As chief of party he has commanded the same loyalty of a majority of the party (on almost every issue) that his predecessors, the Tammany chieftains of eighty years ago commanded.

But there is a major difference, and this is the major difference between the party of eighty years ago and the party of today. Tweed's principal source of strength was his position within the organization, and the sustenance of that power demanded an organizational orientation. Tweed's district leaders were important to him both as executors of his decisions and as his supporters and the sources of his power. Where party leadership is exercised by public officeholders like mayors Daley and Wagner, the leader's principal source of strength is his almost impregnable hold on public office as mayor; the sustenance of that power demands at times, because of our distorted views of party politics, an *anti*-organizational orientation. The district leaders are not the mayor's source of strength; the people are.

And so party leadership becomes personalized, it becomes the chief executive's, and he uses it as he sees fit. But no chief executive can ever be defeated for re-election to *public office* because of the way he exercises *party power*. The issues in a campaign for public office are not internal party issues.

It is part of Wagner's political genius—and he is a political genius, of that I have no doubt—that he recognized these aspects of the modern political structure and has guided himself accordingly. Frequently apparently cornered, he quietly has eluded the trap—because unlike his organization-oriented adversaries, he simply does not recognize the traditional rules of the game, for they are not the rules of *his* game. *His* game is that of every public officeholder—survival at the polls. (See, e.g., Lindsay's and Romney's refusal to endorse Goldwater in 1964 and their consequent survival, while their more party-oriented co-candidates were slaughtered.) In consequence, when the political leaders corner Wagner at the edge of the chessboard, shouting "Check" or "Checkmate," Wagner creates two new spaces outside the traditional sixty-four and moves to one of them, thereby winning the game.

The events of early 1965 provide a good example. Wagner's candidates for majority leadership in the state legislature were defeated in the Democratic caucus. Yet Wagner, by three moves into three spaces created specially for the occasion, won:

Space 1: his minority of Democratic legislators, outvoted 21 to 12 in the Democratic senate caucus and 53 to 35 in the Democratic assembly caucus, refused to accept the caucus choices and refused to vote for the choices of the caucuses;

Space 2: when cornered by widespread demands for a secret ballot among the legislators and a binding commitment by the legislators to support the caucus winner on the floor, Wagner himself joined in proposing the arrangement and twenty-four hours later blew up his own proposal by accusing the state chairman of bribery;

Space 3: Wagner sought and got enough Republican votes to elect his candidates—the choices of a minority of Democrats—as leaders of the Democrats in the legislature.

The point of this is not to suggest that Wagner should be chastised so much as it is to demonstrate the fact that modern political leadership by public officeholders has not only radically altered the game of politics as well as the rules of that game, but also the stakes for which it is played, and the manner in which it is played. That this tendency has militated against responsible party management and growth is a good but largely academic question, since in a party dominated by a public officeholder there is no effective way for the party to restore itself or to assert its own best interests—and these interests are always larger and more representative of what the party stands for than the career of one man ever is.

For years political leaders in New York have talked about how "lucky" Wagner has been. (California's professionals like to talk the same way about Governor Pat Brown.) The plain truth is, Wagner has not been lucky so much as brilliantly adaptable to the new kind of politics which has emerged since World War II.

There are, of course, other political styles and types which enjoy political success.

Adam Clayton Powell, for example, is an unusual mixture of charm, audacity, arrogance, sensitivity to the mood of his voters, and demagoguery. Every story about him seems to illustrate another facet of his remarkable personality. And no brief sketch could hope to describe all of him accurately.

The complexities of his personality are explained, perhaps, to some extent by the fact that in his first year at college apparently no one knew he was a Negro, and he socialized with his white classmates. Later, some of his "friends" discovered that he was a Negro, and most of his newly made "friendships" quietly evaporated.

Many years later a some-time political friend and some-time political foe of Powell's said to me one night: "I've finally figured Adam out. He spends most of his time trying to make a monkey out of the white man, and the rest of his time trying to make a monkey out of the black man!"

Powell has been enormously successful in annoying the white power structure by his anarchistic refusal to abide by any of its standards of acceptable behavior. Every time he does this, however, he expresses the secret and not-so-secret desire of his constituents and he has never lost his contact with his community. When he speaks, he usually speaks the views of his constituents. It is perhaps this capacity to rub the white man's nose in the black man's ugly situation that endears Powell most to those Negro New Yorkers who follow him. He is very good at it. The release, the emotional wallop his brilliant verbal sallies give his adherents can never be overlooked.

His capacity for demagoguery is startling. In 1959, I sat next to him on the platform at a County Committee meeting of some 3,000 committeemen. It was an unhappy and divided meeting. Every group seemed mad at every other one. People were shouting, interrupting the speakers, and there was a tension of developing, inchoate anger.

When Powell was introduced he rose, grinned at me, and said, "Watch this."

He walked to the podium, quieted the crowd, and started, "Before I say what I came here to say," he began, his voice rising in pitch and volume, "I want to register my protest [his voice higher and higher and louder and louder] at the seating arrangements made here TONIGHT" (his voice rising in pitch right through "tonight").

The place exploded. He had found the common denominator of discontent.

He allowed the tumult to crescendo until it seemed almost ready to explode, turned, gave me a wink, turned the other way and gave De Sapio a look which I interpreted as "Don't mess with me. See what I can do." Then he stilled the crowd. The explosion was over, and somehow the tension gone.

One other occasion I remember was at his club's annual dance at a time when Adam was in hot water for some outrageous behavior involving a European trip and unearned salaries to his wife. He was enjoying himself. He introduced his staff, announcing their salaries with their names, to the joy of the multitude, and he declared his intention of returning shortly to Europe on another trip. With relish, he let it be known he was going "first class—*again.*"

The crowd roared.

So long as the Negro community goes through life second-class or worse, it cannot be blamed for reveling in the antics of one of its members who has managed to make it "first class." And, unhappily, so long as the Negro community tolerates Powell as its spokesman in Congress, the rest of New York City's residents will find it difficult to believe that any community that tolerates such a spokesman may, in fact, be brought to the point where its equality with the rest of the community will be actual rather than rhetorical.

This vicious circle is one of the tragedies history has bequeathed us. Powell is one of that history's saddest examples of waste. There can be no doubt that he is a man of unusual ability. Anyone who knows him cannot help wondering, as he must wonder, what he might have achieved if he had not been born a Negro in a bigoted society.

Adlai Stevenson had no political style: he had a personal style that willy-nilly became a political style. Still for him it wasn't a political style or technique at all. It was simply an effortless capacity to be himself. In person and in private, he was much the same man he was in public, thoughtful, witty, personable, somewhat shy. Yet he created a style. In many ways he made John F. Kennedy possible. For the latter's literate and intellectual style could never have secured the public acceptance it did but for Stevenson, who paved the way. And I am sure that for generations politicians who fell under Stevenson's spell will try to produce, and their supporters who remember Stevenson will expect, literate, thoughtful statements on public issues. This is only one of the legacies he has left the politics of our country.

There are also the perennial politicians who survive flood and famine, victory and defeat, but always emerge on their feet—remaining as district leaders even while the districts changed under them. One I privately called "the noblest Roman"—an

Italo-American in whose district perhaps twenty Italian voters reside, but he is still the leader, because whoever and whatever his constituents are, they are *his* people. And although he never finished high school (fifty years ago), every problem that is brought to him warrants at least one—probably three—highly literate and persuasive letters. I know their recipients will plead with a subordinate, in desperation, "For God's sake, take care of this! If you don't, he'll clog the mails and tie up the phones."

Another is a sententious, wise, and silent fulcrum of the opinions of his associates, a man who suffers the indignities of leadership in quiet agony, in the conviction that he will survive until once again a district leader is a respectable and effective participant in the governmental process.

There are also the young ones. They come surely up the ladder, at times paralyzed by their local problems and befuddled by the ideological and doctrinaire atmosphere to which they have been subjected, but slowly feeling their way toward a politics that makes sense to them.

These are real people, struggling with real ideological and practical problems, learning, adhering to principles, basically struggling to make the governmental process work the way they, right or wrong, believe it should work.

As a group they are, with rare exceptions, decent people. And they are part of the incredible variety of political types, who together and in opposition to each other somehow make the political apparatus function.

It takes an extremely talented, perceptive, and able person— not a hack—to make it function as well as it does, especially in the absence of the old sustaining tradition of organizational unity.

Nor is it grim, technical, and unpleasant. Indeed, especially in retrospect, it often seems like a jovial and amusing experience. There are lots of laughs and much amusement at the incredible and inexhaustible variety of knots imperfectly rational men can tie themselves into for good, bad, and indifferent purposes.

This is part of what makes a political leader stay at it, year after year after year, despite the burdens, problems, and opprobium that are his inevitable and principal reward. It's his game and he will play no other.

28.　Political Apocrypha

✿✿

An essential characteristic of the good political leader is a sense of humor. It is hard to say why, but every deadly serious political figure I have ever known has usually been a man so filled with his own importance—and thus with a sense of the consuming necessity for his election and re-election if city and nation were to survive—that he lacked not only the capacity to laugh at himself but the capacity to see himself and the rest of us in anything like a true light. His fixed self-regard isolates him and ultimately becomes obvious for the severe political defect it is. In short order, such a man becomes the butt of political jokes and in due course usually disappears from public office.

Humor is as good a political weapon as there is. There have been many masters of it. Some—like Franklin, Lincoln, FDR, Stevenson, and John Kennedy—have been complex and creative politicians of inestimable value. Others, like Alben Barkley, the Veep, have been beloved figures whose long public careers were spent in honorable service. Some, like James Curley of Boston, were colorful rogues. All shared the gift of laughter and all knew how to laugh at themselves.

Good politicians relax and rejoice in humanity. The spectacle of its sheer cussedness, its capacity for generosity, and especially its outrageous tendency toward contradiction is not lost on them. And politicians like to tell stories. Whether the stories are true or not is not as important as the fact that they are told and retold, generation after generation. Many suffer from being written down. They are meant to be told, not read. They have a flavor, sound, and music when spoken that cannot readily be reduced to print. All the embroidery of the retelling disappears in the transfer to mere prose.

One of the most famous political yarns is the Hymie Shorenstein story. Shorenstein was a Brooklyn district leader forty or fifty years ago whose Yiddish accent was as thick as good sour cream. He ran his district with the traditional iron hand. One year he nominated a young man, who was making his first run for office, for the assembly. Elated, the young man began preparing speeches and practicing them. On club nights he rushed up to the club expecting to be called on to say a few words, but his presence was ignored. Posters went up, literature was distributed, rallies were held—but he was neither mentioned in the posters and literature nor called upon at the rallies.

In desperation he tried to meet Shorenstein, without any luck. Finally, on a club night, he joined the long line of constituents sitting in chairs along the side of the room who were waiting to see the leader. Finally his turn came, and he was ushered into Shorenstein's cubbyhole office.

"Mr. Shorenstein," he began, "do you remember me?"

"Sure," came the reply.

"I'm running for the assembly," explained the candidate.

"I know," grunted Shorenstein. "I picked you."

"But I've been running for six weeks," pleaded the candidate, "and nobody knows it. No speeches, no rallies, no literature, no nothing. What should I do?"

"Go home," said Shorenstein.

"But—"

"Go home," repeated Shorenstein.

As the young man, dismissed, rose and started out the door, Shorenstein relented.

"Young man," he said. The candidate stopped and turned.

"Come back," said Shorenstein with a wave of the hand.

"Young man," he said. "You ever been to the East River?"

"Yes," came the answer.

"You see the ferryboats come in?" asked Shorenstein.

"Yes."

"You see them pull into the slip?"

"Yes."

"You see the water suck in behind?" the litany continued.

"Yes."

"And when the water sucks in behind the ferryboat, all kinds of dirty garbage comes smack into the slip with the ferryboat?"

"Yes."

"So go home and relax. Al Smith is the ferryboat. This year you're the garbage."

There is another Shorenstein story. Shorenstein held the position of recorder (or some similar title) to the Brooklyn Supreme Court. One year, a disgruntled political opponent discovered that about the only requirement for the job was that its holder be literate. Convinced that Shorenstein was not literate, he commenced an action to have Shorenstein removed. In fact, it developed (if it wasn't already known) Shorenstein couldn't read or write a word of English. The problem was only technical, he felt, and so he retained counsel to attempt to save his job.

A young lawyer a year out of law school was assigned to work on the case by the firm Shorenstein had retained. The young lawyer struggled and struggled with the law, seeking a solution, but he got nowhere. Late one night he had a brainstorm. The statute required "literacy" but it didn't say in what language!

It was 1:30 A.M., but the young lawyer was so excited he called Shorenstein and explained.

"I have the solution. The statute says you must be literate, but it doesn't say in what language. You can read Yiddish, can't you?"

There was a dead silence. Finally, Shorenstein said coldly, "Young man, you better stick to the law and leave the facts alone."

Shorenstein lost the job.

There is another story, reputed to be Al Smith's favorite, about a newly elected freshman assemblyman. Immediately after election day, the governor called a special session of the legislature and the young assemblyman packed his bag and headed for Albany.

He arrived and headed for the Ten Eyck Hotel.

"I'm Assemblyman Jones from the Second District," he said, "and I'd like a room."

"Have you a reservation, sir?" asked the clerk.

"Why, no," said Assemblyman Jones.

"I'm sorry, sir," said the clerk, "we're all filled up."

"But I'm Assemblyman Jones from the Second District," said the young man, with feeling.

"Sorry, sir," said the clerk. "Why don't you try the DeWitt Clinton?"

And so Assemblyman Jones picked up his suitcase and headed up the street to the DeWitt Clinton.

There the same conversation took place, with the same result.

Assemblyman Jones was sent from one hotel to another, each one a little shabbier, until he had been to every hotel in town. Each time his greeting, "I'm Assemblyman Jones from the Second District," was delivered with less confidence. By now it was raining, and as the assemblyman stood dripping on a corner, wondering where to go next, a stray dog mistook him for a fire hydrant and raised his leg.

The assemblyman looked down in despair, shook his head sadly, and said to the dog: "Now, how the hell did *you* know I was Assemblyman Jones from the Second District?"

Fiorello La Guardia was the subject of many stories. One of my favorites is about his relations with his commissioners, whom he never hesitated to call at any hour of the day or night. One morning at 4:00 A.M. his commissioner of sanitation, whose main delight and interest in the department were the department's band and baseball team, was awakened from a sound sleep.

"Commissioner," came the mayor's high-pitched voice, "sorry to bother you, but I wanted to check on the department's snow-removal plans."

"Mr. Mayor," the sleepy commissioner replied, "don't you worry about it. It's all arranged. The minute a flake of snow falls the Weather Bureau at the Battery will let me know personally. I have a man assigned to mobilize the forces, and all I have to do is call him. Within five minutes after that first flake drops, the trucks will be manned. Within ten minutes they'll be ready to start plowing. Within twenty minutes all the department's sweepers will be alerted to report for duty. Within thirty minutes the men and the trucks will be on the street."

"Grand," piped the mayor. "That's just grand, commissioner. Now, look out the window!" And the mayor hung up.

The commissioner stuck his sleepy head out the window of his

Beekman Place apartment to see that a full-fledged storm had already piled snow four inches deep on the streets.

Another La Guardia story relates to his refusal to have a phone on his desk. Instead, at the end of the room there was a closet, and high on the wall a pay phone. To reach it, Fiorello stood on a soapbox. There he received and made his calls.

One day he was asked why.

"If there's a phone on my desk, everybody will bother me with phone calls. This way, if I have to get a call, I can, but the calls don't interrupt my work."

"But Mr. Mayor," continued his admirer, "why is the phone so high on the wall? Why don't you have it moved down?"

"Two reasons," snapped hizzoner. "First, anyone who knows about that phone knows how inconvenient and uncomfortable it is for me. So they don't call unless it's essential, and if they do call they make it short.

"Second," he continued, his voice rising in pitch and intensity, "all phones should be high on the wall. Otherwise, the bookies [louder] write down their bets on the wall above the phone. This way [triumphantly] *they can't do it!*"

And then there was the young man who attended a long debate at a meeting of the Young Democrats. The subject aroused intense emotions, and the speeches went on and on as the young man vainly sought recognition.

Finally the chairman announced that the debate would close after two more pro and two more con speakers were heard. At last the young man was recognized.

"Which side are you on?" the chairman asked.

The young man stood, stunned, silent. Finally, he figured out the answer:

"I don't know," he said. "I haven't heard what I'm going to say yet."

Or the story of the leader who had lost favor with his captains. They called a meeting and invited him to attend. When he arrived, his captains grouped around him, shook his hand one by one, and led him to the front of the room.

Then his opponent rose, and on behalf of the assembled

multitude presented the leader with a radio set. The speaker explained that the leader was going to have a lot of free time on his hands and that the captains didn't want to see him get bored.

Then all sang "Auld Lang Syne," and one by one they said "So long, chief" to the recipient of the gift—who realistically and graciously accepted the farewells—and the radio.

James Michael Curley's autobiography, *I'd Do It Again,* is loaded with delightful political stories, many of them of dubious authenticity, and the temptation is strong to borrow at least one. Curley wrote the stories with such an outrageously delightful style that somehow they almost capture the spirit in which politicians delight in exchanging stories.

Thus, Curley tells us:

As the 1921 [mayoralty] fight drew to an end, Murphy pulled no punches, and I countered with jabs of my own. One night I was addressing a Roxbury audience, most of whom were Roman Catholics.

"Where was James M. Curley last Friday night?" I asked. "He was conducting a political meeting in Duxbury. And where was John R. Murphy last night? He was eating steak at the Copley Plaza."

Murphy spent a few nights on the stump trying to clear himself of that charge, while my camp followers embarrassed him further, launching a playful propaganda campaign in my behalf. Masquerading as laborers in the Lord's vineyard, and carrying prayer books, they walked around Charlestown and elsewhere informing groups what a disgrace it was that John R. Murphy had renounced his Catholic faith and had joined a Masonic order. It was also bruited about that he intended to divorce his good wife and marry a sixteen-year-old girl. This news shocked many of the patrons of saloons, according to reports.

Meanwhile, another group of my supporters—some of them reputed to be Boston College students—posed as members of the Hawes Baptist Club in South Boston and went about the neighborhood urging the good people to vote for John R. Murphy. And, unfortunately, this "Baptist" endorsement in many cases proved to be the kiss of death for poor John.

Thurman Arnold, whose wit is Western and in the great dead-pan tradition of Mark Twain, recalls in *Fair Fights and Foul* his election to the Wyoming state legislature.

This was in 1920—the year that Warren G. Harding swept the country, and when the smoke all cleared away I was the only Democrat elected to the Wyoming House of Representatives. When I got to Cheyenne the Republican representatives were in a great dither about who was to be elected speaker. The deadlock lasted for days. Finally one faction won the controlling vote, but the price was that a ranchman from the Big Piney was made speaker pro tem.

On the fateful day the legislature assembled to elect a speaker, there were a number of flowery speeches made for the leading candidate. After they were over and the question was about to be put to a vote, I rose and said, "Mr. Speaker, the Democratic party caucused last night, and when the name of Thurman Arnold was mentioned, it threw its hat up in the air and cheered for fifteen minutes. I therefore wish to put his name in nomination for speaker of this House." I then sat down, but I got up immediately and seconded the nomination. I said, "I have known Thurman Arnold for most of my life, and I would trust him as far as I would myself."

Everybody laughed except the speaker pro tem. My nomination was not on his carefully prepared agenda, and he did not know what to do. People were waving at him from all directions. So I rose a third time, and said, "Mr. Speaker, some irresponsible Democrat has put my name in nomination and I wish to withdraw it." After that, the train got on the track again.

This story is too good to be true and too perfect to question by checking against the records of the Wyoming legislature. I am unable to resist it and so accept it verbatim. It rings with truth of a kind that life, to improve itself, learns to imitate from art. All well and good, though one can hear Arnold laconically interjecting that to suggest that his story is in the slightest degree apocryphal is only a fancy way of calling him a liar.

Sometimes the apocryphal story is used as a political tool. In 1962, for example, there were five Supreme Court judgeships to be nominated by Manhattan and the Bronx. The first question to be decided was how many should come from Manhattan and how many from the Bronx.

For years the bulk of the judges had come from Manhattan, because its population was the larger of the two counties and it had far more legal business. By 1962, however, the Bronx population was almost as large as Manhattan.

One of the five vacancies was created by the retirement for age of a Republican Manhattan judge, three by Manhattan Democrats, one by a Bronx Democrat. By traditional rules, Manhattan should have selected four judges and the Bronx one.

But the population shift plus Manhattan party disunity gave the Bronx practical control of the convention. The Bronx had 108 well-controlled delegates, Manhattan had 116 uncontrolled ones. Anyone with five delegates behind him could join the Bronx's 108, and the Bronx could take four judgeships and give one to the Manhattan defector.

In this context I met with Charlie Buckley, the Bronx leader, who was then seventy-three years old; I was thirty-seven. I was prepared to concede two of the spots to the Bronx, keeping the three Manhattan Democratic spots. I did not see how I could answer the population-growth argument I expected.

But I never got it. Instead Buckley told me he thought it was time to redress an old wrong. Years before, according to him, the Bronx county leader had met to discuss the same subject Charlie and I were discussing with one of my predecessors. Buckley charged that my predecessor got his predecessor drunk and, at a Turkish bath where they were recovering, my predecessor persuaded his predecessor to surrender a Bronx judgeship to Manhattan in order to help the Manhattan leader solve some local problem.

To make matters worse, I was told, the position thus surrendered in the spirit of camaraderie generated by stronger spirits was later given by another predecessor of mine to the Republican Party! And *that* was the Manhattan Republican spot now open!

Charlie made it clear that he wanted that spot back! Overwhelmed by an argument I could never have anticipated, I was glad to do justice by surrendering any claim to my predecessor's ill-gotten gains—especially since we never got into the touchy question of population changes.

But political apocrypha rarely have such political utility. Usually, a story is told when the occasion demands or justifies it, or when it seems impossible not to yield to the impulse to tell one.

29 ✴ Grounds for Laughter and Pride

✴✴

The basic stuff of politics, as the banks now say of their business in the ads, is people. It is the activity of people, not policy or program, not graft or maneuver, that is the substance of urban politics. It would be wrong to portray the politician as a computerized agent making antiseptic judgments based on statistical information supplied him by "scientific" polls. It would be equally wrong to permit the impression that politics is some sort of behavioral science through which the politician may readily manipulate men and women into whatever position it serves his party interest to put them.

Political activity is one of the warmest kinds of human activity extant. Good humor, warmth, sardonic self-deflating attitudes, ridicule of power and pretense, pervade the entire process.

It is, for example, hard to communicate the incongruous hilarity produced when a network of walkie-talkies is inadvertently used by one group at a convention to keep the opposition posted on all of the group's secrets. But it happened at the Syracuse state convention in 1962 during the nomination of the United States Senate candidate. The supporters of Paul O'Dwyer, by and large New York County reformers, had observed the supporters of Bob Morgenthau, the nominated candidate for Governor, roaming the convention floor armed with walkie-talkies during the balloting. Some two dozen of them were all in touch with a central command post, manned by Morgenthau's campaign manager. Through this network, the candidate could run down or quash rumors and keep in touch with every friendly delegation during the balloting.

Observing this operation, the reformers were impressed. And

so they hired *one-half* the same set of walkie-talkies and set up a similar network. Hearing of this, one of their opponents rented one of the remaining half set. All the radios were broadcasting on the same wave-length. And so O'Dwyer's opponent tuned in.

But he heard nothing worth while. For, like kids with a new toy, the O'Dwyer forces were busy relaying trivia to each other from one end of the hall to the other. The hall was half empty anyway, so there was really nothing to report.

But one grizzled veteran listened in. He heard:

"Willie, Willie—this is Henry."

Willie: "Yes, Henry, I'm here."

Henry: "Where's here?"

Willie: "Near Nassau."

Henry: "What's going on?"

Willie: "Nothing. What's going on elsewhere?"

Henry: "Nothing."

And so it went.

The grizzled veteran watched and listened, and ambled over to me.

"Notice how quiet it is?" he asked.

"What do you mean?" I asked.

"No reformers bothering you?"

"Not in the last few minutes," I answered.

He pointed to his radio.

"They're all on the raadio [the Al Smith pronunciation] talking to each other, saying nothing," he said. And he let me listen in.

"Take my advice," he said, as he walked away. "Buy them some toys when you get home. Keep 'em busy." And he walked away.

I still don't know who he was.

For a time it looked as if there were more communicators than delegates. But the communicators were happy in that empty hall, while the people they were watching were casting votes for a full delegation while all but one or two of its members had gone home.

There was the time when a leader begged me for help for a

blind constituent. The only open job I knew of was a corporation-inspector position—"hole inspectors," as they were known—whose job was to check holes in the street created by Con Edison or some other utility, and to report whether they were properly filled in when the utility said they were. The job paid $1,800 a year, and was a notorious nonworking job.

I remonstrated, but the leader with delectable logic beat down my every objection to recommending the man. The man's sister would go with him and check the closing of the holes. Most "hole inspectors" never bothered checking anyway. This guy would take no chances. He'd go. If his sister told him the hole was closed, I could count on its being closed.

After several months of this, the leader finally said, "Listen, who the hell do you think you are? If City Hall will approve it, who are you to stand in the way of a blind man? At least you could send the name in."

Figuring City Hall would kick it back to me pronto, and end the argument, I relented.

To my amazement it went through. The name was forwarded to the appointing agency.

By then I was intrigued with the whole thing. Was it really possible that a sightless man would be appointed as an inspector?

But the phone rang. An apoplectic agency head screamed, "Eddie, you're not serious! Eddie, think of what the press will say!"

Feeling a little like a successful Diogenes, I acknowledged the validity of his point of view, and then advised the district leader of the result.

He sighed, "Well, I tried," and then added, "I guess we finally established *some* qualifications for that job," and hung up.

There was the night that Carmine De Sapio was defeated for the second time, in September, 1963, by Edward Koch, by all of 41 votes. Koch invited me to his club late that night to join in the victory celebration.

Never a favorite of his club's members, I nevertheless went. Koch, with a degree of courage and courtesy which I would never have requested but which I appreciated, rose to introduce me. Before a hostile group, he said that he had invited me, that I was a friend, and that I had contributed to the victory "in many ways which you will never know." He alienated some of his supporters by doing this.

As we were leaving, one of the spectators, a young man of dubious sex, accosted one of my party, who was walking down the stairs behind us.

"Keep your hands to yourself," I heard my friend's voice boom out.

His rebuffed accoster shouted, "Go ahead, you Tammany hacks —you and Costikyan, with your $300 suits."

It is true that our clothes looked, compared to his, as if they had cost $300 at least, for both of us made a habit of having our clothes pressed from time to time.

The sharp reply snapped back: "Listen, buddy, I was a reformer long before you were ever a fag."

As we left, roaring with laughter as the young man screamed obscenities at us, the whole experience was somehow weirdly and wildly funny.

At the Buffalo state convention in 1958, some of us learned a real and, in retrospect, amusing political lesson. That year the future reform wing of the party was firmly committed to Thomas K. Finletter for the United States Senate. But Finletter's organization was not prepared for what happened. Expecting the blessing of the governor, the staff had made no preparation for the traditional convention hoopla. No demonstrators were hired, no band was hired, signs for demonstrations weren't there (instead balloons were made available, each of which lasted about ten seconds before enthusiastic opposition delegates popped them).

Finletter was nominated in a bitter, low-key speech by a New York County delegate. The convention band, hired by the convention officials, had been paid $35 by Finletter supporters to play for the Finletter demonstration. When the nominating speech ended, the band struck up a tune and a sad group of around forty demonstrators, carrying balloons, started down the aisle. All of a sudden the demonstration sort of evaporated and was absorbed—

The balloons were burst;

A seconding speech for another candidate began;

The band stopped playing after two bars of "Happy Days Are Here Again." (Apparently that's what $35 buys from someone else's band.)

I got up from my delegate's seat to find out what had happened. I was told that one of De Sapio's friends had paid the band $100 *not* to play, and was asked if I had any money.

"What for?" I asked.

"Well, if we can raise $300, we think we can buy back the band."

Meanwhile the convention was moving full speed ahead and the roll-call was about to start. It was too late.

I always regretted that. I have wondered how much band music $300 would buy in such circumstances.

The political lesson, of course, is *Always Bring Your Own Band.*

Loyalties in politics are also part of the humanity of the process. There is, for instance, a businessman in New York who met a young Minneapolis mayor, I believe, right after the war. The New Yorker, Marvin Rosenberg, and the Minnesotan, Hubert Humphrey, became friends. Marvin became known as "Hubert's man in New York." Marvin tapped everyone he knew, and many he didn't, for contributions year after year, whenever Humphrey had a campaign.

In 1964, Rosenberg was a delegate-at-large at the national convention. He was on tenterhooks as he sweated out the decision on the Vice-Presidency.

On Wednesday, rumors were flying fast, low and high. It *would* be Humphrey. It *wouldn't* be Humphrey. But finally the word was out—the President was coming to tell the delegates personally of his choice.

By the time the President arrived, we all knew it was *supposed* to be Humphrey, but we weren't quite *sure.*

Someone—I don't know who—arranged for Rosenberg to sit in the front row of the New York delegation that night. He looked alternatively worried, lest something go wrong, and beaming with joy.

The President arrived, the ovation began and ended, the President spoke and finally uttered the words "Hubert Horatio Humphrey" and the hall exploded. Our state chairman, Bill McKeon, looked down the line, saw Rosenberg's ecstatic face as his friend, the next Vice-President, stood on the dais, and barked out: "Marvin, you want the standard?" And Marvin Rosenberg ran down the row of seats, took the fifteen-foot high New York State standard out of its pail of sand on the aisle, lifted it high and danced up the aisle to juggle it up and down right under the dais as the demonstration went on and on.

I saw Humphrey as he recognized that the man carrying New York's standard was "his" man, his old friend from New York. I think Hubert was as happy for Rosenberg as he was for himself. And Marvin pushed the sign up and down for fifteen minutes while the demonstration wore on, a look of bliss on his face, as the friend for whom he had worked so hard and so long received the adulation of the delegates.

When the demonstration ended, Rosenberg returned the standard, a happy smile on his face and sweat on his brow.

Someone said, "Hot work, Marvin." Someone—it may have been Rosenberg, but I'm not sure—answered, "Yeah, hot, but happy."

Beyond the fun and the good humor and the sardonic deflating of the self-important, there is the spectacle of firm courage, and often the making of decisions at personal cost in deference to some more important value.

I remember, in 1964, when the leaders from the Twenty-second Senate District met. The incumbent state senator, Jerry Wilson, was up for renomination. One of the leaders, Joe Erazo from the Sixteenth Assembly District South, was himself a candidate. His opposite number, Frank Rossetti, leader of the Sixteenth Assembly District North, was the assemblyman from the Sixteenth Assembly District.

When the voting took place, Erazo made it clear that, if Rossetti supported Wilson for renomination as state senator, Erazo would oppose Rossetti for renomination as assemblyman and give him a primary fight.

Rossetti was the last to vote. With his vote, Wilson had a

clear majority. Without it, Wilson might have a tie, since one of the leaders was absent and had not voted.

Rossetti made a quiet appeal to Erazo not to force a party-dividing issue. Erazo refused, and made it clear that Rossetti would have to vote for Erazo or face opposition himself.

Rossetti looked Erazo in the eye. "So you want me to vote, despite what I've said?" he asked.

"Yes," said Erazo.

Without batting an eyelash, Rossetti said, "Okay, I vote for Wilson."

He had previously told me he thought Wilson had done a good job and deserved renomination. This being his view, Rossetti showed no hesitation whatsoever in putting his own office in jeopardy to vote for Wilson.

And Rossetti did get the primary fight—but it evaporated before primary day.

How many people are there who would deliberately put their own positions in jeopardy in order to do the right thing for someone else?

My own club has a warm spot in my recollections of political courage. We early learned to stand on our own feet—before there were any CDV's or Herbert Lehmans or Mrs. Franklin D. Roosevelts spreading their wings and blessings over fledgling politicians.

In 1957, our little club stood up to Carmine De Sapio and the remnants of the old Tammany and won. That year we went through every catastrophe imaginable.

I was running for re-election to my second term as district leader. My first campaign manager effectively sabotaged the launching of the campaign by failing to notify the captains to come in to pick up the designating petitions. Available on a Tuesday night in late June, the petitions were still in the club-house on Thursday night. My campaign manager's explanation was that the captains had refused to come in.

I got on the phone. None of them had been told the petitions were available. By midnight the petitions were in the captains' hands and the campaign manager was removed.

The next week and a half I spent quelling a movement within

the club led by my co-candidate to launch a club-expulsion procedure against the ex-campaign manager. I insisted we could wait till the campaign was over, and that meanwhile we had to devote all our energies to the campaign. I finally prevailed, but it almost split the club wide open.

For a week or two I was my own campaign manager. Then I persuaded one of our old captains to take on the job. We got things rolling again. Then a week before the primary, he came to see me. He gave me a complete rundown on the status of the campaign. He had been told to "get out of town," by unnamed but powerful individuals. He never told me who, and I never asked. And, for his own safety, he intended to do so.

He was scared, and by then so was I.

I asked the Lexington Club to lend me someone to help keep the campaign rolling, and they did—Jim Ottenberg and Dick Brown, two expert political managers. Somehow we kept going. Every night my now out-of-town manager called to check, to advise, to suggest—always from a pay phone and never identifying himself.

On primary day the district was inundated by regulars from all over town. Over-sized empty barrels with placards on them appeared on every street corner. The placards, and many others stuck up over the district, announced that my opponent was the "regular."

By 5:00 P.M., at least five workers per election district had descended on us. (The polls closed at ten.) Every street corner was occupied by literature distributors, and opposition workers, members of the union headed by my opponent, and regulars from the district to the south of us.

As dark fell, the invaders, not knowing whose doorbells to ring and lacking effective direction, congregated in doorways. The district took on the aura of an occupied territory.

By 6:00 P.M., I was scared—the only time I ever was frightened in politics—because I was afraid my people might get hurt. I dispatched a friend and law partner to stay with my wife to keep her out of trouble (she was captaining her district) and to make sure she would not be the subject of any violence. Earlier that day she had been threatened with arrest because she had got a camera (without any film in it, to her chagrin) to take pictures of some of the invaders she recognized. The policeman said my 5'4", 110-lb. wife was "intimidating" four or five hulking Irishmen; both she and I knew them; they lived in another district, and were ashamed of themselves, but had been ordered in by their leader.

I took off on a tour of the polls at a little after six and found chaos. The doorways near the polling places and the polling places themselves were jammed with the strangers in our midst. In the increasing dark, they looked like hoodlums. Our far fewer, smaller, quieter captains and workers were outnumbered three to one; the noise in the polls was incredible.

All our people were a little scared, but they stayed at their jobs. I spread encouragement, muttered words to allay fears, but I got even more worried. I remember muttering to myself over and over, "I hope to God nobody gets hurt." After all, only nine years earlier there had been a killing of a captain during a political campaign only forty or fifty blocks to the north of us.

By eight o'clock it was quite dark, and the doorways of closed shops were filled with silent, huddling figures. Walking to the polls was a scary experience for the voters, as many of them told me. But they walked and voted.

Our white-faced, outnumbered, and by now angry captains and workers pulled in the voters—one by one—and our vote, as we later learned, quietly rolled up as the time for closing the polls approached.

We had one or two lawyers assigned to each polling place, ready for the count. At 8:30, I made my last tour of the polls, checking with the lawyers and trying to assure our people that everything was okay and praying that it was.

The captains launched their last-hour operation of getting all known favorable voters who hadn't yet voted out to the polls. This is the worst hour for the candidate. His work is done, but the issue is still in doubt.

Gradually the doorways emptied as their occupants silently moved into the polling places to watch the count.

I returned to the headquarters and prepared a chart to record the vote, district by district, and my own projection of the vote, district by district. My out-of-town campaign manager quietly and surreptitiously slipped up the stairway into the headquarters—nervous and obviously himself afraid he had been seen. He made his projection and we compared them. They were almost identical. And then we waited for the polls to close (at ten) and the first telephoned returns (10:40 P.M. or so).

I later learned that the scene in each polling place was more frightening to some of the captains than anything else all day. The doors were locked, and the polls filled with "watchers" (far more than legally permissible, but no one raised the question). At each election-district table the paper ballots were opened, and spread out.

Each table was ringed with the opposition workers, their faces, as I was told, pyramided three deep around the tables, as our outnumbered captains quietly—locked in with these strangers —watched the count.

As the count progressed, the polling places gradually quieted from a roaring, shouting uproar to sullen silence. Initially, each recorded opposition vote drew a cheer. (There were two to six tables in each polling place and they were all noisy.) But as more and more of our votes were tallied and the trend became clear, a tense quiet settled—and then suddenly the tenseness evaporated, and these strangers in our midst were stumbling, defeated mercenaries quietly heading for the doors and going back home—never to be seen again in the Eighth Assembly District South.

By 10:40, we received the first call at headquarters—three election districts—all ours, and by the margin we needed to win the whole district.

Five minutes later, three more districts. Our projection was holding, and we knew we had won and we brought out the liquor. My out-of-town campaign manager smiled for the first time in a week.

But the isolated election districts did not know the results, and heated, violent, emotional arguments over the counting of ballots continued until 11:30 and 12:00 and later.

And then, one by one, the tired, emotionally drained, gray-faced captains and workers made their way back up the stairs to the club, clutching their tally sheets, proud of their courage and their victories and hoping it had all been worth while. As each arrived, a new explosion of greetings and congratulations and reports on other districts took place.

My exhausted wife, still accompanied by my law partner, rushed in, waving the tally sheet for her E.D.—91 for me and 11 for the opposition—and everyone kidded her for letting 11 votes get away.

I remember many of the others, slowly and hopefully climbing the stairs, looking up to the faces at the top for a sign—grimness or happiness—as to how it was going. Peppery 59-year-old Tillie Miller, from the First Election District, a district with thousands of steps to climb—and she had climbed them all again and again during that hot summer. She had won her district again. But her drained face showed the cost.

And Bill and Freda Barlow (Bill had been in charge of the six polling places at one schoolhouse—his technique for dealing with noisy and obstreperous opponents was to yell louder and longer until the police told everyone to shut up); Freda's district was 4 to 1. And Jean McCabe (who later became my co-leader), Howard Amron (who succeeded me as leader), Toby Wherry, Gen Sparling, Angie and Joe Novellino, Stuart Greenfield, Joanne McQuillan, Christine Volkmar, Alex McDonald, Marty and Meryl Evans, Arthur Levine, Pete O'Connell, Helen Buss, Gert Spilberg, Ben Gardner, Bob Haft, Ed and Mary Reed, Tony Morrello, Hazel Hull, Pegeen Robinson, the Santomassinos—and finally John and Jeanne Laidler, whose district we had hoped to hold to a 2 to 1 loss, and which we split 50–50.

Do the names sound like a "cross-section"? They were—and so were the people who have them.

They came up the stairs one by one, or in pairs, looking hopeful and listening with satisfaction and then delight and then exuberance to the report of victory.

That's how the day ended.

But it has never been forgotten by those who participated in it. For each of them demonstrated his own brand of courage and each had disregarded the very real and perfectly legitimate fears that had been generated during the campaign.

Our club was never again the same. For we had demonstrated that, although we were amateurs, we were more professional than the professionals, and that we could win, on our own, despite every obstacle placed in our way.

To see ordinary citizens acquiring this kind of confidence, this kind of professionalism, this kind of determination, is a rare experience in this day and age of easy conformity and complaisant acceptance of the powers that be.

It is the kind of experience that completes the theoretical postulation and analytical dissection of political activity. It is this kind of experience that gives the skeleton of political theory the flesh and blood of substance.

It is this kind of experience that can make politics a wholesome, idealistic preoccupation or occupation.

It is this kind of experience that shows politics at its best—when it brings out of its participants the best they have to give, and makes them better people for what they have done. Any true picture of the political process must include this element—the human element of laughter and fear and elation and dejection and courage—and people trying, according to their own lights, to make the political process work.

30. "I'd Do It Again"

No one knows how to explain the essence of his fascination with something that exerts a permanent hold on his life. This does not mean that there are not explanations, only that they are insufficient. If one says that the taste for politics becomes an addiction and that once addicted you can never quite kick the habit, a confession has been made, not an explanation. All addicts will understand, and those who have no addiction will never understand no matter how many words are used.

I was drawn to politics in the first place by some instinct. I left it in less than a year—in the spring of 1952. That summer and fall Adlai Stevenson emerged as an ideal of what a politician might be. And I found myself back in politics within a year.

For my political generation especially, the spectacle of Stevenson in the 1952 Presidential campaign was a transforming experience. That great sequence of speeches in which he "talked sense to the American people," and did so with compassion, humor, and an unfailing commitment to expose the hard truths of our national situation, somehow made it necessary for many of us to become involved in the politics of the party he loved— and which we came to love.

But Stevenson's example is not sufficient to account for what kept me in politics. This is where the mysteries of addiction come in. The kind of daily practical political activity that increasingly took my time was different from the campaigning and the speeches that took Stevenson's time in 1952. Of course, it had to be.

There was the problem of how to translate the inspiration of Adlai Stevenson into what the political marketplace required.

The Stevenson inspiration got many of us to the political market-place, but it did not tell us what to do when we got there. For me, the pathway was to join a newly organized Lexingtonian local Democratic club (which had been organized by others) and to go through the routines of the internal political process.

The process is not dirty unless you want to make it dirty. It is, however, grinding, and many dropped by the wayside. The reasons for the high drop-out rate are many. Politics is costly in time and money and in the expenditure of energy and emotion.

Despite the Tammany myths, movement up the leadership ladder within the Democratic Party in New York County does not make you rich. In point of fact, it has been a costly venture for me. Because—at the end—I spent half my time on political activities, my income suffered. Time spent in politics is not compensable, as is time spent by a lawyer on his clients' affairs. Overworked partners cannot fail to take into consideration the frequent absences of a junior on political gambols. "A voice on the other end of the telephone" is the way one key partner described me. My share of the firm income was fixed accordingly— although fairly, since my partners were prepared to "carry me" in my political venture to some extent.

Moreover, to avoid any criticism once I was county leader, I made an arrangement with my firm so that I would not share in any fees involving dealings with the City of New York— another cut off the top.

Finally, there were direct political expenses—tickets, trips, conventions, carfare, lunches. Prior to my election as county leader, like most district leaders I paid such expenses myself, completely. After I became county leader, the expenses increased but I rarely charged them to the county organization until the end of my last year, because the county was beset by a substantial inherited deficit, which I was determined to liquidate. Moreover, its income was scanty. In my last year, over and above the reimbursement I received of some $450, I spent well over five times that amount of unreimbursed after-tax income on politics—my checkbook showed over $700 in tickets to dinners and political affairs alone.

There was no corresponding increase in clients as a result of political activity. Most prospective clients, I assume, who heard of me through politics, must have assumed I was a full-time politician. In any event, I had little extra time available to take on new matters.

There was one incidental material benefit: those who knew I was a practicing lawyer were reminded of my existence with some frequency. I was not just one of a number of anonymous partners in a large law firm, but someone with my own identity.

On a strictly material cash-accounting basis, the political account shows a substantial debit balance that will be difficult to redress. Such a debit is not an uncommon phenomenon among politicians and it is willingly accepted by them. It is one of the costs of living with a political addiction. So much, then, for the material aspects.

On an over-all accounting, however, including the intangible values, my fourteen years of political activity shows a substantial credit balance. The experience was incomparable. Crises, struggles, arguments, opportunities to make a difference, if only a small one, were a common, even a daily occurrence. The pressures of all kinds to which I was subjected, I think, gave me a capacity to deal with practical problems which I would never have developed in any other way.

When I started out, I was a young lawyer hoping to be a good trial lawyer. The opportunities for young lawyers in large firms to make arguments and try cases in court are limited and delayed. And one doesn't learn how to make an argument except by making it.

By the time I tried my first jury case, I had made so many arguments in my club that the jury looked to me like a small club meeting. Indeed, one of the jurors was a member of my club—a fact he acknowledged on examination of his qualifications, but my adversary disregarded this. The next morning I told the judge and my adversary that not only was the juror a member of my club, but, as I had assumed they knew, I was the Democratic leader of the district and the club. Since I was then thirty-one years old, the judge looked up in amazement and muttered: "You? I thought the guy I heard about must have been your father."

Argumentation in court and argumentation in politics involve basically the same arts. The training in one is interchangeable with the other. But the training in political activity is far easier to acquire, far less costly to clients, far more intensive in amount and in variety.

Other than the development of skills—which to a considerable extent is a materialistic consideration—the rewards of political activity are intangible.

My wife once pointed out that politics is one area in which its participants have the repeated opportunity to make serious moral and intellectual choices between competitive alternatives, although in one's daily life such choices are relative rarities. This is true. We early learned that every decision seemed to involve a choice between competing principles and values, not a choice between principle and no principle, or value and no value.

The very first issue which divided the New Democratic Club provides an excellent example of choosing between competing principles. In 1953, the club supported Casper Citron as a candidate for male leader in the Eighth Assembly District South. During the campaign, he somehow managed to take positions or actions that angered his supporters. Captains quit and were replaced or cajoled back. The law chairman walked out one night in protest at what he regarded to be improper handling of petitions. The first night I went up to the club, I found people arguing on the sidewalk outside the headquarters, arguing inside on the ground floor, arguing on the stairs, and arguing upstairs. As one of our members later remarked, our candidate, when under pressure, had a genius for creating discord wherever he went. Nevertheless, after a major blow-up over something or other, everything settled down, Citron corrected some earlier faults, and the captains came back and went to work. On election day 29 county committeemen pledged to Citron won—according to our count. (A later recount showed we had won 31 committeemen, but we didn't find that out until later and it wouldn't have made any difference anyway in the light of what happened.) Since there were 58 committeemen elected in the entire Eighth A. D. South, and since the committeemen elected the leader, we were one short of a majority.

The other 29 committeemen were divided—22 for another candidate, and 7 for a third. On paper no one had a majority. Of course, if a meeting of the 58 committeemen had been called, the likelihood was strong that due to absences among the 22 or 7 committeemen pledged to other candidates, our 29 committeemen would have been a clear majority and Citron would have been elected.

No such meeting of the committeemen from the Eighth South was ever called. Rather, a meeting of committeemen from the entire Eighth Assembly District was scheduled. By custom, the committeemen from the Eighth North, some 150 strong, should have voted for our candidate to be leader of the Eighth South, and our committeemen should have voted for the candidate of the northern committeemen to be leader of the Eighth North. But the leader of the Eighth North had an intense personal dislike for our candidate, and privately made it clear that unless we dropped our man and came up with someone else, he would vote to seat no one.

We stood fast, and *no* one was seated. But it was made clear that the door was still open and that if we substituted someone else for Citron, a new meeting would be held and the substitute would be seated.

Meanwhile, the pre-primary unrest and unhappiness over Citron flared up again. Charges and counter-charges were made. Repeated club meetings were held. Tempers ran high and a special committee was appointed to attempt to seek peace.

The competing principles were clear. On one side many captains and members sincerely felt Citron ought not to be elected, that he was unpredictable and the source of dissension, that we had been wrong when we (successfully) urged the voters to support the committeemen pledged to him, that it was essential for the club to be part of the regular party organization (which it would be if it selected an acceptable leader), and that the success of the club was far more important than the success of any one of its members. On the other side, many felt that we had told the voters they should support Citron, that the voters had done so, that Citron had the capacity to be a good leader especially if he got the necessary help, guidance, and support from the club, that the leader of the Eighth North had no right to tell the Democrats of the Eighth South who their leader should be, and, finally, that we had persuaded the voters to support Citron and no one had given *us* the right to reverse or overrule the decision of the voters.

The battle raged for three months. Ultimately the Citron supporters won in a club meeting, 91 votes to 3, and the prevailing principle was that the voters had decided and we had no right to substitute our judgment for that of the voters as expressed in the primary.

Almost every other political decision I have participated in involves similar competing principles and values. In 1960, for example, our club, torn by its loyalty and devotion to Adlai Stevenson, the recognition of the futility of the effort to nominate him, and its growing attachment to the man who was in many ways a new, more politically trained and sophisticated Stevenson, John F. Kennedy, finally compromised by advising our delegates to the national convention in Los Angeles that the nomination of either Kennedy or Stevenson would be gratifying. Since we were convinced that Stevenson was not a serious candidate, we viewed the resolution as a statement for Kennedy that avoided needlessly hurting an old and beloved friend.

For loyalty and gratitude are values that play as significant a role in many political decisions as do other more practical considerations. And they should. Politicians are very human, and usually the more human they are, the better the brand of politics and government they produce.

In addition to learning about competing principles, and what they were, and what values should be attached to them, my wife and I learned a great deal about appraising the characters of our associates. We made mistakes—fewer as we got more experience—but we acquired some understanding of people, and their ambitions, and their prejudices, and how to distinguish erratic brilliance from genuine quality.

We made many many close personal friends, white and black, Jew and Protestant, Catholic and agnostic. Indeed, I know of no better way than politics to break out of the insulation of a New York apartment and to meet and know and to come to have genuine affection for all kinds and conditions of men and women.

We have a far greater tolerance for the foibles of others. We listen to some of our liberal friends expounding upon what is right and what is wrong about government, knowing they have never raised a finger for or contributed a penny to a young candidate hopefully on his way up, or to a political club or to a political campaign.

At cocktail parties we occasionally hear someone holding forth on what's right or wrong with a government official whom we know and respect or think incompetent.

We hear simple blueprints for solutions to problems whose complexity we are only beginning to understand. We sometimes must listen to attacks upon politics and politicians as the devils in the governmental process when we know better, but must keep silent because there simply isn't time to explain the whole complexity of it. And there's really no point in starting an argument—although that too has happened sometimes when it's just been too much to take.

We are both different people. We are both happier people. I hope we are better people. I wonder how many experiences there are in this life that can justify such an appraisal.

The choice of "I'd Do It Again," the title of James Michael Curley's remarkable autobiography, for the title of this chapter is deliberate. By using it I hope one politician may salute the zest of another and pass it on. For different reasons—deeply different reasons—but from the same addiction, I must echo the colorful Bostonian. For I am wholly convinced that politics, as it was for Adlai Stevenson, is a worthy occupation for people who want to make it worth while.

And for that reason, if no other, I must echo James Michael Curley's words.

Government?

For the first 165 years of this country's existence, the manner in which our cities were governed remained a local problem. The majority of our people lived outside city limits. Legislative apportionments conceived in an earlier, largely agrarian society insured rural domination.

Both of these conditions have changed: the majority of our citizens are urban and not rural, and recent United States Supreme Court decisions require that their votes be counted on the same scale as those of rural residents. In the years ahead there will be an increasing predominance of urban and suburban voters, and an increasing national interest in adequate city government.

I have no blueprint for better city government, merely some tentative propositions. This book has not attempted to formulate such a blueprint. Rather, I have been concerned with attempting to analyze and banish some myths about city government which my experience has taught me amount to little more today than mortmain—to little more, in truth, than a collection of dead myths that, when they are permitted to masquerade as reality, defraud those who in a reformist spirit accept them as a reasonable guide to urban political life. Reasonable they were for our grandfathers. Not for us. They must not be accepted as keys to reality any longer if genuine political reform is to be sustained in New York (or, I suspect, in any city at all comparable to New York).

Of course, the first step in the evolution of a new and better form of city government must be an honest appraisal of where we are, and a critical analysis of the assumptions that are supposed to lead us to the promised land.

If I am correct that the anti-political-party orientation of traditional reform doctrines is the product of the mistaken assumption that an early symptom of bad government was its cause, my conclusion, however correct, does not in itself provide a blueprint for tomorrow.

But it does suggest a hypothesis.

If anti-political-party good government has not achieved good government, would it be possible for a party-oriented theory of good government to achieve more progress?

I think it would. I would like to see it tried.

It must not be forgotten that the existence of the hierarchy of party officers has always acted as a check upon and balance to the power of the public official. The problem with party officers is never their existence but always their quality. The existence of such power in reliable hands can achieve the same kind of balance and consensual government the federal government has achieved through the Constitutional system of checks and balances.

Certainly, with a growing civil-service bureaucracy, which is increasingly dominating city government, some counterbalance is necessary. Indeed, the growing political power of the civil service has reached the point where the civil-service unions have almost filled the power position formerly occupied by the political parties. As Professor Theodore Lowi, of the University of Chicago, pointed out in an unusual speech to the New York League of Women Voters on May 27, 1965:

. . . the *Legacy of Reform is essentially the ushering in of the bureaucratic state.* The bureaucracies in New York City government—that is, the professionally organized, autonomous agencies—are the New Machines. We may all like these better than the Old Machines, but they are Machines just the same. As with the Old Machines, the New Machines are based on fraternal loyalty, on trust built up over long years of probation and testing, on slow promotion up through the ranks, and on services rendered to members and to the public. As with the Old Machines, you have to join up before you can hope to have any influence. (Therefore the same words define each type of Machine.)

The New Machines are different in that there are more of them, in that they are functional rather than geographic, in that they do not depend upon votes for their power, and in that they probably minimize graft and corruption. But these differences only help to explain their success as machines!

To a political scientist, the New Machines are machines because they are relatively responsible structures of power: that is, they shape the important public policies, yet the leadership is relatively self-perpetuating, and they are not readily subject to the controls of any higher, popularly based authority.

Bureaucratic power unchecked by any countervailing force has been able to dictate public policy over the objections of all other interested parties. For example, in New York the issue of civilian determination of charges of police brutality has grown and grown in importance. One political and civic group after another—including the New York County Democratic Party, the Liberal Party, the CDV, the Association of the Bar of the City of New York, the New York County Lawyers Association— pressed for a change in the system, which vested jurisdiction over such complaints exclusively in the police.

In 1965 every mayoralty candidate but one (Mr. William F. Buckley, Jr., of the Conservative Party) came out for some form of civilian review. Why did the city administrators resist these proposals? Professor Lowi again supplies the answer:

For some time now the Police Department has been suffering from acute illegitimacy in some impressive quarters of the community. As a consequence, the killing of the Negro boy by an officer last July touched off the worst Harlem riots in twenty years. A large part of the credit for stopping the violence goes to the formation of the Unity Council of Harlem Organizations and the demand of that organization for a review board totally independent of the Police Department. Considering the widely accepted rights and practices of legislative oversight of administrative agencies in Washington and the state governments, and considering such independent investigations as Hoover-type commissions and the like, the demand of the Negro leaders seems relatively modest. But not to Commissioner Murphy, who threatened to resign if such a board were set up. He cast the issue strictly in terms of the integrity of his organization, arguing that such intrusion would destroy police morale.

Here is a 25,000-man organization, praised by Mr. Murphy as "one of the finest municipal departments in the world." Nonetheless it is too weak to withstand questions as to whether it is sufficiently close to the most pressing problems of the city.

Mr. Murphy's strategy was one I call "totalism." It is a vital strategy in bureaucratic warfare, and it is also used by rational conservatives the world over.

. . . . .

Mr. Murphy resigned even at the faint effort of the City Council to set up a less independent *legislative* review. At all costs the professional agency must be left to itself to decide what is the public interest. All the mayor can do is to "regret" the passing of one bureaucratic boss and see to the appointment of the next, with the usual promise of "no interference."

So, here is the spectacle of New York politics today. On the one hand you have an array of bureaucrats who believe in their respective organizations, and leaders and who follow an established policy line especially when the organization itself is at stake. *The strength of each bureaucratic agency lies in its cohesiveness as a minority in the midst of vast dispersion of the multitude.* (Once these words fit the Old Machine to a T.)

There are countless other examples of the civil-service bureaucracy deciding important questions of *public* policy. In addition, in the vacuum created by the absence of any viable party structure, the civil-service establishment has increasingly assumed both the policy function and the political function of the old machine. I would today rather have John DeLury's sanitation men with me in an election than half the party headquarters in town.

This again is a natural phenomenon. For the party organizations existed in response to a functional need for what they could provide—the machinery to elect a candidate—in return for which the party expected to be heard by the people it elected.

It seems clear to me that there should be checks and balances upon the power of any chief executive, but that this restraint should be exercised by an organization over which the voters have control—through the power to select the officers of the organization in primary elections—rather than a civil-service union responsive only to the demands and special interests of its government-employee members.

The result of combining the party-leader role and that of the chief executive has been to prevent the party from performing its legitimate governmental function. Mayor Wagner's administration, in fact, demonstrated both extremes of an undesirable power relationship.

Until 1961, too much power in public areas was in the hands of party officers. Fluoridation, for example, could not pass until the party leaders lost their power to control the Board of Estimate. Until 1961, when Wagner toppled them, they controlled enough votes on the Board of Estimate to prevent a decision on the question. This condition existed in large part because of the historical relationship between the party and its mayor, and partly because the current mayor believed as a matter of policy that he should keep strictly out of questions of internal party leadership—until 1961.

After 1961, the balance went the other way. Party leaders were hobbled in making *their* decisions because the mayor exercised all party power. The designation of candidates for all major public offices, for judgeships, and even the selection of people to fill party offices such as county leader, was made by the chief public officeholder. The result was that the party officeholder became no more than a first sergeant executing orders. The party organization more and more came to be at the disposal of one man—the mayor.

The mayor in turn suffered from a tremendous diversion of energy as he became more and more involved in internal party maneuvering. His *party leadership* role, it should be remembered, was immune from any control. For mayors are nominated and elected, after all, to run the city, not the party, and in a primary the mayor's party activities are hardly an obviously relevant, let alone an effective, issue.°

° The role of the President of the United States as leader of his national party is an entirely different phenomenon. For there is no national party in the sense that there are state and county political parties. The so-called national party is in effect a loose federation of state parties with no independent existence at all. It is either the political agency of the incumbent President or

I believe that the mayor, however, honestly felt on the basis of his experience and education that his course was the proper one. I do not think he was seeking the political leader's power for the sake of having more power (although he enjoyed exercising it), but rather because he believed it was essential *for the cause of good government* that he, and not the party officials, control the party structure.

In taking this position he was standing firmly in the anti-party, good-government–fusion tradition of reform. But, the reform movement he embraced, and which helped elect him, had moved beyond that old doctrine of reform to the party-oriented theory developed in the 1950's by the Lexingtonian clubs in Manhattan.

No small wonder that the mayor and the CDV were constantly at odds.

There was extensive speculation in the press and political circles when I resigned as county leader in December 1964 as to whether my resignation constituted a political split with the mayor. It didn't. I resigned because the practice of law and the practice of politics, both at the same time, had become too demanding. I had to choose which main road to follow. I chose the law.

But the mayor and I did have a basic disagreement as to the function of the party organization. The disagreement was never fully discussed between us, or even understood by me—at least not until after I had resigned and had an opportunity to reflect upon and analyze my experiences. But I had perceived some aspects of the disagreement while I was in office. At my club's annual dinner in June 1964 I spoke about it. Only a few people understood what I was talking about (the mayor was one of them). What I said was:

Twelve years ago we were on the threshold of a great new development in the Democratic Party. Almost alone and almost

a caretaker for the next Presidential nominee of the party that is out of power.

It has none of the other attributes of a political party on the state level. It is not an independent fund-raiser, it controls and makes no nominations, and it simply fails to exhibit the characteristics of a continuing political institution.

always lonely, this club forged its way as a pioneer in the drive to make the Democratic Party a better party. We believed in organization, but in better organization. We believed that the work of the Democratic Party and of party workers was *good* work for *good* men and women who believed in *good* government. Our principles were simple:

Political organization is a force for good government when good people staff it; and

Good people do not become bad ones because they are active in politics or have political power.

And so tonight we stand, almost as we did twelve years ago, at the threshold of a new struggle. This struggle is between those who believe the party organization is bad or at its best a necessary evil and those who still believe that better organization of good Democrats devoted to good government is a good thing.

It is a struggle between those who wish to weaken and divide our political party because they honestly believe the Party is a menace to good government and those, like ourselves, who believe that a strong organization is healthy, desirable, and an affirmative force for good government when it is staffed with good people.

Where do we stand in the coming struggle between those who would destroy party organization and those who would restore it in improved form?

I think the answer is clear. The same principles which have motivated this Club through twelve years of activity in the battle we have fought and won must lead us to join forces with those who believe that party organization is a good thing. For we have not done all of the work that we have done over these many years just to keep an evil—whether necessary or unnecessary—alive.

This conflict will increasingly affect city government in the years ahead. In more and more cities, the elected public office-holder is also the party leader. The civil-service establishment and other nonpolitical power structures (like the "public authorities") are becoming increasingly powerful both on the policy and operational level. At the same time, more and more citizens, on a part-time basis, are involving themselves in internal party politics. And yet this development brings with it its own contradiction. As Professor Lowi pointed out:

On the other hand, you get the remains of a party, progressively absorbing individuals who have been taught that it is good *not* to believe in their organization. They have not been prepared to follow any established policy line, even when their organization is at stake. In fact the leadership enjoys only their distrust; there is heroism in this distrust, even when a truly distinguished, modern type is in power—for example, Edward Costikyan. So, the need for central leadership is greatest at the time it is becoming progressively weaker. And the situation is not likely to change as long as each new generation is trained in the old myths.

On the basis of my experience I cannot say with certainty that I am right and that Robert F. Wagner was wrong. A return to party government may conceivably bring with it a return to the old abuses as the former mayor feared (although I doubt it). From his point of view, he apparently believed he could not take the risk.

But I believe the risk is worth taking, given the nature of the changes in the composition of political parties since Boss Tweed's day, the kind of people now involved in party politics, the control the voters have over the party through direct election of party officers, and the failures of present-day city government.

While no one can prophesy with certainty the results of a new form of party government, and while it is clear that *no* form of government will achieve utopia, I am sure that some new departure is necessary if city governments are to serve their proper function in the coming decades. I am also sure that the potential to be achieved if party organizations played their proper role in the governmental process has not been properly perceived or appreciated.

And so I offer as a hypothesis for achieving good government, a new form of party government. I believe the public office-holder must play a major role but not a dictatorial role in the party, especially on policy questions. I believe the party office-holder must play a major role, but not a dictatorial role, in the area of candidate selection—an area incidentally in which the public officeholder's views are to be taken with some skepticism since today's assemblymen, state senators and congressmen may be his competitor for higher officer tomorrow.

When a state the size of New York must look to Massachusetts for a candidate for the United States Senate, as New York's Democrats did in 1964, it is conclusive proof either of the failure of the party to nominate the right kind of people to lower office ten or fifteen years ago or of its failure to develop them properly. In my judgment this failure is both that of the party leaders *and* of the public officeholders, who were not anxious to encourage future competition for themselves.

I also believe there is a role to be played by the party officeholder in government. For example, in personnel recruitment, there has been an unfortunate separation between the two arms of government. Political sponsorship of an aspiring public servant is often as much of a liability as it is an asset.

"Quality" public officials are not supposed to come with political connections or recommendations. Three times I enjoyed the experience of learning of the appointment of an active member of my club to high office by reading about it in the New York *Times*. I could have found all three of them a lot faster than the city government did, if I had only had the opportunity to look.

Why shouldn't the party be asked first? Why not choose a man whose devotion to the party's positions on public issues has been evidenced by some prior political activity? Why ignore, in other words, the fact that good men have attached themselves to the party because of what it believes, because of its program? Why not encourage the participation of the right kind of public servant—or potential public servant—in political activity by using the political organization to the extent it can be used to recruit personnel?

This is not a plea for a return to the spoils system. It is a plea to encourage rather than discourage political participation by good citizens.

A second neglected area is that of information gathering. The political parties are well qualified to report on what the standing and the new major and minor governmental problems are. There is no good reason why they should not contribute to the agenda of government. They know, usually with an intimacy the public officeholder cannot command, the problems the people face each day. And more often than not they have responded to these problems long before the problems have reached the press, the government bureaus, the City Council, or the mayor's office— long before, that is, they have acquired names like "juvenile delinquency," "*de facto* segregation," "urban blight," and the rest. Such party services as these are rarely used by government. They should be.

Finally, the party organization can play a major role in explaining governmental problems and policies to those affected by them. Sometimes an early explanation of why something can't be done immediately, with some indication of when it can be done, goes a long way to forestall the build-up and explosive expression of public resentment—a combination of factors that only makes government's job harder.

The results of the 1965 municipal election in which Republican-Liberal John Lindsay was elected mayor have relatively little impact upon the validity of the hypothesis I have been suggesting. To some extent, at least, the campaigns of both major candidates recognized that some of the functions the parties formerly performed were both valid and necessary in order to achieve good government, although neither suggested that the political parties should once again perform them.

Thus, both Lindsay and Abraham D. Beame, the Democratic candidate, urged the creation of "local City Halls"— neighborhood offices to be staffed in part by volunteers and in part by city employees. It is clear that these offices were to perform some of the governmental functions which I have suggested the party should once again perform—information-gathering for the use of the mayor, and explanation to the voters of what their city administration can and cannot do, and why.

While neither candidate suggested that these local offices also act in the area of personnel recruitment, I believe that function will inevitably be assumed if these local offices effectively perform the other functions assigned to them.

Neither candidate, of course, suggested that the city-financed "local City Halls" were substitutes for the "machine," but they must have recognized it. And no one gave any attention to the impact of creating a political machine (inevitably these local offices will become local political headquarters in Mayor Lindsay's campaign for re-election, as he himself recognized in one incautious interview after the election) financed by city funds, immune from democratic control, controlled by the mayor, and staffed in part, at least, by city personnel.

If this is the only viable alternative to a system of party government—and no other alternative has as yet been suggested —then the argument for a new form of party government becomes that more compelling.

Otherwise, the election left the validity of the hypothesis I have suggested untouched.

Certainly the voters expressed no clear commitment to the old anti-political tradition of good government. For they elected Lindsay by a narrow margin, and a Democratic president of the City Council (the number-two man in city government), a Democratic comptroller (number-three), and a Democratic City Council by a large margin. Lindsay's was a personal victory, not a victory for a theory of government.

Clearly, the end result—a Republican-Liberal mayor surrounded by a Democratic administration with 16 out of 22 votes on the Board of Estimate and a veto-proof City Council does not appear to offer any likelihood of effective nonpartisan government. Nor does such a solution appear to offer any formula for good government.

It is perilous to leap to conclusions about the meanings of elections. Nevertheless, I believe it correct to say that the 1965 municipal contest in New York did not resolve the most important question facing New Yorkers:

> *Will responsible party government or "fusion" government serve the city best?*

The result of the election might be summarized in a sentence: The voters chose Lindsay but not "fusion," and they took out a Democratic insurance policy against what Lindsay might try to do.

In these circumstances, Professor Lowi's hypothesis, enunciated before the 1965 municipal struggle began, in the same speech quoted above, remains as cogent as ever:

A new type of *party machine* composed of responsible partisans is highly desirable, if attainable. There is nothing to *fear* in this, because the conditions for the *abusive* Old Machines no longer exist. Moreover, it is also necessary. The party machine is necessary not only because it is a prerequisite to democracy but because the organized popular base offers the only chance of forging a *balance* among the specialized bureaucracies. The bureaucracies ought to be left to run the city. The party ought to be restored to help *govern* *them*.

Professor Lowi conditions his hypothesis on the question: Is such a new type of party machine composed of "responsible partisans" attainable? If the myths of the past are banished, and regular participation of good citizens in the new type of party machine encouraged rather than discouraged, who can say such a machine cannot be built? The conditions for its creation exist today.

And if such a new machine can be built, as I believe it can, why should it not play a major role in the government of our cities? The tradition that cities are ungovernable is as false as the myth that political parties are necessarily corrupt. What *is* true is that cities and the political parties within them decay from the same kinds of citizen contempt and external and internal neglect. Neither the government nor the party rot because of any immutable law of life.

I believe we can save our cities and our parties if we want to, but I do not believe we can save one without saving the other.

Index